KT-478-139

After winning 2015's *Great British Bake Off*, Nadiya Hussain has gone on to capture the hearts of the nation.

A regular columnist for *The Times*, she has also presented many BBC shows, including *The Chronicles of Nadiya*, *Nadiya's Asian Odyssey*, *Nadiya's British Food Adventure*, *Nadiya's Family Favourites* and *Time to Eat*.

Her cookery books include *Nadiya's Kitchen*, *Nadiya's British Food Adventure*, *Nadiya's Family Favourites* and *Time To Eat*. Her three books in the bestselling *Bake Me a Story* series, one of which was shortlisted for a British Book Award, are published by Hachette Children's Group, as well as her first picture book for younger readers, *My Monster and Me*.

Born in Luton to British–Bangladeshi parents, Nadiya now lives in Milton Keynes with her husband, Abdal, and their three children.

To everyone with a voice.
Those in pursuit, for a voice, lost.
A voice they dream of having.
The voice they wish they had.
Because life happens.
And with it we lose, we gain and grow.

It is there somewhere.
I've found it today. It may be gone tomorrow.
But for now I have it.

This is for you. This is for us.

To the loves of my life.
Abdal, Musa, Dawud and Maryam.

Contents

Introduction xi

1. DAUGHTER *1*

2. SISTER *29*

3. GRANDDAUGHTER *71*

4. WIFE *99*

5. DAUGHTER-IN-LAW *133*

6. MA *171*

7. EARNER *213*

8. COOK *245*

9. USERNAME *275*

10. WOMAN *301*

Acknowledgements *331*

Index *334*

Recipe Index *338*

Introduction

This is a book of stories untold, tales I have grown up hearing and ones my children will listen to in the future. Stories of lessons learned, memories saved and things that have made me the person that I am today. This is not an autobiography in the sense that it is not my tell-all, hear-all, reveal-all. Instead, it is a memoir of sorts. Within these pages you will find snippets of my life, ones that I am happy to share because these stories are mine. From then to now. From the moment I was born to the moment that I typed these words out.

Each chapter in the book takes a title of one of the many roles I play in my life: Daughter, Sister, Wife, Mother and so on. Along with the stories you will find within these pages, each chapter starts with a poem that I wrote, dug up from my decades-old back catalogue, and ends with a recipe that means something to me, that brings back a memory, an emotion, a sense of who I am. Because along with the people in my life and the roles that have defined me – somewhere in between all of that – lives a love of poetry and the sheer joy that food brings.

If I step back and think about the twists and turns we all take in life, I look at my own journey and it has been far from a straight road. In fact, it has been quite the opposite – one step forward, two steps back, off the road, sat nav on the blink and I've forgotten my glasses. That is my kind of road and, frankly, I wouldn't have it any other way. Because this is the road that has led me through life: sometimes standstill, stationary, stuck; other times flying at 70 mph with the windows open.

So what prompted me to write this book?

Well, there are girls out there who are quiet, just like I used to be. Who are allowing their lives to be steered in the hope that one day they might find their happy and, with that, their voice. Who are growing up being told 'it's not appropriate', 'no you can't', 'it's not the done thing'. With this book I want to show that, actually, who cares if it's not appropriate, you can and it *is* the done thing!

We all have a voice. Yours might be loud and strong, or quiet yet insistent. I have always tried to use mine for the right reasons, to make myself heard, to tell those I love how much they mean to me, to shine a light on the important issues of the day. But I wasn't always like that. In fact, occasionally, even now, I find myself forgetting I have a voice and have to find ways of locating it all over again.

Whatever life path we are walking, whatever God we follow, or not, whatever choices we make along the way, we all have moments when we stumble. And somewhere in those stumbled-jumbled thoughts and life choices, it's easy to lose this very important part of what makes us who we are.

Whether you decide to use your voice to change the world, to retaliate, to say 'I love you' or to drop the 'f bomb', it is yours to use how you wish. But life can have a funny way of sometimes muting it, dulling its passion.

As the third girl born into a large Muslim family, having a voice didn't always mean anything to me. Sometimes I had to be silent in our family line-up, to accept what my life was meant to be – occasionally without question, but mostly with. I always talked too much. My dad would say, 'Nadiya, why so many questions?'

The answer, quite simply, is that girls matter, women matter, we matter. Wherever you come from, whatever your story, whether you relate to the words in here or not, we are linked by this. We matter. You know that and I know that; it's just time we started believing it.

It took me a while to find my voice. With it, I may not change the world; I may not make a difference. But if you are still hiding your voice, if it's buried away at the back of your head, or it's just out of reach on the tip of your tongue, then I hope that reading about my experiences will help you to find it. Because voices are meant to be heard and questions are meant to be asked. This book shows how I found my voice and, with it, I hope I help you to find yours. Be heard. Because someone will be listening.

DAUGHTER

Door to where?
Door to here.
Right here. Right now.
You and this door to somewhere.
This, door to where?
Your door to here.
Your door to somewhere.

There are some stories that stand the test of time, no matter how many occasions they are told, repeated or re-enacted. These tales, the ones that we hear again and again through life's ups and downs, are the very best kind of stories. The essence is identical on each retelling: the same beginning, the exact same middle and the very same end.

There was always that single story, just the one, that I would crowbar into the conversation with a carefully planted question. As young children we would sit together on a midweek afternoon. Dad would mostly take his occasional days off work on a Wednesday or Thursday. These were the slow days so sometimes he would take one day off, very rarely and only every few weeks. We like to call our dad the S.P.O.F. – a tongue-in-cheek nickname that stands for 'single point of failure'. He charmed and entertained at his restaurant but all the while he forgot he had books to balance and bills to pay, which meant that despite his best efforts his business sometimes suffered. He wanted to be all over the lot: the kitchen, the food, the floor, the customers, the takeaways, the bar, the folding of the napkins, the temperature of the poppadom-warming machine thingy. The lot! So on the rare afternoon that we did see him, we did not want to let him out of our sight. Deep down we all knew he had a niggle (or two) in the back of his mind about whether the tablecloths had been delivered or if the ice machine was overflowing. But when we did have him . . .

'Go on, Dad, tell us about the day we were born.'

To each of us in turn, Dad would tell us about the day he became a father for the first time, second time, third time, fourth time, fifth time and, of course, the sixth. On each retelling, his stories have become lighter in detail and heavier in sorrow with the realisation of how life has moved on.

Nothing much has changed these days. Except we are children no more. We are still our parents' offspring, of course, but now with the odd wrinkle, stray white hairs and the strong smell of caffeine and musk of curry wafting through the air, marred with a hint of cigarette. We are no longer the plucky children eagerly waiting at our father's toes ready to hear a story we have heard a million times before. We are his six adult children, some with bigger hands than his, though just one taller than him (total medical anomaly; everyone else in our family is vertically challenged so Lord only knows how my brother managed to reach six foot – as a child of '95 it must have been all the pesticides in his diet). Some have the loudest voices (that would be my big sister: big in title, tiny in stature – but her voice makes up for it), while others do not speak at all. We are his children with our own children. Every story interrupted with refereeing a fight or two or six, cleaning pooey bottoms, mopping up a spill, wiping a snotty nose or simply shouting, 'DO NOT put that in your mouth!' We are his six children, with eleven of his grandchildren in tow, eleven and counting.

It is an important story. This story. For all of us. The one where we came into the world. The story of the moment we arrived. The second where we come into existence, a presence. An actual person. This was the moment I breathed my first gasp of air. Innocent, dependent, sinless, clean. A human. So, as the story goes . . .

My mum was in quarantine in hospital with me near the tail end of her pregnancy. The weeks, vague. I could tell you exactly what week during my pregnancies I had heartburn. But this was the eighties and I was in the womb of a woman who once lived in a country where pregnant women climbed trees even at full term. Back in Bangladesh, the place my parents call home, women ate what they wanted during pregnancy. There were no rules. They did not have scans or check-ups. If the painters and decorators did not arrive you were pregnant and if you were pregnant you were like everyone else. You worked, you ate, you lived; nothing stopped, not even for the carrier of human life. German measles was not about to get my mum down, let alone go anywhere near her child.

'How sick were you, Mum? Were we both going to die? Did we cheat death?'

Now that's a story! But no. We were not cheating death; Mum was in quarantine, but she was out of hospital again soon enough. I'm sure she had been grateful for the rest. But knowing my mum as she is now I am nearly certain she would have been restless – if not a little testy – and keen to get back to her daily routine. She had other children to get home to, after all – a two-year-old and one-year-old, to be exact. If I were in her sandals I would have milked it, for sure. I would have given myself a few extra days at least to be waited on hand and foot. Would you care about how the hospital food tastes? As long as you are not cooking or reheating it yourself for a few days, why on earth not make the most of the break? But the year before my birth, Mum had my second sister and the year before that, my older sister. So, she was a busy lady; she did not have time to be taken down by some European disease, not her, not my mother.

So as the story goes, Mum went into labour and had to go back into hospital again. My nan looked after my sisters during the labour. In those days, Dad told us, men did not have to attend the birth of the child. Which feels like madness today – I mean, you put that baby there, after all; the least you can do is watch it come out. But Dad, luckily for Mum (I think), wanted to stay with her for the birth. Having done it two years in a row, he considered himself an expert in the field, so he went out for a quick fag before facing what could be an uncertain few hours. 'This baby will be ages,' he declared.

Every job always started with a quick fag. There was nothing quick about it. Every fag was the same size and every fag took the same amount of time to smoke. How was it quick, if it was the same every time? I'm pretty sure I was rolling my tiny eyeballs from the edge of my mother's womb. I certainly do it now, in full force, right in front of him. On his way outside, before he could even reach the end of the corridor, he was shouted down by a gaggle of midwives who flapped their arms and called his name, 'Mr Ali, Mr Ali!', waking a few babes in their excitement.

'What did I have?'

'Congratulations, Mr Ali, you've had a bouncy baby girl!'

'Bastard!'

Enough to make even an untidy, minutes-old, newborn baby offended. I never tire of my birth story. I ask to hear it over and over again. It's already the best, right? I'm relentless in my pursuit to understand it. I am not averse to a little profanity occasionally, if I'm in the mood or the situation is appropriate. But never during the birth of a child, my own or otherwise. A new baby, a time to rejoice, a time to celebrate, a time to dream of where life will take you next. But expletives, never: I cannot, if I rummage through my cluttered and preoccupied brain, even think of a celebratory explétive if I tried. I mean, what the actual f***! I don't know about you but this feels like the right time for a foul-mouthed tirade. Wouldn't you agree?

As a child I remember being slighted, saddened, by this part of the story. Even as a grown-up now, I feel a pang of sadness for those words along with an equal measure of hysterics. It is amusing when I think about it . . . then I really think about it. Bastard! I mean, really? I always questioned my dad and his choice of word. I mean, seriously, imagine for a second how those midwives felt when they heard him. I'm sure as the middlepersons in the delivery of life, someone else human, they would have been presented with plenty of peculiar and intriguing scenarios and a wide range of vocabulary. But had they ever met a dad who shouted the word 'bastard' upon the arrival of the fruit of his wife's womb? I doubt it very much! The chat after work . . .

'So anything interesting happen at work today?' Apart from delivering humans.

'Yeah, so a baby flew right out of her mother's bajiji, like lightning, she flew right out, we told the dad he had a baby girl and he said, "Bastard!"'

I think it's a tremendous story to tell over the dinner table. They probably thought I was doomed. They were not entirely wrong.

'Then what?' I would ask my dad.

As I got older, it was not the first portion of the story that interested me. It was the subsequent part that really got me every single time. A husband, a father, shuddered at the thought of calling his relatives to announce the birth of his third daughter. Not one, not two, but three. How was he going to break the news? Was the news that dreadful? My dad always maintained that he was happy that he had a healthy little girl, but I know that secretly he wished, longed for that little boy. An heir to his throne – or stool more like. The carrier of his surname (the same surname that was meant to bring bad luck, of which more later). He knew all too well that life would have been a lot easier if he had just had that baby boy. The phone call to his parents-in-law, for one, would have been much less difficult, as everyone waited with bated breath for the news.

I asked him how he felt. 'Were you nervous, Dad? Were you pooing in your pants like your new baby, Dad? Did you ever consider not ringing the family at all and just waiting to show them what sex I was during a staged nappy change?' Of course, like any good parent he always protested; he said he was happy – but he knew his family would not be. Having a boy would have been easier, he said. For who, though, easier for who? The madness still makes my head spin. I repeatedly find myself wondering about the fact that these days you can find out the sex of your child. Would my parents have gone down this path if they had had the opportunity? And if they did find out they were having a third girl, would I be here today? I don't think I would. That is just a really big, totally unnecessary guess, of course, but naturally one does wonder. In a community so hellbent on creating alpha males, I might not have stood a chance. No way, no how. Thank goodness the choice did not exist then. But it does now and I know the problem of wanting to breed a boy still does too.

The pressure was on for my old man. He had to make that call. What I think made it more challenging and painful was my uncle, my dad's brother. My uncle, just a few streets away, with four strapping young boys. His wife revered and loved. Practically worshipped. Whenever she was asked how many children she had she would puff out her chest and say, 'I have four sons.' She was everything every woman in our community wanted to be. All they wanted to do was puff out like a proud brooding bird, ruffle their feathers and speak of how many boys they had made. My mum never answered that question in the same satisfied way as my aunt. I think she feared that question.

How was he going to break the news? He had to. He may not have wanted to. But he had to. News that should have been met with cheers was met with a morose 'never mind'. The same response my mum would get when she told people she had six children, four girls and only two boys. 'Never mind, at least you have two.' The more I heard those words the more invisible we became.

I figure if my sisters were old enough to receive a phone call (which they were not at one and two years of age), they would have let out a collective whoop at the news of my arrival. Maybe even tears of joy. Who knows? Is that a little presumptuous? I'm hopeful. But Dad called my nana first (my maternal grandad), telling him he had a nathin (which means granddaughter). The problem was that the word for grandson is nathi. Not great if you are hard of hearing. But my grandad was not, he can't have been, at least not in his late forties, and even if he was, I am not having it as an excuse! So, anyway, my dad started his conversation quietly with a coy:

'You have another nathin.'

'A nathi! All praise be to Allah!'

'No, you have another nathin.'

Dad got louder. My grandad got deafer. Dad became even louder still. Were my grandad's ears hearing what his brain desperately wanted to tell him?

'A nathi! All praise be to Allah!' he cried to my grandma as she waited apprehensively next to him.

'Nathin, nathin, nathin!' Dad repeated. My grandad heard this time.

'Okay,' he replied. 'Well, that's good!'

Okay? Was that it? Good? That part of the story, the point in the line when you read a book and it gets you, right there, right in your centre. Right there where you think words can never reach you. 'Bastard' did that to me, or at least I thought it did till I heard the word 'okay'. Bastard suddenly felt like a compliment. Maybe I will take bastard.

No I won't. I don't want either.

That is how I came to be. So quick to make an entrance, so desperate to get into the world, that you won't even get a chance to get your fags out of your pocket, let alone light one.

If you don't have words then just give me a curse word, the best you have; be certain that nothing will ever top bastard, until someone says okay. Okay, bastard.

Nadiya Begum on my birth certificate. Born at seven pounds and ten ounces, that was what made me a bouncy baby girl. That is good going. The name Nadiya was an idea my dad's Russian friend had. I never met the Russian friend; my dad had acquaintances, people he would hang out with, but no actual friend stood the test of time. Neither did this Russian guy, whoever he was, wherever Dad met him, wherever he was going. Thanks for the name. Although I am slightly dubious: my sister, the one born the year before me, is called Sadiya. So somebody, whether this elusive Russian guy or someone else, someone rhymed our names. Easy enough, I suppose. Those rhyming names made us instant pairs. There are two more where we came from, but that's for another chapter.

When my big sister was pregnant with her first and we were researching names it was the first time I even considered finding out the meaning of my name.

What does Nadiya mean? In France, it means hope. In Spain, it means hope too. In Russian it means hope again. I'm liking where this is going; everyone wants to be hope. I want to be hope. It does not last. In Arabic it means moist, tender and delicate. What am I, a roast chicken dinner? Funny though, at seventeen. All the jokes! In Swahili, Nadiya means caller. That's the Nadiya I want to be, the call for hope. What with the Arabic meaning I did not have a hope in hell. So I am sticking to the first and last meanings and getting rid of the yucky filling of the bad name. Now it is a good name filling-less sandwich.

Nadiya: I like that. I like it a lot. Thanks, never-seen-before Russian 'friend' with the ability to rhyme like a primary school kid. Thanks a bunch.

Surnames were a whole other issue for me, growing up. My dad is an Ali. My mum is a Begum. My sisters, all Begums; my brothers Hussains. I think I only really noticed the difference between our names when I was learning to read. I started seeing my parents' names on the post; that is when I longed for us all to have the same surname, my mum included. The people I grew up around, all extended family, just like me, just like us, had a variety of names in their families and that felt, actually, like our normal, whatever that was. But I for one was not having it; I could not understand and so to me, even at the tender reading age of five, I did not like it, not at all, not one tiny bit. I wanted to have surnames that matched, like English families did on the television. That was the kind of normal I wanted, an ordinary, blend-into-the-crowd kind of normal matched name. Like the Dingles in *Emmerdale*. Like the Fowlers in *EastEnders*. Like the Shadwicks in *Brookside*. Oh, just to be typically average and ordinary in every kind of way. No chance.

'I want us to have the same surname, we sound so dysfunctional with so many surnames.'

Turns out you can have the same surname and still be dysfunctional, but at least such families are all publicly identified with each other despite their defects. Isn't that what all families are about, being maladjusted but with the same surname so their imbalances can be identified in the form of one unit?

As a kid I used to imagine scenes out of Bollywood. A perfectly elaborate fist-fight outside our street: *dishoom!* That's the sound the soft-skinned cheek flaps of the enemy would make when they met with the fist of his unlikely assailant, a five-foot-five bearded man, Ali, my dad. My dad would single-handedly destroy thirty men and when he was done, the enemy and his goons would be all bloodied and writhing around in pain. Not a hair on his head would have budged, despite the punching with one hand, the other in his pocket, in a choreographed fight that included four costume changes, two songs and several one-handed dance moves. The enemies would crawl away and say, 'Don't mess with those Alis! Or are they the Hussains? I think they're Begums . . . No, I'm sure they're Hussains.'

Do you see what I mean? Scrap the Bollywood scene, the singing, the dancing, the costume changes, the lot. There is something magical about saying we are the (insert name here). I knew that we were never going to change our surnames, so we are the Ali Begum Hussains! It's not strong, punchy or forthright, in fact it's muddled, wordy and a mouthful, which says everything about who we are and that is actually perfect.

The story, as it goes:

My dhadha (paternal grandad) warned my dad that the

name Ali was bad luck, so although that was my dad's surname, he was instructed by my dhadha not to give any of his
children that name. I imagine an elaborate story of witch-
craft and a gruesome death led my dhadha to that conclusion,
but who knows? None of us will ever know now. He was a
firecracker who knew his mind, so when he gave an instruc-
tion, everyone did what they were told. I would have asked
him; he quite liked me and I quite liked him. He would have
told me. But for some reason I never did and sadly he has now
passed away, so I still don't know why that name was bad
luck. My dad agreed to the change without a fight. But let's
just say the surnames that we were given, however they were
picked, did not give anyone much luck either. My brothers
became Hussains, which means 'small handsome one', and
we were Begums, which is the title of a married Muslim
woman, equivalent to 'Mrs'. Some research perhaps would
not have gone amiss here.

I asked Mum, 'Why that name in particular?'

'Because it's my name.' It was the name she had had since
birth – there is no tradition of taking a husband's surname in
our culture. Couldn't really argue with that. Damn.

'Why not Dad's name?'

'Because your grandad said no, it's bad luck.' I couldn't
argue with that either, because no one was willing to argue
with the old grandad.

'Do you know what it means, Mum, Begum? It means
wife! How can a kid be called wife?' I was slightly self-
satisfied with my questioning.

'Well, that is what you will become one day.'

Floored. I think that may have been my first experience of feeling offence. That was the moment I decided I did not want to be anyone's wife. I was not going to become a wife by surname or by relationship.

A first of many labels: stuck, waxed and sealed on me and my sisters from the moment we were born. They – they being Mum and Dad and everyone else, being the extended family – did not really understand what it meant; they just gave us the name without really thinking about it too much. But it was a bugbear that stayed with me from the moment my Year 6 teacher Mrs Kookoolis said we were to research our surnames. Bearing in my mind most of the class were Ahmeds, Khans, Begums and Butts, this was the only time we could copy each other's homework and feasibly get away with it. As long as someone got the answer, we were all sorted. I was envious of my teacher. Imagine having a great mouthful of a name like Kookoolis! I mean, just say it: Koo-koo-lis! Break it up and say it in three parts! That's the kind of name that starts and stops conversations. That's the kind of name that you know everyone asks her about, every time she says it. I can imagine she must have sat through several pots of tea and packets of Garibaldis talking about her name and who she inherited it from. Was it her married name? If so, her lucky husband. Was it her name from birth? A name like that would make any potential suitor nervous. You wouldn't want to change your name after marriage with a name like Kookoolis. It is the kind of name that if you put it into a search engine it would spew out reams and reams of information. Just imagine: births, marriages, deaths, family trees, immigration, travel, the works!

I was stuck with Begum. How could I be a wife, or at least be called one, even when I was still defecating in plastic pants? When I could not walk, talk, or even hold my head up, why was I a wife? We had the Begum barney for years and years more to come. I hated the name. They hated that I hated the name. I hated that they hated me for hating a name that I hated. It never ended.

My dad is known as Baba. Traditional in his approach to some things, he asked us to call him this. While everyone else's kids were calling their dads Abba or Dad, he wanted to be addressed as Baba. That's what he called his dad. That is the title that everyone in the village addresses their fathers with. Being 5,019 miles away from his home in Bangladesh meant he worked extra hard to recreate his village for his family in Luton, Bedfordshire. Recreating the tranquillity and resourcefulness of a rural village in the centre of an urban hive in a small town outside of London was never going to be easy. There were always going to be struggles. Many more than he ever anticipated. In fact, knowing my dad, he wouldn't have anticipated or expected any problems. He always struggled to find the balance between the modernity of Western life and the traditions of a life he never really lived himself back in his very rural village in Bangladesh, given he left there when he was very young. We certainly did not make it easy for him. Cue the child inside me letting out a little laugh, loud enough for me to feel and Dad not to hear.

No bad words at home. All parents know that is a rule. We all have certain taboo words. We say trump instead of fart. I have young kids and a husband who is a little kid in a big kid's disguise who say and perform trumps often. It's like an orchestra. So we use the word trump a lot, although that is a word (name) that should be banned all over the world. But let's not get into politics yet. Maybe later. We also don't use words like stupid or dumb or kill. We have a plethora of words that are banned. Simply not allowed.

Well, when I was growing up, we had one particular bad word we were not allowed. Dad. Oops, I said it.

'I am your baba, not your dad,' Baba would proclaim if we ever said it accidentally.

'But you are our dad, what's wrong with calling you Dad?'

'You are Bangladeshi and you should be calling me Baba. I don't want to hear the word dad, you are not English.'

I thought I was as English as my Mauritian neighbours next door who used to yell at each other so loudly I could hear their distinct French through the very thin walls. I thought I was as English as my Pakistani neighbour on the other side of the terrace. His kids called him Dad.

'They are too modern,' Dad would say.

'I want to be modern like them and call you Dad, I think.'

I'm still not sure. I never knew where my questioning would lead me or what trouble it would get me into. But I carried on anyway.

'So you want me and your mum to be divorced?'

'Well, no, but maybe a little bit yes. It's not like you really like each other anyway.'

I was obsessed by the thought of my parents being divorced. What an absolutely morbid thought! My kids see single families and dread the thought of my husband and me separating. Yet here I was, willing it on.

I used to peek over the fence of our neighbour on the right side. I can't have been that old or tall. Not much has changed except for the old bit. I remember standing on my tippy-toes trying to look over. But to no avail. I would attempt a running jump. I'd seen my cousins do it. It couldn't be that hard, could it? The garden was not that big and was filled with an exotic veg patch, backing on to train tracks. Lack of space meant my running jump was more of a scamper and hop. Eat your heart out, Greg Rutherford. I would hook myself on to the fence with the folds of my belly and stay there till the pain of the splinters digging into my gut was unbearable. It gave me five seconds and I'm being generous here. There I would watch our neighbour, an 'uncle' by no relation who used to go to school with my dad. Or baba. He would have his kids stay with him very occasionally. I may have only ever seen them in the garden a handful of times. He would buy them bags of toys that would be all strewn across the garden. 'Dumb girls,' I would say to myself. 'If I had all those toys I would look after them.'

'Dad!' they would scream. They were never scorned. He would come out running with a fag vibrating at the edge of his lip, tearing himself away from the cricket on the TV, set at the highest volume. Either his remote was broken or he was deaf.

'Daaaaaaad!' I would scream in turn. I was met with silence. He never responded if we said Dad. Not ever. Come hell or high water, if you wanted his attention of any kind, saying Dad was the wrong thing to do. Did that stop me? Sometimes I would say Dad just to see if he reacted, mostly when he was watching snooker. Propped on the edge of his seat, surrounded by a cloud of cigarette fumes and gripping a cup of tepid tea. That's how he drinks his tea. That's how I drink my tea. Tepid. None of the snooker and not the fag fumes for me. Just the tepid tea, in the hands that look just like his.

He always went silent when I called him that. He hated it with a passion. Now imagine that you have six kids and all six at some point during the day manage to accidentally or sometimes on purpose (that would be me) say Dad. Multiply six by four and you get twenty-four times being called Dad. That's a guesstimate.

One day he lost it. He came charging out of the kitchen.

'How many f****** times have I told you not to call me Dad? It's Baba!'

That is when I realised how much he hated it. But I still didn't know why.

We had a grapevine at the back of the garden that yielded the most beautiful purple grapes. I can appreciate them from my memory as a child and would give away a small fortune for an established grapevine in my garden now. It was his pride and joy and when he was mad he would head there. So that is where he went after his foul-mouthed outburst.

We were not allowed to say Dad. But we could throw in a f*** and we wouldn't be sent to bed without dinner. That's what made my dad mad but cool. At least to my friends. 'You can say the word f*** and you don't get a slap?' They would celebrate. I didn't want to say the F word but I did want to say Dad. I felt sorry for myself; I felt sorry for us. It didn't make sense. Neither did he.

I watched Dad pull up his lungi (a traditional skirt worn in Bangladesh), storm down to the shed at the bottom of the garden and walk out with a pair of shears. Then I watched him hack away at this poor unassuming grapevine that did not know what it was in for. I plucked up the courage and ran down to the bottom of the garden. The poor, poor grapevine. Bald in the spot where he had taken out most of his frustration. What did the grapevine do? It was being punished for something we had done. I hated that vine as a child. Spiders hid in it and fell on your head when you walked past. It grew so many grapes that my dad didn't know what to do with them, too many to eat and not enough to give away. So we were made to drink skin-crawling, eye-wateringly tart grape juice. I hated that grapevine my whole life. But that day I felt sorry for it.

'Baba, why do you get so angry with us when we call you the D word?'

He stopped, took a breath and brushed with his fingers

the footstool he'd been standing on, flicking the fallen vine leaves to the ground. Then he sat on it. He started to talk. At first I did not catch one single word. Just the rumbling of the earth beneath our feet and the movement of his lips. We lived with train tracks at the back of the garden. I hated the sound. It was so loud and earth-shattering it felt like the train was going to tip on its side and fall on both of us, squishing us into patties in its wake. But as much as I didn't want to be there, I stayed. And eventually I could hear what he was saying.

'I have been here all my life.'

He had; he moved long before he even turned ten.

'I dream about saying Baba, every day. I love my dad and I don't get to say it.'

My heart was beating rapidly. It was the first time I had seen him vulnerable. Who was the child? Because suddenly it wasn't me any more.

'When I hear my kids say Baba, it reminds me of my baba.'

I got up off the brick I was sitting on and hugged him tight. I think he said 'Baba loves you' – I'm not really sure, a train was going past – but I'm guessing that was the sentiment.

'And I love you, Baba.' A pause. 'But can I call you Dad one day?'

He smirked. 'No!'

Always pushing the limits.

I was his daughter and he was my baba. Now I don't call him Dad, I call him Baba, because that is what he is. My baba, a man too soon. With nothing of a childhood to look back on. He told us stories that make my stomach churn as I picture my children's faces in his second-hand, two-sizes-too-big for him, stuffed-with-tissue shoes. There he is, peeling garlic for a part-time job after school, eyes stinging with sleep and the astringent fumes of the allium. All he wanted to do was go to school the next day and not fall asleep. He would watch others dress up for Eid in their suits and finery while he tugged and tucked his ill-fitting clothes, embarrassed by his attire. I can't bear it. If I could turn back time, I would tell him: 'One day you will feel love.' Encapsulated in a hexagonal-shaped embrace, with love streaming six ways.

The word baba was not just a word to him. It was a longing, a word he could say but with no one to say it to. I imagine him saying it to himself. Maybe he did. When you don't say a word for long enough you forget how it will roll off your tongue. Was he scared that the less he said it, the less his dad would exist somewhere in his heart? So he needed to hear it from us. I wish he had more chances to say baba and have his father at the end of that word. But that was not to be. I know now we keep his baba alive every time we call him that name.

In the spirit of keeping things alive, let's talk about some-one who died. Seamless link.

My nana (maternal grandad) died in the November of 1987. We get told the story of how he was on his way to pick up my big sister to take her to nursery. A story that is thirty-something years old, ageing with my big sister. When I see her I think of him. She was to become five years old the November my nana died. Mum was occupied with three of us still at home and her hands must have always been full; at this point she now had four children. Us younger ones were nearly four, nearly three and one, and there was another on the way.

'My dad helped me out a lot, he could see I was always busy,' my mum says when she tells the story.

My big sister was the apple of his eye; he loved her a lot. But his real love was his girl, my mum. That's what she told us. We never saw it ourselves, but if she said it then she must have felt it. I don't remember him at all but this particular story makes me remember a man I never knew with a strange sense of fondness. There he was, on his way to nursery, and he fell and died on the corner of his street. They say it was instant, a ruptured spleen. I always wonder if he lay there for an age and died slowly. Was he in pain? Was it raining? Was he cold? It was November; it can't have been warm. Did he know that he would never make that school run? Questions that I will always have and I will never have the heart to ask my mum. Because I know these are questions she will have plagued herself with. Some questions are better left unasked.

He never made it to my mum's. Never made the school run. Ruptured spleen at fifty-two. Gone. That day, when he died, he left behind his daughter and her madness and my mum has never really recovered from the loss of the love she will never feel with any other man. He was her dad and she was his daughter. No other man could ever replace that, no brother, husband or son. Despite years of watching her try, nobody will ever quite fill the hole he left in her soul. Some are too big for that blank space, others far too small.

I think I remember the night his body was flown to Bangladesh for burial. I was jumping between beds. We had a few beds lined up with a gap of a foot between them. I must have been no older than three and I have this vivid memory of mum curled into a ball in between these beds. She was seven months pregnant, lying in a foetal position in a space smaller than a foot wide, with a foetus inside of her. I could not see her face but I could hear her cry. I caught a glimpse of her puffy tear-soaked cheeks every time a car passed, the light shining in the dark room reflecting the net curtains' elaborate pattern onto her acne-scarred face. She cried for hours, or at least it seemed like she did. But what are hours to a nearly three-year-old? Can a nearly three-year-old even have memories? I don't know the answer to that; all I know is that I remember that night so clearly.

Eventually she sat up and moved onto the corner of the bed, still sobbing uncontrollably. I walked up to her and wiped the tear that had rolled down her beautiful rounded cheeks, a tear that had come to her chin and stayed suspended. That was my first taste of tears, or at least someone else's. I'm sure I had tasted my own after a fall or tantrum. But this was different. It was salty.

She looked down at me and cupped my face. 'Is your nana dead?' she said in Bengali. I understood. Though I am fairly certain that even at three I did not know what being dead was.

'Let me feed you children,' she said, turning to my sister, and she disappeared into the badly lit hallway. There she stopped for a moment and took in a deep breath before going down the stairs. I carried on jumping, as the room filled with the smell of tenga. Now, every time I cook tenga I picture my mum's tear-soaked face. Eyes so puffy she could barely see through the slits. All those hopes she had for her father to watch us grow. All gone. But she had to feed her kids. How does a mother lose the one man in her life who truly loved her, grieve and carry on being a mum?

I always keep that memory of my mum sobbing while curled up in a ball, on the floor, in the dark, in my head. Tucked in the back of my memory. It reminds me that she too is human. Like the rest of us. Even though she felt like a bloodshot-eyed, fire-breathing, knife-tongued tyrant at times. I am her daughter. She was the lioness who lost her dad and, heartbroken, she wiped her salty tears. Walked when her legs couldn't really take her. Stood when she wanted to fall. Carried on even though her carrier was gone. She was human; she too was someone's daughter, like I am hers.

I was sitting with her not long ago. 'Mum, do you realise you are older than nana now?' You know me, sensitive as ever. Her face dropped and the guilt rose to mine. I went a perfect shade of burgundy and there was no hiding it. I thought it was a fact she would have realised at some point.

'You're right, I am,' she said, her voice too shallow and her eyes looking up to the sky. 'He died so young. My dad died so young.'

What do you say to that? Nothing.

'I don't want to die young like him. I want to live so I can see you live.'

Complete silence as we both cried.

'Don't cry,' she said, as she wiped one tear and walked to the sink. 'Shall we eat?'

That's my mum.

'Yes, let's eat.'

So we ate.

I am their daughter. They are me. I am my baba's stubborn backbone and his great brows. I am my mum's resilience and wide birthing hips.

I am that little bouncy baby girl that didn't care what time it was. I was coming because making an entrance waits for no man. Even if he needs a fag. Not even German measles will stop me or my mum.

Bastard, you say? I'm thirty-four now, I've heard worse. Bastard is a compliment these days.

I am my grandparents' nathin, not nathi, and for anyone hard of hearing that means I'm a girl, woman, lady, female, lass, chick – and a badass one at that. I can say badass; it's dad I can't say.

My name is Nadiya, and it's the best name no matter who picked it, Russian or otherwise.

I still hate the name Begum and so spent an age being called just Nadiya, like Madonna, Sade, Prince, Adele and suchlike. But there is nothing wrong with being a wife or being called one; it didn't define me then and it doesn't define me now.

The name for our next pet will be Kookoolis; that's how spectacular that name is.

I have a hatred for grapes, which is entirely my dad's fault. So in this book I'm calling you DAD! I'm sorry, don't be angry, Baba.

I am their profanity, their nerves, their traditions, their hang-ups, their loss, their tears. I am their human, their child, their daughter. They made me. They have broken me. But they are mine and I am theirs.

TENGA

This is the dish that permeated out from under the kitchen floor and crept up the stairs and in through our bedroom door. This is the aroma that reminds me of my mum, my grandad, her loss, her salty tears and her dynamic strength. When I was learning to cook, this is the one I asked to learn first. It fills me with joy that it is now a favourite with all our kids too. Sometimes I cook it to remind me of my mum and her love for the real love of her life, her baba.

Feeds 4

You will need:

6 tbsp olive oil
10 cloves of garlic, minced
6 tomatoes, quartered
1 chilli, split lengthways
1 tsp fine salt
½ tsp ground turmeric
½ tsp chilli powder
3 cod loins (roughly 375g), chopped into small chunks
Handful of fresh coriander, chopped

How to make it:

Add the oil to a hot pan and add the garlic, turning down the heat so the garlic doesn't burn. When the garlic is brown, add the tomatoes and cook till they are totally mushy and broken down.

Now add the chilli and salt and cook for just a few minutes more. Add the turmeric and chilli powder and cook for another few minutes.

Add the chopped fish and put the flame down to a really low heat. Pop on the lid and leave for about 5 minutes, just long enough to make a cup of tea.

Take off the lid and the fish should be cooked. Add 300ml of warm water. Mix and cook for just 5 minutes with the lid off.

Take off the heat, add the fresh coriander and serve with hot rice.

SISTER

This is a club. An exclusive one
For members only.

Clubs come with rules.
The rules are as follows.

Protect, no matter what.
At your own detriment.

You are friends; some feuds are allowed.
But for a maximum of eleven minutes.

You don't always have to be brave.
It is desirable. Pretend if you have to.

Try to stay alive.
For as long as is physically possible.

But if you have to die.
Which you do.
Die in the order you were born.

It's only fair.

If I think being a daughter is difficult – challenging mostly, easy occasionally – I should say being a sister, a teammate, a piece of the puzzle, is, or should be, a piece of cake. Not the kind of cake that requires fifty-six eggs, two ovens, wooden dowels, a second-hand chainsaw and a small refrigerated Transit van to transport it. More like a Victoria sponge, a simple Victoria sponge, uncomplicated and easy. Being a sister is like that kind of cake: effortless enough, easy, uncomplicated and straightforward. Till of course you realise you only have one tin that is two sizes too big, the oven works (just about) but the light is on the blink again, so you know that as soon as the door is shut, the light will go out. You will be left waiting, wondering, 'Can I judge if my cake is ready just by the way it smells? Because I sure as hell can't see if it's ready!' Not to mention you've forgotten to take the butter out of the fridge and it's so hard, it feels like it has been refrigerated on top of Ben Nevis, and you just dropped the only egg you have left on the concrete floor. It's that kind of Victoria sponge: simple and easy, in theory. Till the universe decides to teach you that you can have your Victoria sponge, but not without a fight.

Who is Victoria anyway? I don't much fancy her sponge.

I am one of six. One of six kids. I am number three of six. There are so many of us. So many, that we have to address ourselves like the numbers of a page, like the pages of a fax machine, like the footer of an email trail. I mean, I say there are so many of us. But I only really think it or say it when I am in a 'British' situation, which I am often, which inherently means when I am around white people. When I say I am one of six and I get: 'Wow.' I always back it up with, 'My parents didn't own a telly.' They did; of course they did. We are no different to the Smiths or the Joneses of Britain. We were just the Alis or the Ahmeds. Everyone played catch-up, everyone wanted what the neighbours had, but better. We had a telly; we had two. But they just did what everyone else did round our way: they got married and had kids. Nothing wrong with that; they just watched telly in between. In between life, living and six kids under the age of thirteen.

If, however, I'm speaking to Bengali people or ethnics like us, it is entirely normal to hear the numbers range from five to twelve. That's the highest I have ever heard. In which case six felt like the British equivalent of two. My dad was one of fourteen, two of whom passed away, leaving their family with twelve. My mum was one of eight, four of whom died, leaving them with just four. I am feeling very British as I write this, almost slightly 'judgey'. Saying it out loud confirms how gargantuan our family really is and certainly how it has grown over the decades. The sixteen children went on to have their own kids, making us six of fifty-nine grandchildren. That's not counting the ones that died. Fifty-nine! Talking of fifties, that is around the age bracket my paternal grandma died, in her early fifties. Which now, as a thirty-four-year-old, feels scarily young. I am convinced that having fourteen kids played a part in her demise. Maybe she died to get some much-needed respite. Who knows, but I am utterly convinced that my dad and his thirteen siblings had their part to play. The poor woman's uterus must have been worn out.

'Mum, do you think Dhadhi died so young because she had fourteen kids?'

'Yes.' That's that answered.

Imagine if she had to deal with fifty-nine grandchildren! Luckily she didn't have to because some of us were thousands of miles away in the UK.

Where I went to school, in Luton, it was easily almost 100 per cent brown faces. I don't know the exact figures but it was close to the hundred mark. I remember only ever seeing a handful of white faces and boy did they look white in the sea of coffee, cinnamon, bronze and chocolate. I had never met anyone who was an only child. The numbers varied but there were almost always more than four siblings in each family. I had friends who had sisters in the year groups above and below me, who were friends of my sisters, who were friends of our parents. Everyone knew everyone and everyone knew everyone's sister and everyone knew everyone's parents or uncles or grandparents or neighbours.

It was one big cesspool of sister incestry! You could not get away with one bad word about any of your siblings. Someone would find out. I didn't even think bad thoughts around them, for fear that someone would hear.

Growing up in our culture we were never allowed to use our siblings' names. It was the 'rule', and I use that word firmly. The rules ARE the rules: commandments, still very much alive and kicking. You were not allowed to address anyone older than you using their name. Every brother or sister older than you had a label of some variety and if there wasn't a label, someone would find one, no matter how obscure or silly.

And this rule extended out to everyone! Parents and grandparents I could understand, even aunts and uncles if you have enough to count on one hand. But what if you have more uncles and aunts and cousins and relatives than you have fingers and toes? And hairs on your head? How many labels can anyone create? All I'm saying is, they always found a title.

'That's just stupid, Dad, why can't we just use their names? What's the point in having names if you can't use them?'

Oh, the look on my poor dad's face. When he faced questioning and he didn't have the answers, he deployed my mum and addressed me as her daughter. Not taking his donation into account for that precise moment. Funny that.

I would repeat this interrogation whenever possible, if I wasn't sent away to my room and told to stop with all the questions. Who knows where that conversation went when I shut the door behind me and stormed up the stairs? I heard a few faint Bengali swear words, but nothing too sinister.

I always asked the wrong questions of my parents, the kind of questions they never really had the answers to. When they reacted like that – with a stumble, no answer, me sent away, profanity and secret conversation – I would store that question in my back catalogue, in the secret part of my brain. So I could bring it up again. Timing is important, but a stored-up, precarious, revisited sticky question is the way forward as a teenager.

'So stupid' were the words that would ring in my head. I couldn't say them out loud and so the words translated into the rolling of eyeballs. I would get caught or tattled on. Safety in my head: 'so stupid'.

What was the point in the hierarchy? What was the point in the labels? More importantly what did these traditions achieve, apart from confusion? They're the rules my kids follow now, what I do, what my parents' generation still do, and my grandparents' generation did the same. That is just what each generation did before them. The hierarchy is still alive and present now. So if I get faced with the same question from my kids, I might just send them to their room, or better still I will have an answer.

'Actually, guys, I do not have a clue. But you know what, it's not harming anyone.'

One of Six

My big sister. I won't even give her a name because I think it's far more amusing giving her a connective number sandwich as a first name. Although Jasmin is much more gracious and delicate, it's less amusing than One of Six. I love calling her my big sister because she is so far away from the adjective, it's hilarious. She is the eldest in our family and boy, does she know it. She is top dog. We have to listen to her, even if she's wrong, but there is a secret group chat on which we can air our grievances about her quietly and obediently. I'm sure there's one for all of us individually. I have come to accept that. I imagine mine would aptly be named 'too big for her boots'.

Being at the top came with lots of responsibility and choice phrases.

'You are the eldest.'

'Everything you do, they will do after you.'

'You have to be the best example.'

'You are responsible for all of them.'

The sad thing is, I don't think my parents realised that they themselves were up there, right at the top, as the best examples for our young, easily influenced minds. It seems important to highlight the hierarchy of good examples, as we are on the subject. But somehow my parents' minds managed to erase that top part of their hierarchy system. It always started with her. Never them. I seem to always relay this, back and forth in my own pre- and post-pubescent mind. They are up there, above us all; we saw that, they conveniently did not.

A slight lady: I call her that, because that is what she is, perfectly polite, helpful and sociable. She gags at the thought of wearing tracksuit bottoms. She wears shoes and heels. I mean, she is proper. Behind closed doors, however, she is a totally different person with us.

'I just realised you never wear tracksuit bottoms when you're out.'

'And I never will.'

I'm glad we had that chat.

I always felt a tiny bit sorry for her as a kid, balanced out with intense jealousy. The scale tipped slightly more towards jealousy, being the more substantial end. Mostly jealousy. She was, she still is, incredibly beautiful. Slight, slim, with skin so fair, only she could play Snow White in a panto full of brown kids. I know, blows my mind too. I'm brown, same parents! How? She was so fair she even had pink cheeks. Actual pink cheeks! When I blush my cheeks look like someone has punched me in the face. Like a black eye, purple and blue, has slipped down onto my cheek in my sleep. She was perfect. She seemingly had everything. She was smart, skinny and white.

'You have everything, you're perfect.'

'No I'm not.'

'Yes you are.'

'Fine, I am.'

The perfect formula to find a husband. Or at least that is what we were reminded of regularly. Not like a weekly email or a Post-it note or a reminder on the phone. Just words, conversations, things we heard in passing, when really we should not have been listening. If it was loud enough for us to hear, maybe it was loud enough so we *could* hear? 'You will find her a nice husband.' Not that I wanted one of those, but it would have been nice to be thought marketable. It's nice to be wanted, even if you don't care to be wanted. I came with a shedload of PR; she, however, needed nothing. She could sell herself, in the least vulgar and most befitting arranged marriage sort of way. 'We will not be short of proposals for her,' I would hear. I always heard it. It rang in my ears. What I never really thought about was that she was hearing it too.

Professedly, she seemed to have everything. The one thing that she didn't have, however, was a penis. She was reminded of that her entire life. She was perfect. But she was born with the wrong genitalia. So often she would be showered with praise for being all of the above, but there was always a sting in the tail. 'Imagine if you had all of that and you were a boy.' Imagine being all of that and still not being enough? To be honest, I'll have that. What I would have done to have had all of that. I was willing to be all that she was and still not be enough. It was better than being nothing at all.

'It would have been great if you all had a big brother.'

That was what we heard and that was what we repeated. Anyone and everyone, every generation, grandparents, parents, family, extended or otherwise; I would not be surprised if the postman was in on the action. Everyone said it. They thought it and they always allowed it to catapult out of their mouth. I never met anyone with enough tact to keep it locked shut behind their teeth. They said it, we heard it and we pined. For years on end we craved an older brother, a brother we never had. A brother we were told we should have had. Even though biologically we could never have one. Because even modern science could not reverse time and give us an older brother.

Lying in bed at night. We shared a room. We shared our thoughts.

'I wish we had an older brother.'

Everyone agreed. Except for her.

'Well, you're stuck with me.'

'If only you were our big brother.' How ridiculous!

It was never really said with any thought of how it affected her. She heard that day in day out for years and I never thought about how that must have sounded to her.

I remember one particular night. I shared a double bed with her and the others were scattered around the room in variations of beds, bunks, singles and suchlike. We must have been small: you could not get us all in one room sleeping like that now. We come with so much excess baggage it would be near enough impossible. We have grown, as have our numbers. On the scales and in our ancestry! There was a bothersome clock in our room that ticked so loud. Tick tock tick tock all night. It was only when the batteries ran out and nobody replaced them that I realised how much I needed that annoying ticking to get to sleep.

Everything was still, with no clock to count down to. I was wide awake, but my sister's conversation had tailed off and I thought she might have fallen asleep. We had run out of chat, which we often did. But the best kind of silence is the kind with a sister. Nobody is judging. Nobody is waiting in anticipation for the other to spark a new subject. It was the best kind of least awkward silence you can get. If there was a kind, that was the best kind. I could hear the water running through the pipes under the floors as Mum turned on the heating downstairs. I heard her footsteps lead out of the kitchen, as she closed the door behind her. That door was in desperate need of some WD-40. She had light feet for a well-built lady. I imagine she would have made herself a steaming cup of tea made with freshly boiled milk. That's the way she liked it. Her gentle footsteps led to the television. All I could hear now was the muffled sound of a Bollywood movie, *Dilwale Dulhania Le Jayenge*. I knew the words to every song; I wished she would turn it up. My ears strained to hear the drums, the beat, the costume changes, but she reduced the volume every time she detected a hint of movement. So I lay still, singing along in my head.

She muted the box every time she heard a car go by. She was waiting for Dad. He was the only one not home, working late as usual. I knew she was waiting for an argument. He knew he was coming home to one. Like all parents, sometimes emotions boiled over between them and every stored grievance would get an airing.

The sound of keys in the lock and then a banging on the door. She had locked him out and she was waiting to let him in or not let him. The latter was always desirable. But the latter she never did. The beat of my favourite song was quickly drowned out by the sound of two adults yelling. As one got louder, the other's volume increased in turn. They never realised how much the noise travelled.

I thought everyone was asleep. I dared not look either side. For the fear that the argument would penetrate itself into our room. If one parent came up, so would the other. Which meant it would be in front of us to see and hear. I had witnessed it often enough to know I never wanted to see it again. If I didn't see it I could pretend it wasn't happening. But I was awake and so was my big sister. As I lay on my back with my covers right up to my mouth, tears ran down my face and filled my ears. I would occasionally turn my head to empty the cavity. She used the corner of the blanket to wipe them away.

'If I hold your ears, all you have to do is pretend that they are not fighting.'

I didn't say a thing. She sat up beside me and held me tightly, with the palms of her hands firmly pressed against my soggy tear-soaked ears.

What is a big brother? It is a notion, an idea of a protector, a leader. Yet if I step back and look around me at everyone who had a big brother, those big brothers were the total opposite. They didn't protect and they chose not to lead. So why the consistent need to plant the idea that big brothers were what all families required, when family history suggested otherwise?

I had a protector, a leader, a confidante. The kind of person who would sit up all night covering my ears. She fell asleep eventually, she must have, but not without hearing everything she drowned out from my lugholes. That is protection. That is a leader of a pack . . . and all without a penis. Totally possible! My big sister. If life didn't give her a big brother and she didn't need one, why did I?

I don't. She is enough.

Two of Six

I think the universe wanted us to be twins. She is undeniably far more athletic than I am, so it comes as no surprise that she won the race to the egg before I did. Forgive the unfortunate image! She was born exactly 365 days before me on Christmas Eve and I was born the following year on Christmas Day. If that wasn't already one clue from the universe, I can give you a second reason. I am called Nadiya and she is called Sadiya. See what I mean? And another: we are both brown with the biggest, most unruly hair you will ever have the misfortune of seeing. Do you get what I am saying? The universe, the stars, wanted us to be twins and it just never happened.

I'm glad we were not twins. Whose face would we share?

I don't want her nose and she doesn't want my caterpillar eyebrows. If it's all the same, I quite like not being a twin.

But growing up, we felt one and the same. So although we're not twins we felt like we were. We shared birthdays; I celebrated on her day and she celebrated on mine. We had a two-day birthday that we orchestrated all on our own. We never had a birthday cake, so we made Frosties sandwiches. Most people had cake, so we found a way. Picture this: lashings of butter on white bread, topped with a thick layer of jam and then sprinkled over with Frosties, the sugar-coated cornflakes, the kind you could eat back then without the fear of being judged. That kind! Squashed down. That was our thing. It was like a sweet crisp sandwich. If crisp sandwiches are your thing, this might be too!

We had birthdays in the holidays so we never stood up in assembly to be serenaded by 300 out-of-tune kids. We did it at home instead. We sang the 'Happy Birthday' song to ourselves. Once on Christmas Eve and once on Christmas Day. Twice. Nobody else celebrated it, so we celebrated together. That was our thing.

It did not always stay that way. I don't know what happened between eleven and seventeen but I can't say I saw her much. I mean, she was there and so was I. But I didn't see her very often and she didn't see me. We lived in the same house. We shared the same floor for dinner; we used the same toilet. We 'lived' together as all families do. We even still met each other every year on our birthday. But we didn't celebrate in the same way: we sang 'Happy Birthday' but barely once, let alone twice and we never made Frosties sandwiches again. Ever.

I found her again. In the college toilets. I was in my second year of college. I was crying into my hands. I was also in the wettest toilet cubicle in the history of time. I mean what had people been doing in here? Why was it so wet? What was this unidentified liquid? I couldn't sit. So I stood against the door. Head in hand. Hand against the cubicle door. She walked in with her friends, I recognised her voice and she recognised my muffled sobs. I could hear her usher her friends out. She had a way about her. She commanded respect in the most hostile of manners, but it worked for her.

'Are you crying?'

'No.'

'You idiot! I can hear you.'

She could and let's face it, there was no hiding it at this point. She could also see my Adidas Campus trainers sticking out the door. That might have been the giveaway! My crying had gone from gentle tears falling off my chin to a stream of snot across my cheek with the occasional grunt to release the sheer frustration I was feeling.

'No, you *grunt* can't!'

'Okay, I'll leave then.'

I unlatched the hook and rushed out. If she said she was doing something, she was doing it there and then. I hugged her. She has always been a few inches taller than me. But I make up for my lack of inches in wit and humour. She will confirm that, I'm sure! It was something I always made sure to remind her of. She was a good under-arm hugger. I felt safe and protected in her hug. I felt intact even, if just for a second, in her firm embrace.

'My friends lied to me. They made plans without me and then lied to me to cover it up. Can I hang around with you for a little while?' Trivial now as an adult. But a big deal as a teenager.

'Course you can.' Famous last words. She said I could. So that is exactly what I did.

Break time, lunch time, free periods, before college, after college, literally every second of every single day. For almost six months. Not to mention the drive in to college and then the walk home afterwards. Then there was dinner. Her single bed was right next to mine. Her single bed with a gap shy of one foot. We watched each other sleep, for God's sake!

One night, just before lights out, I sat on her bed.

'Get off of my bed, that's my bed. And those friends are mine too; I don't have to share everything with you.'

I knew it. I had felt it. I had been feeling those words coming for weeks. I had tiptoed around her in fear that she would say it. Sweetening her up every time I thought she might utter those words. But finally they were there.

I stopped facing her that night. I turned and stared at the peach wallpaper on the other side. Risking my dad's disdain, I began peeling it at the seam where the two bits of paper met. Maybe this way he will decorate this monstrosity of a room, I thought. He never did. I knew it. It niggled me. I felt it. I was a nuisance. I was the third wheel on a perfectly functioning bike. I was not needed or wanted. I was getting in the way of what seemed like a seamless motion.

I stayed away. It was the loneliest . . . well, I want to say weeks, but it was about two periods' worth of loneliness, which all in all adds up to two hours, if that. I made an excuse and got myself out of my English lesson to go to the loo. When you say the words 'periods' and 'cramps' to a thirty-something-year-old male teacher, it's funny how they excuse you before you can even finish the sentence. I had used the same excuse twice already in the same month but he was too shy or clueless (or both) to even question it. I sat on this less wet loo. I found myself in the same place, crying into my hands. A place I was becoming all too familiar with. Then I heard a knock on my cubicle door.

'I know you're in there. I checked your timetable and when I saw you were not in English, I knew you'd be in here.'

That's how attached I had become. I had given her a copy of my timetable, for goodness' sake. Who does that?

I didn't say anything. My pride was bruised, my ego battered and my heart sad.

'I'm sorry.'

Silence.

'Fine, I'm leaving.'

I found myself almost lifting my cheeks off the seat. But I didn't. I stayed put. She didn't leave either, despite her unusually empty threat. Her ears were no doubt glued to the other side of the cubicle door. That's how I imagined her desperation for my friendship! Eventually I walked out. She waited, perched by the sink. She didn't say a word. She didn't have to. She draped her gangly arms round my short shoulders and pushed the heavy toilet doors open, accompanying me out into the corridor. Where all her friends waited. Where OUR friends waited.

'You skipping English?' Well, that cramp was suddenly feeling much worse.

No friendship of mine has ever really stood the test of time. Life has meant distance, in so many more ways than one. But what my sisters and I have is a friendship connected by kin, that is built on the firmest foundations. The materials sourced to build the actual house were bought at cut price. So the building occasionally suffers some damage, through wear and tear, through lack of maintenance, through unforeseen weather conditions. It falls apart and gets put back together. Sometimes not the same as it was first built, a little rough around the edges, a little worn. But still standing.

She is friendship. Even when she didn't need it or want it. She knew I did. Friendship is sacrifice; it is quietly putting up with something that is much bigger than the rules that come with being a link in a chain. She is my friend.

Three of Six

I am number three of six, so officially the middle child. Given that I have Middle Child Syndrome, I am writing a book about me, me, me! So we can skip this tiny bit out.

Four of Six

He was our first-born boy. Can you imagine the rejoicing at his arrival? A boy, an actual real-life boy with a pee-pee and everything! The sacrifice of an entire cattle herd would not have been enough. Thank the Lord. To be provided with a young boy child, to carry the weakly connected surname of Ali, the name of his father and (perhaps) his forefathers . . . what better thing to do than to give him a different surname altogether? Jak HUSSAIN it is then! If *The Lion King* were a thing in the mid-eighties, that moment when the blue-arsed monkey lifts the tiny sleeping curled-up lion cub high for every man and his dog to view in awe, that scene would have been the enactment of my brother's arrival into the world.

Except, he did not quite get that reception. He was born with bilateral hare lip and cleft palate, which meant he had the meat and two veg, he was definitely a boy, but he was still not quite good enough. That's what they told my mum and dad. By whose standard? Everyone's. Because community mattered. Family whispers mattered. Their opinions mattered. I don't know why. I still don't know why. But it did. If they said he wasn't enough, almost everyone else started to believe it too.

My mum tells us we were very excited to have a baby brother. I was barely two; I have no recollection. I doubt it mattered much to me either way and at two I'm sure I didn't really care. Who has a memory as early as two? I certainly don't. If anything, I bet our parents don't want us to remember things from when we were that young. The things they said and did; I have memories from when I was five that I would happily erase.

When my brother was born, he didn't come home straight away. On his eighth day in hospital he had his first operation. His first of many. He was born to a life on a doctor's table, being poked and prodded. Put to sleep and woken up again. In and out through those revolving doors. He would walk in and be wheeled out. These are not my accounts; these are the stories we were told.

'We want to bring your brother home, but we don't want you to be scared,' our parents said.

My big sister replied, 'We won't be scared, he's our brother.' She remembers it well.

So they brought him home. I don't remember the day he came home. My sister does. We have a Polaroid to prove it. He was pretty lovely. There was nothing scary about him. In fact he may be, to this day (and I have had my own kids at this point), the cutest little human I have ever set my eyes on. We were not afraid of him, but it did not stop the world from being afraid.

As he grew up, his stories after school were a familiar collection of sentences. On a loop. Every day.

'He called me a monster.'

'He said my face was disgusting.'

'She won't sit next to me, because she doesn't want to get what I have.'

'He said Mum and Dad should have killed me when I was born.'

The list could go on and on. Parents and children alike had nothing but nasty things to say. He was watched, stared at, jeered at, pointed at and it was all topped off with the worst of the many remarks I have heard towards him: 'He's making me feel sick.' The more surgery he had, the more time he had off school, and the more at home he felt in his hospital ward with his poorly peers. So every time he heard a remark he had heard a million other times, it cut us like a knife. And if it cut us, imagine how it penetrated his tiny little soul.

It was another one of those days. Only a few weeks after surgery, which meant he was a little puffy in places we could see and sore in places we couldn't. He missed so much school he was always eager to get back, despite the comments. He wasn't allowed to play sports, or swim, or really do anything that could mean potentially getting smacked in the face. So he spent a lot of time doing arts and crafts, lots of time taking things apart that didn't need disassembling and then he would happily spend a whole afternoon reassembling them. Not always successfully, but he was starting to get really good at making things work like they used to before. Activities that kept his head down; I get it now.

That day, he came running out of school in floods of tears, a common occurrence.

'He said my face was like a monster.' He pointed to a man standing in the playground, waiting for his own children.

Dad didn't often make the school run; for someone's

misfortune, he had done so that day. My dad's anger rose; I could literally see the red rise up like a faulty jam thermometer. Dad got on his knees and whispered something into my brother's ears. He nodded profusely.

What was he saying to him? I knew if Dad was hatching a plan it was going to be dynamite.

Jak turned to me, held my hand and said, 'I'm scared.' I squeezed his hand back and he led me and Dad to the grown man who just minutes ago had said to a minuscule frightened eight-year-old: 'Your face looks like a monster.'

I remember watching the scene with my heart racing. Dad stood directly behind Jak. 'Go on, say it,' Dad urged him, holding his shoulder.

My brother's chest rose up and down. It looked like a hollow breast of the most malnourished pigeon, one that hasn't been to Trafalgar Square yet. The words minced around in his mouth; he swallowed nothing as he prepared to say something, but what?

'If you're man enough, say that again, in front of my dad.'

The man stood there, pale-faced. He wasn't a stranger. We knew him well; he was a regular in the playground. So I knew that the shade of grey he was going was not his usual skin tone.

Dad prompted Jak again, with a tiny pat on the shoulder. He repeated his line.

'If you're man enough, say that again, in front of my dad.'

Nothing. I saw our opponent go a shade I had never ever seen before. What I didn't know then but I know now, is that

I would never see anyone turn that colour again. It was an ability only my dad has ever possessed. No painter, my dad, but he could turn a man grey.

This time it was dad's turn. 'Go on, say to me what you just said to my son.'

The man's lips moved but before words could even make it out, he had Dad's bulbous fist in his mouth, swallowing whatever phrases he intended to spew. He lay on the ground. I would say his ego was more bruised than his face, but Dad had done quite a number on his now black and blue features.

We walked away. My brother held my hand even tighter now, but this time when he looked up at me he smiled so hard I could barely see his eyes.

'That's what you get when you're mean to monsters.'

In his thirties now, nearly twenty-something operations later, I see the wobble occasionally. When he looks like he needs a hand to hold or to squeeze again. These days he looks down at me and not the other way round. Once upon a time he needed a dad to throw some of the punches. These days he throws all the punches, in all of the right places, and not a bulbous fist in sight.

He is the epitome of brave.

Five of Six

I woke up and found myself bolting for the stairs. I was always up first. And I was always the first to fall asleep the night before. Literally the second my head hit that pillow, I was out cold. Not a heavy sleeper, but asleep. Nothing much has changed. I can pretty much get to sleep within seconds of my head hitting my synthetic stuffed pillow.

'People who sleep so fast have no stress in their life.' My mum's words.

No, perhaps we just fall asleep because we are so stressed, overworked and tired that our body's natural reaction is to sleep? Maybe not as a kid, but certainly now as an actual grown-up. Either way, I was always up first, and I would give my sister Yasmin a tiny wee prod and she would be up, not too far behind me, with her slightly shorter legs. I would bolt down the stairs and she would race behind. First job: get those letters. There were always letters, headed in red: 'read immediately', 'action immediately', 'open immediately'. What was with all the rush? They were the boring letters; I would hand those to her to pass to Mum and Dad. Imagine being woken up to a pile of final notices before 6 a.m? I never understood the need for the raised voices as she ran out of my parents' room and the door was slammed shut behind her. She would come out panting. She panted all the time anyway; well, mostly – her little heart worked harder than ours. But her morning visit to my parents always made her pant a little harder. As grown-ups now, neither of us would want to be presented by final notices before the sun has come up. But then again, we pay our bills so there is a slim chance of that happening. It is one of the few things we learned from our childhood. Pay your damn bills, people!

Once we found a Topic bar in the post. It was some pro-
motion thing, perhaps, and it came through the post in the
form of a celestial offering, packed in a cellophane bag with
a tiny note. I don't even remember what the note said,
because all we wanted was that Topic bar and that's what we
did; we had it. The only way we knew how: six ways! If we
had one of something, nobody, and I mean nobody, ever ate
it alone. Even if you found a penny sweet in the bottom of
your pocket, covered in fluff, even that one manhandled
penny sweet had to be shared. Once I found such a sweet and
ate it; I thought to myself, 'So what's going to happen if I eat
it? They won't know.' They didn't know, but I knew and the
guilt nearly killed me, so I never did it again. We waited for
another one of those Topics in the post for years, till we
forgot about it.

Amongst the letters, there was often one letter stamped
in a sketchy blue, the kind where you know the ink is low,
but someone in the post room tried to take it to its last leg.
Sketchy, but it was there. 'NHS', it said. Before I could hide
it, she, my little sister, Yasmin, would be looking over my
shoulder, panting, breathing hard, hopeful for a Topic, dis-
heartened a little, again, but then she would see the envelope
in my hand. She recognised those three letters better than
the rest of us. NHS. Those three letters were the organisers,
the directors, the executives of her life. That letter would be
the summons, still is the summons, that would reveal her
plans for the coming months. They dictated ours too.

When that letter was printed and stamped and posted,

there was no thought as to where it was going and what it meant when it hit the cold, worn, £5-a-square-metre carpet of our house. It meant destiny. It was hers and she lived it and she feared it. I would see it in her expression for just a glimmer, just long enough to see the tears gather in the wells of her big Bambi eyes, saturated to bursting. One blink and a tear would plummet to its doom, tumbling down her plump Cabbage Patch Kid cheek, and then she would run straight into hiding. She never hid well. She would sit in front of the television. Switched off and black. I would look at her reflection in the dark screen, illuminated by the sliver of light that escaped the thick, patterned curtains. She would cry, her tears flowing freely now, the ones she seemed to have on reserve for occasions such as this. Her face wet, dank with dejection.

'Not again.'

'We don't know what it is, it could be good news.'

It was never good news. I knew that. She knew that. She knew I was lying, consoling, deflecting.

'I don't want to open it.'

She never did. Someone else always did it. We all had different ways.

Mum would leave it for a few hours. She knew that from the moment she opened that letter, it would dictate where she would be and for how long. It was an unwanted, unplanned holiday. She got away from looking after five other kids, but all the stress of childcare was concentrated into one. My sister's heart was broken but mum's heart broke a little more every time her daughter's was a little more fixed. She needed a good cry and some amateur dramatics to go with it whenever we received one of those letters. Once that was out of her system she was ready to open the envelope. 'What can I do if you die?' Never a helpful thing to say to someone who is about to be lying on the butcher's block.

Dad would rip it open furiously. So much so, the envelope would be torn to pieces. Like a small untrained puppy had been at it. He would rip, shred and lacerate it, and all the remnants would tumble to his toes. Leaving a very buckled letter in his wake. He would read it and stare at it for such a long time. Despite 'What does it say?' being repeated in various voices, he would ignore us. He would either read it over and over, in quiet repetition, never moving his lips, or he was just staring at it. Either way we didn't have the guts to approach him; we just waited for him to come out of his NHS-induced temporary trance. 'I bet he can't even read.' I always said that in my head, never managed to gather the bollocks to say that one out loud. My thought stayed back with all of our feet. He needed space and time. 'Just another one, like the rest of the operations.' Denial is useful at times like this. But was it denial or was this just his normal now?

When we opened the letter – by we I mean any of us children old enough to do it – we would switch between babbling a pep talk to our younger sister and slowly tearing one tiny bit of the lip of the envelope. Stalling? Most definitely. None of us really wanted to see what was in that letter. Yasmin would eventually just take it right out of our hands and open it up like a normal person. No ripping to shreds, no delaying, no stalling. It was her inevitable and she knew that better than anyone. So she opened it, robust and receptive. She knew what was what and this was hers. She faced it.

'It's just a stent.'

The thought of having a pipe shoved up my thigh into my heart and a balloon put into an artery . . . well, that just scares me. Scares me something mindless. But for her it was *just* a stent. After having had your chest opened up and your heart fixed outside of your body, a stent really did feel like a walk in the park to her.

She had courage. And she gave us a molecule of her spirit, to help us through, whatever the procedure, big or small.

I took her one time. She was fifteen and I was eighteen. It was my first time on a train. I may as well have been on the butcher's table myself, I was so stressed about the journey. So overdramatic, I know! But it felt like it would have been the easier option. I sweated profusely as I tried to appear confident in getting her there without being late. In my head I had concocted a plan: if I was late, I would take her around London and show her the sights, the ones I had never seen before. Then if the fear of getting told off was too high, we would live out the rest of our days in London. I would get a job at a cafe, resorting to petty crime if need be. I would have to drop out of college, because there would be no time for that with a teenager to provide for. I would enrol my sister into school and that's how life would go. My parents would forget we ever existed because we were such disappointments and that would restore the balance of love/hate and revenge/ forgiveness and all would be good in the world.

Luckily, I did not have to resort to a life of beverage-making and petty crime. We got there, sweat patches and all. She was none the wiser that I had no clue, that I wished she had never got that letter. It was that letter and my big mouth that had got me into this monumental, tacky, perspiring, putrid mess. My transport-related problems seemed bigger than hers, just for a while. Totally selfish! Till we walked around the corner and in the distance we could see the name of the building appear: Great Ormond Street Hospital. I let out the biggest sigh. 'We made it.' I was filled with a sense of triumph and gave myself a metaphorical pat on the back. She was met with a sense of impending doom. We had to meet somewhere in the middle – in fact, forget the middle. I had to meet her wherever she was and it wasn't a happy place.

By fifteen she had been in and out of hospital so often, I had lost count. But she always left from the house. We said goodbye at the door. She left. We got on with our day. We waited for the call to say she was out of surgery. We waited to hear that she hadn't died. That became the routine. This time I was there. I got to see the in-between.

'It can't be that bad, surely,' I told myself. 'You come in, they do their thing, she leaves.' But she wasn't a pet; this wasn't a vet. She was a human. A human to them and a sister to me. This was much more. I had not realised how much more and what I had really signed myself up for. I regretted volunteering myself, selfishly. I knew from the moment we walked under the air conditioning unit that blasted our heads at the entrance of the revolving door, from the moment our nostrils filled with the smell of sanitisation and unease, I knew this was something I had not prepared for.

How did my parents do this every year?

She stopped being my sister from the moment she was nil by mouth. The operation would take place in the morning. I slept through the night on a chair beside her. In and out of sleep, she bleeped the whole night through. Disturbed by a friendly nurse, with a face of caution, who woke us both. We hated her for it. She knew it. From the moment my sister woke it was a blur of white coats, swabs, needles and signatures.

'Would you like to be with her when we put her to sleep?'

Absolutely not, no way in hell, I can't watch her be put to sleep, it would be like watching her die, no way, no how, not happening. That's what I told myself.

'Yes.'

I walked into a room, my hands and feet covered in plastic, top to toe in white. My sister lay there, eyes wide with fear. In a cold room. She was so cold. Someone turn up the heat, for God's sake! Why did it feel like a morgue? Why did this place feel like the end?

'You mustn't touch her face or body, but you can hold her hand.'

I held her cold, purple-tinged fingers.

I couldn't touch my own sister. I couldn't wipe away her tear as it trickled down her Cabbage Patch Kid cheeks and into her tear-soaked hairline. I wanted to tell the doctor to f*** off.

'I'm scared.'

'I'm scared too.' I tried furiously to hold back my tears and failed miserably. I felt a hand on my shoulder. Reassurance.

'But I will be here when you wake up.'

'What if I don't . . .'

She was asleep. I'm glad she never finished that sentence.

'What if she doesn't wake up?'

She woke up.

'Hi Affa [meaning older sister], am I awake?'

'Yes, you are.'

And alive. She didn't die. The epitome of life.

Six of Six

I looked at my hands. Fingers extended out in front of me. Like when you have your nails done, inspecting, making sure you got what you paid for. My nails were painted all right, just not the shade I had picked. In truth I didn't want them painted. Dad never let us paint our nails. He hated it and so we never did. Doesn't stop me now, though!

'Please can we paint our nails, Mum?'

'No, you know your dad will have me and you lot if we paint our nails.'

I wish she had wavered. Painted our nails and then taken the varnish off before he got home. Opened up all the windows to get rid of any hint of the acrid remover liquid. She never did though.

Now my nails were a shade of ombré, two-tone tie-dyed black and blue with a hint of purple. All the rage if you're on the receiving end of a pair of bullies' rage. I never called them that at the time, but that is what they were. They painted your nails for you, no charge. The more I extended them, the more they throbbed. So I extended them as much as I could bear. If I felt the pain now, it would go away faster. Strange theory, but that kind of theory makes sense when you're ten.

It had been just after the last lesson of the morning when it happened. Our form room was in a small, stiflingly warm Portakabin-style makeshift classroom. The kind that probably would not be allowed now, for various health and safety reasons. They cared less in the nineties and here we are in the twenty-first century and it feels like we care too much about the wrong things. I wonder if there was ever a middle ground, did I miss it? Damn if I did!

I don't know why they picked me. I asked myself often, 'Why me?' Various reasons, I told myself. I was the only girl bold enough to wear trousers and not a shalwar kameez – traditional as it was, it was faffy and I was not going to wear it. I was the only girl with hair cut like a boy. Not in a cool pixie crop: I had curly, frizzy, unruly hair, which never had the pleasure of meeting a bottle of conditioner. I didn't like it. I wanted long hair like all the other girls; I wanted to put bobbles in it, bows and suchlike. But I think having my hair cut like a boy made my dad feel like he had another boy –

except I wasn't; I was a girl and on occasion I wanted to feel like one. So trousers suited me; at least I looked the part. Imagine having hair and clothes like a boy, but being a girl? Not so accepted then as it is now. Maybe I set the trend and didn't know it!

As I walked out of class to go to lunch, they waited in the gap between the Portakabins. I had become used to looking over my shoulder. Because no matter how much I tried to hide, they were there. They came in a short-sighted foolish double act. The kind that thought that they were really amusing but they were the act and they were their own audience too. My previous attempts to ask for help had been futile.

'Miss, I'm being bullied.'

'Ignore them and they will go away.' I ignored them and they never went away.

So I stopped ignoring them. They were there. So was I.

As I walked out that lunchtime, one of the dopey double act – always the same one – gave me a greeting with a willy, peering out of his grey trousers. He would wait unzipped, ready to show off his wares. I know now as an adult that he would have worked on it, waiting for my imminent arrival, to get it into the aroused state. As a mother of two sons who have surpassed that age now, I often wonder what led those boys to become so vicious, so damaged, to behave in such an intimidating and sullied way. Were they not told that they were loved? I never grew up being told 'I love you' but I wasn't flashing my vagina to people I disliked. What happened to them?

I wanted to tell my parents but their minds were preoccupied with two sick kids. I get that. Perspective is hard to learn when you've only just got used to double digits. But we had no choice except to learn and to live. My problems were never going to be bigger than life or death.

'Look at it,' he said as he pulled out his manhood.

Disgusted, ashamed, embarrassed, I turned away. 'You're disgusting.'

'You're disgusting, you black bitch!'

He grabbed my hair. The only time I have ever been pleased to have hair so short you couldn't grab it from the back. But enough hair to draw some blood. Then they held my hands down into the hinge of the Portakabin door I had just walked out of, carefree in the knowledge that I was going to enjoy my pizza, mash and beans. Maybe even a slice of farmhouse cake with pink custard. But no. I was going to eat my words for lunch. My hands in the hinge, being held down, I couldn't fight them off. I had tried weeks before when they flushed my head down the boys' gammy toilets, but to no avail. I wasn't even going to try this time. I lie. I tried. But they were strong and I had accepted that this was going to happen whether I liked it or not. Two of them, one of me.

I couldn't even count it down in my head. They slammed the door onto my fingers three times. It hurt the first time, but the second time – when you know what it felt like the first time – it hurt a tiny bit more, and by the third time I told them, in my head, 'Please stop.' They stopped. I got off my knees and ran with the faint sound of 'ugly black bitch' in the background to mix in with the pounding of my heart and the throbbing in my chest. I cried because it hurt. So much. My fingers, everything, it all just hurt so much.

I remember being back at home, later that afternoon, sitting on the side of a bed – whose I don't know, though it could well have been my own. My feet didn't touch the ground yet, so they dangled. Everyone was downstairs. I could hear the faint sound of the television and my mum's Singer sewing machine rattling occasionally. Some talking, some laughter, some telling off. I had taken my dad's pack of paracetamol from a box my mum kept in the living room. These days we keep medicine in high places, out of reach. Back then, not so much. Perhaps the fear of an overdose or taking medication that isn't yours wasn't a worry in those days.

I sat there and patted my pocket. I knew they were in there, all one hundred of them. Barring the two missing that dad had taken for a headache. So ninety-eight. I thought back to the conversation I had overheard a few weeks back. My cousins were all boys and they lived in their own alternate universe. From what they wore to what they ate to what they laughed about – it all felt alien to me. I didn't much like boys anyway. So there was no appeal there. One of my cousins spoke about a guy who killed himself after having a whole box of paracetamol.

That's what I had: a whole box. In my pocket right now. I didn't know what death was. Not really. All I knew was that it meant not living the life I had now and I didn't like my life.

I didn't want to be in it. So I wanted to leave it. I had never swallowed a tablet, not ever before. 'Dying is easy, everyone does it,' I thought. 'Why wait? I can just do it now. Then I don't have to go to school tomorrow.' I didn't want to go back to school.

Would I have to eat the whole box of pills? I could do that. I had seen my mum take pills her whole life; she always took paracetamol to get rid of her headaches and if I had the whole box it would take away my problem too. I took out six paracetamol tablets. I figured that would be a good place to start. It had to be; that was about as many as I could manage to extract from the tightly sealed plastic and foil casing. Some whole, a few crushed from the struggle of trying to release them.

I tried to swallow my first. It was harder than it looked. No amount of tilting my head in every angle helped to get that pill down, but by the time it did it had partially or mostly dissolved itself in my mouth, leaving the most bitter taste. Even more bitter than having fingers slammed in a door. This was not going to be easy. I chewed the second one and the third and then I ran out of water. My stomach bloated, full with liquid from my feeble attempts. The universe needed me to go downstairs, I know that now. It had a plan I knew nothing about.

Not feeling quite dead yet, I was excited that I was about to do this. I was not going to get bullied tomorrow. I, without any help, had found my way out. I felt quite the grown-up. But first I just had to go downstairs to fill my empty glass.

As I walked across the living room, I noticed everyone was huddled around my mum. What was going on?

'Tell them, tell them!' Dad said to Mum. She had something to announce but she was not about to say it. She looked angry, disgruntled even, sitting at her sewing machine.

But Dad was going to tell us; he wanted to tell us with or without her permission.

'Mum's having another baby!'

A roar of excitement. An actual baby!

I joined in with the celebration at the thought of another sibling. Quickly reminded by my empty glass that I had a job to do. I filled it up and went upstairs. Every step leading up to that room felt heavy. I jumped onto the edge of the bed, feet still dangling. Then I paused to think.

'I will do this, but after the baby is born.' I had to meet this baby; after all, he or she was my brother or sister.

I packed away what was left of the tablets and quietly left them in my parents' room. I drank what was left of that water.

My brother Shak was born on 6 August. I held him in my arms: tiny hands and feet, a little squashed nose. He looked up at me. I had never seen anything so small or needy.

'I can't go anywhere, I have to stay for him. He will need me.'

So I stayed. The epitome of a new life in more ways than one.

*

Jasmin and Yasmin, Sadiya and Nadiya, Jakir and Shakir. We used to hate the pairings once upon a time, not so much any more. I think it's rather cool, despite the lack of creativity, or maybe it was just meant to be.

My siblings and I protect one another; we are our very own friendship circle. We have room for more but we are not currently recruiting. We are brave for the weak amongst us, when we suppress the weakness into the most guarded parts of our soul and cover it with bravery. We are life – the reality, the harshness, the truth that is life, we are it. Because we live it, we breathe it, we are it. Hope: when there is a glimmer left, we find it and capture it, and if we lose it, we look for it again.

The protection, the friendship, the bravery, the life, the hope – these are the threads that make up the bulletproof vests we wear. They are mine and I am theirs. When those bullets are fired they ricochet off each of us.

'What if we stop wearing our vests?'

I live in fear that one day someone will take that vest off. I certainly have, on occasion. 'But what if one day someone takes it off and never puts it back on again?' All those bullets that ricocheted off us will finally penetrate.

It's okay to be scared, to feel fear, but what fear doesn't know is that I have them.

TUNA PATTIES

This is the recipe for our tuna patties. We made this when we were not practised enough to make samosas properly and didn't have access to the internet for long enough to learn how to make the delicious salt cod Jamaican patties we would buy from the indoor market in Luton town centre. So this was what we made instead. Shortcrust pastry – easy enough to buy – a can of tuna, onions, spices and we're not far off a samosa-slash-patty hybrid.

Makes 8

You will need:

1 pack shortcrust pastry, ready rolled – if we're going
    to cheat, let's do it properly
4 tbsp vegetable oil
2 cloves of garlic, grated
1 medium onion, finely chopped
1 tsp salt
1 tsp chilli powder
½ tsp turmeric
1 tsp ground cumin

1 tsp curry powder

1 can tuna (145g) in brine, drained and moisture
    squeezed out

1 can sweetcorn (198g), drained

Small handful of fresh coriander, finely chopped

2 tbsp full-fat mayonnaise

1 egg, lightly beaten

How to make it:

Start by making the filling. Be sure that your pastry is chilling in the fridge, defrosted if it's come out of the freezer.

Add the oil to a small non-stick pan or frying pan. When the oil is hot, add the garlic and stir around for a few seconds, making sure that it doesn't burn.

Drop the chopped onions in straight away along with the salt and cook on a medium heat, stirring all the time, until you have soft, light brown, translucent onions that will be lovely and sweet.

Lower the heat and add the chilli, turmeric, ground cumin and curry powder. Mix through and cook out for 5 minutes on the lowest heat.

Now mix in the tuna and sweetcorn – remember, all this is already cooked so all we need is for the flavours to mingle.

After 5 minutes, take off the heat and transfer into another bowl. Stir in the chopped coriander.

Wait for the mixture to cool completely, then add the mayo and mix through.

To make the patties, start by lining a baking tray with some baking paper and pre-heat the oven to 180°C/gas mark 4.

Unroll the pastry till you have the whole sheet laid out, then make 8 even squares or rectangles using a sharp knife or pizza cutter. Separate them out a little so now you can work on filling them.

Divide the filling between all 8 squares, making sure to put the filling on only one half as we need to use the other half to fold over the top and encase it. Leave a gap round the edges too. Be warned: it is really easy to overfill and you will know if you have when you go to encase the first one. Don't be deterred if you have some left over – it makes a mean jacket potato/ toastie/sandwich filling.

Brush the pastry edges very lightly with the beaten egg on the half that has the filling. Now fold over the other half and encase.

Use the end of a knife or fork to seal around the edges. Pierce a little hole in the top to allow some steam to release itself and pop onto the prepped tray. Brush the remaining beaten egg all over the top. Do the same for all the other patties.

Bake in the oven for 23–25 minutes, until you have a lovely golden top and the base of the pastry is no longer soggy.

I like to eat this with ketchup and it is as simple as that really.

⟶⟍⟋⟵

GRANDDAUGHTER

Your hips punished from birth and death.
Mine remain rounded, limber, intact.

Your hands crusted, rough with the labour of love.
Labour of duty.
Mine are soft, nourished.

Your eyes worn from what they have witnessed. Hopeless.
Mine still gleam. Hopeful.

Your feet sore, from the path they have taken. Bare.
Protected, mine sit pretty.

Your back bent.
While I stand tall.

Your dreams stopped somewhere.
I see mine grow.

One day your journey will end. Somewhere in the road.
Mine will keep going.

I will take your punished hips,
Your crusted hands,
Your worn eyes
Your sore feet,
With your bent back and stop on the road too.
Just like you.

I scurried back from the cloakroom with my bags in tow. I said goodbye to my clown picture next to my hook, like I did every day. He was a creepy kind of clown but he smiled so I always smiled back and propped myself onto my knees to rub his big, red, slightly faded-in-the-sunlight nose. I walked up to the line of children, tuning into the swooshing sound of my corner-shop carrier bag against my shell suit, all made louder by the raincoat scrunched into the bag. One step forward, followed by the next step. Till I reached the end of the line, right next to my friend. I stood beside her. My arm against hers – attached was the way we liked it.

Mum was in hospital, with my brother.

The line got shorter; the crowd outside got smaller. The playground quieter, the nursery airier. As the wind whistled in the playground, the teacher's steps echoed in the classroom. My friend and I stood there, arms still attached; if her mum was coming, then so was my gran. They lived on the same street, so their paths always led to us. There she was in the distance, my friend's mum. Her face filled me with dread because my nan's face did not precede hers. I looked past her and still no Nan.

My friend glanced over at me. She knew that I would be alone. I could see it in her face and I think she saw it in mine. She was going to leave me. If I wasn't holding her hand on the way home, swinging forwards and backwards till our sockets felt like they would dislocate, whose hand would she hold? She looked at me as she was wrapped up extra hard by her mum, top button fastened, nearly taking out her lip. Then she was dragged away, her arm in the air, into the empty playground. With an attempt at a hopscotch manoeuvre, she was promptly ushered to the right and she was gone. My arm felt lost without her.

'Who's picking you up today? Mum?'

'She's in hospital.'

'Is she not well?'

'She's in hospital with my brother . . . he's having another operation.'

That shut her up. They never really knew what to say.

My teacher ushered me along to a table and that triple rustling sound, of shell suit against carrier bag against raincoat, whooshed in the empty room. It was loud. I walked over and sat at the table. I was handed a piece of paper with some jumbo crayons. I didn't want that yellow one because I once saw a boy shove a yellow one up his sticky nose. So this picture was not going to be sunny.

I watched her stand, with her arms crossed, peering over into the distance, through the glass. She tiptoed onto the balls of her feet and her heel pinged out of her shoe. She rubbed her crossed arms and squeezed her upper arms tight. As a grown-up now, I realise she probably had a family to get to – children, a husband maybe, a dog to pick up from the sitter, a long drive home out of town, a hair appointment. That's what grown-ups do; they make plans, and she probably had some that were being scuppered by the tardiness of my primary caregiver.

I didn't know that then, but I certainly felt her anxiety, her frustration, as she scowled at me every time she walked away and walked back, only to see nothing but the same in the distance. An empty playground.

'Is she here yet?' I asked. I could feel my heart racing now. Colouring seemed like a feeble task as my mind wandered wildly. *Maybe she's dead, like how Nana died in the street, maybe she's forgotten, maybe she doesn't know to pick me up, maybe she's dead, she has to be dead.*

'No, she is not,' my teacher snapped.

I resorted to using the yellow in the end; after all, what is a picture without some sunshine, even if it is mixed with a little bodily fluid?

'Is she here yet?'

'Will you just be quiet and colour!' There was annoyance in her voice and in her words. She stomped across the room to a telephone, situated out of reach above our pegs. It almost never rang, but when it did, the classroom would become instantly silent. She dialled furiously and spoke to someone. Her face getting redder and redder by the second. I never saw faces this red. Only the white faces of the teachers at school got red. Everyone I knew became their own unique shade of burgundy. At school they went from pink to red to blistering and she was blistering.

Maybe she had a child to pick up. I suppose I will never know.

I looked up and there she was in the distance, her camel-coloured coat billowing in the wind. She had failed to do up her button, because her rice-twice-a-day stomach never allowed her to. The geometric lining was visible with every gust. She ran. I had never seen her run. She was either stationary or moving at an even speed. Her face flushed, out of breath. She knew she was late, and as she rushed in, her headscarf was blown clean from her head. I watched above me as she said 'sorry' in as many intonations and accents as she could. The palms of her hands held together at her chest, in the perfect namaste positioning. She apologised profusely as she tried to catch her breath.

'Why are you late?' Nan looked at me to translate. But before either of us could remove our eyes from each other, my teacher had scurried out of the classroom and pushed us with her. Slamming the door shut behind her, she locked it furiously, then flicked her wrist at us to move us along. Her arms flailed around as she swung her coat on. I hope she made it to her appointment, or to pick up her kids, or to the salon, or to her hot date, or to dinner. I hope she made it to wherever it was she had to go.

Nan, still out of breath, secured my hat firmly and gave me a little flick on the nose with her nose. That was her kiss. That was her thing. Her nose touched ours, with a tiny little flick at the end as she breathed us in. Holding my hand, she walked across to the other classrooms, picking up the remainder of her grandchildren, meeting one furious teacher after the next. Her sorry becoming more and more frequent and excessive, her posture changing; by the end of it she could no longer look any teacher in the eye. At each one it went from bad to worse. With nothing but upraised hands to ask for forgiveness, it was not enough of an apology for taking up their time.

She cried on her way home. As she gradually got her breath back, she wiped her tears.

'Do you think Jak's dead?' I enquired.

'Don't say that!' I got shot down.

'Why are you crying?'

Why was she crying? She didn't cry because she was late. She cried because she was lost. In a country she had to live in for the sake of 'opportunity', when all she longed to do was to go home. To feel the sun on her face. To go to a place where she could understand the muttering of the people that walked past. So she could speak, smile and relate. Here all she had was sorry. She was always sorry and she was always thankful. That was as far as her vocabulary extended. Sorry and thank you. But maybe she wasn't always sorry.

What she wanted to say that day was: 'Sorry I am late, but I am never normally late and today was a one-off. I have misplaced my keys and I couldn't leave my door unlocked, but I have anyway, because I know I had to pick up my grandkids. Sorry for keeping you, but as you can see I am out of breath. When I realised my attempt at relocating my keys was proving feeble I weighed it up and decided that I could not expect you to keep my grandchild longer than you needed to. So thank you for waiting. I am sure you have plans and if I have in any way destroyed them, I can but only apologise and I promise it will not happen again. I'm so sorry. I will have my grandchild now and be out of your hair so you can get on with your evening. Good day.' That would have shut up my teacher good and proper, but she saw just another immigrant lady amongst all the other ladies who picked up their kids and felt it fair to give what she knew could never be returned.

Nan and I walked all the way to the end of the road and turned the corner to her house. Her neighbour, a big burly black man, towered over his tall hedge as he trimmed it with his clippers. With every swipe the wind blew the cuttings into Nan's tidy, modest little driveway. She looked at it where it had settled as she scurried past.

'Don't worry, I will have that cleared up in no time, once I've finished here,' the neighbour said in his strong Nigerian accent. She smiled and nodded coyly as she walked through the unlocked door, ushering us in. We were met by the smell of her lemon chicken as it boiled gently on her cooker, wafting into my nostrils, making my stomach growl with anticipation. Not understanding a word the man had just said, Nan slammed the door behind her, wedging a chair in its path for safety.

'Look for my keys,' she instructed, and together we turned her neat house upside down. There they were on the windowsill beside her glasses. Relieved, she turned her attention to preparing the food, scraping the remains of a salad onto a large plate, then mulching it with her hands. The best kind of mulchy onion and tomato salad you will ever taste. But only *her* hands and *her* salad. Mum's never tasted like hers. She used the same ingredients – she practically had the same hands – and still hers was never quite like Nan's.

With onion-stenched hands she locked the door and dragged the chair back to its rightful spot. Right below the boiler unit that would injure anyone above five foot six, although luckily for our family there were very few of those!

As I waited to eat her lemon chicken, she prepared her mulchy salad and rice. She was tiding us over, before the chicken was ready. Those were not the days of a packet of crisps or a biscuit. It was rice and curry, rice and curry or rice and curry. They were the options. So it was a treat when she opted for rice and salad. Out there! I stood on her bouncy, camel-coloured, striped chairs and lifted myself up with the support of the windowsill to see if her neighbour had, as promised, taken away all the scraps of hedge. Turns out he had. As I sat back down she asked, 'Has he cleaned up the leaves?'

'He has,' I answered.

'He's good for a black person,' she replied. She would never get away with saying something like that now. She would be pulled up and questioned.

'He is,' I replied. 'If he was white he would never have cleared that up.'

'They don't like us brown people,' she said. She carried on mixing her rice on a large plate, in a circular motion that was almost mesmerising in its action as her wrists circled the rim. Her husband had not long died and his memories were still raw. His presence no longer there. He had been the man of the house. The guardian. He cared for her like a keeper of something valuable. He fed her, watered her and she gave him his children, his heirs. Her memories of him, his stories, changed; they tasted more and more bitter the older she got, and when she surpassed his age they became more bitter still. But she often spoke of the day he got beaten and left for dead by a pack of white men coming from the football. 'I never loved him, but nobody should do that to anybody, he did nothing wrong.' She didn't need education or language or a sense of belonging to understand that humans don't do that to humans. Her hatred for football remains. I am with her on that. I dislike football for various reasons but perhaps the violence it induced and her story of that night always stayed with me. After over fifty years in the UK, she has grown to quite like 'English people'. Anyone with fair skin is English as far as she is concerned. Always wary to begin with, she seems to warm up, welcoming a visitor in the only way she knows how, with a gesture and the other word she knows very well: 'tea'. She is more British than she cares to make out.

Sometimes she looked after us at our home and sometimes we stayed at hers. She lived just a few streets away, three minutes in the car, fifteen minutes on foot. She had more space at hers, a passageway big enough to use as a whole other room for playing amongst all the shoes. The novelty of not living there meant everything about her rooms, her things and the things that hid behind her cupboard doors, were all ours to be explored, even though we were not allowed.

I was always curious. I used to think the built-in cupboard at the end of her bed was where my grandad's body was kept. So when I shared a bed with her I would be transfixed by the cupboard door as it sat there ajar, just slightly open. I would peer into it, just for a few seconds, and imagine my nana was staring right back at me . . . and in that moment I would hide under her betel-nut-fragrant covers. My fear gluing my eyes shut for long enough to force me into a slumber. Being looked after by Nan in her house was an adventure, but it also meant it was a short trip. A few days, a small operation, same faff around the patient, just for a shorter time – and then we could go back to 'normal', whatever that was, until the next NHS-stamped letter fell on the bristled front door mat. Our normal was this, not the other.

When she stayed with us, she came packed with her things. Not much. She was never a woman of material possessions. She rotated two outfits. One that she wore and one that she washed. She washed herself five times a day but had a full bath on a Friday, before Jummah (special Friday prayers). She would quietly instruct us, as she handed over the remote, 'Put the television on and watch TV.' She would cover us under a duvet, which acted as the lock. We stayed under it.

'Don't get out from under the blanket,' she would say as she carried her belongings into the bathroom. 'I will be in the bath, I won't be long.' The bathroom was on the same floor at the end of the house. We could hear sloshing about. She would wash the bathroom, then she would wash herself and then she would use her bath water to wash her clothes. Despite us owning a perfectly functioning washing machine, she didn't see the point of turning it on. I think she never actually knew how to turn it on. She said she was being frugal; she was not wasting the water. Using a single bar of Imperial Leather she would wash her body, then it doubled up as soap for her clothes.

I could hear her wringing the clothes out as the trains on the track at the bottom of the garden flew past, shaking the core of the house. That train went by every fifteen minutes and I would count four trains. She was in there a long time. I would watch TV and imagine what it would be like to have no adults, just us! Like Kevin out of *Home Alone*. We could do the shopping, watch movies and gorge on treats and have no adults telling us what to do. Though I didn't fancy the bit where he got robbed. I daydreamed about being completely alone. Oh, the things we could get up to. That dream was shattered every few minutes when I heard the echo of her sloshing away in the bathroom. She was right there and we were never going to be alone. Although sometimes that's exactly what it felt like.

'Nan, are you not finished?' I would say, tapping on the door.

'Get back under that blanket!' she would scorn, in the least scorning type of way. She never raised her voice, ever. Instead she did a weird angry eye thing that made her look like she was going to vomit. That always made me laugh, though never out loud. She felt sorry for us; I could see it. She was our granny. She didn't sign up for this but she did it anyway. Because that's what mothers do for their daughters and that's what nans do for their grandkids. I see it in my own mum now. She is my nan and I am her. I call on her when I need her without a thought of her plans and she always says yes.

'Why do you always say yes, Mum?'

'Because you wouldn't ask if you didn't need me and you need me because that's why you're asking.'

She's not wrong.

'Plus I love my grandkids more than my kids now.' Also a truth.

I put the same question to my nan a few years ago. 'Nan, why did you always look after us when Mum was away?'

'Because she is my daughter.'

'Someone else could have done it.'

'As long as I'm alive, nobody else is doing it.'

Weeks would come and go. We would hear news of how they were doing. It was either my younger brother or sister in hospital. Or both at two ends of the country, leaving my mum nursing one and pining for another, torn between hospital and heart. Dad worked long hours and when he was home he was tired. When he was tired we stayed out of sight, herded away by Nan to stay quiet, giving Dad just enough sleep to recharge. So he could get back to his job, because his day off was about visiting the hospital. Replenishing supplies, taking clean clothes to be replaced by dirty ones. To leave optimistic and come back looking like he had seen a ghost. Another prognosis, another diagnosis, another insight into the future that seemed the same as the present. Full of travel, toil, worry and wariness. Long nights and sleepless ones too.

On a Sunday, Nan would turn the heating right up, which meant we had to get ready for our weekly bath. She would fill it right to the top. Mum never filled it to the top. But we always told Nan that she did when she assessed the level. Someone would need a wee and we'd have to turn the tap off while they flushed, till the Armitage Shanks had had a mouthful.

We would settle into the hot bath. As the water rose, we would float on the top, too light to settle on the bottom.

'You lot soak here while I make chapatis.' We would soak like little raisins in this hot stewing liquid, till the water would have the reverse effect on us and crinkle our fingers. It wasn't like we were going anywhere else. The water getting colder, she would be busy making her chapatis. The smell would waft into the bathroom just a few yards away from the kitchen, the charred smell of the flour. She would walk in, her cheeks pink from the fierce heat of the gas hob. Her face lightly dusted in flour. Dishevelled from the kneading and rolling, she was in a battle with the chapatis and it looked like the chapatis had won. Never, not if Nan was making them!

'Is this the shampoo your mum uses on your hair?' she said one night as she gestured to the half-empty bottle of green Fairy Liquid in her hands.

We laughed at her. 'No, that's for the dishes.' She was not having any of it. Not that day.

Squirt, squirt, squirt and squirt she went on each of our heads. Fairy Liquid, I know you claim your stuff is kind to hands, for which we are all grateful. But your stuff is not kind to the eyes. In total fairness to you I know that you probably have not tested your product on human eyes as that is not the purpose for which it was created, but my goodness does it burn! Nan lathered and lathered and lathered and the sheer weight of the foam weighed down my head. As she furiously tried to wash it out, we cried as the bubbles burned the corners of our eyes. To no avail she washed, drained and refilled the bath, hoping to wash out this soapy disaster. I could see the panic in her eyes, through the fireballs in my own. After a final rinse under a freezing cold tap, she sat with us as we huddled in front of the gas fire. Naked, with just the wet towel for warmth, we dried ourselves, Nan giving us an occasional rub of the back to check how dry we were.

We shivered at first, and I could feel my hair get frizzier till my towel began to do its work. She sat on the floor and said, 'Nani sorry,' followed by a full explanation in Bengali about why she had done it and why she wasn't sure and now she knows she won't do it again. She worried. We were her grandchildren but we were someone else's kids, albeit her own daughter's. She had a job and I could see in her eyes that she felt the weight of responsibility. She tore off a small piece of warm chapati, pinched a tiny bit of her spicy egg omelette into it and fed us one by one. Each of us swallowing faster than the other, ravenous after the longer-than-anticipated bath, until we were full to the brim.

Next she warmed up some olive oil in a pan and brought it to us. One by one, in a production line of clean little bodies, she moisturised our dry, ashy skin, and with every stroke of her warm, oiled hand she rejuvenated new life into us. Our skin turned from ashy to gleaming olive. One by one we ran upstairs naked, picking up the pyjamas she had tucked into the radiator to get toasty. Warm at the thought of our day, full-bellied, I lay in bed, for once not worrying about what was happening on the other side of our four walls. But that never lasted long.

One night I woke, scared suddenly, realising where I was. At home, but Mum wasn't home and neither was Dad. He was at work. He was always at work. Mum was always in the hospital. I missed Mum. I didn't care much for her when she was there. But I didn't like it when she wasn't. Everyone was gone. I looked over in the dark, straining my eyes to catch a glimpse. They were all gone. I ran over to the bed and tapped the covers. My sister wasn't there. I went to the next bed; my other sister wasn't there either. Where was everyone? I ran to the next room, where my brother slept. No one. Dad's room – he wasn't home either. I ran downstairs, my heart racing hard in my chest and my face hurting from resisting tears. She lay on the floor, with three extra bodies on either side of her. I sat by her feet; I touched her feet. I didn't want to wake her as she slept peacefully, but I stroked her foot gently in the hope that she would. I got up to walk away. They were not upstairs but I wasn't alone, so with some relief I got up to go away.

Her voice came out of the darkness. 'Are you missing your mum?'

'No.' Confident that she would believe my lie.

'Your brother and sisters miss her too.' She squashed my brother further into her chest and made room for me beside my sister. I quickly lay beside her and tucked myself into the blanket against her warm back and held onto Nan's hands as they remained splayed across the small sleeping bodies. She wasn't Mum, but she smelled like her and that was enough. She was enough.

My dad still tells the story of that night. He had had a late one at the restaurant. I don't know when he ever had an early one, there was always a customer who came in at midnight and needed feeding. So it was always a late one. Mum was in hospital and he walked in on Nan sleeping on the floor with four of us tucked up beside her. He described the scene as a litter of kittens with their mama cat. All huddled for warmth or comfort or instinct. Or whatever the reason that cats and all other mother-and-child combos do that. He felt sorry for Nan: not a contortionist by trade, she looked uncomfortable.

Gently shaking her awake, he asked, 'Shall I take a few of them upstairs?' It seemed the right thing to do with beds empty and rooms hollow of people and there we all were on the floor in the cold. But she refused to move so as not to disturb the slumber of her grandchildren, who had one by one left the comfort of their beds because they were home-sick in their own home. He attempted to peel my half-asleep brother out of my nan's arms and he point-blank refused. 'No, if I close my eyes I can imagine Nani is Mum. Please let me stay.' Dad placed him gently back down and took his pick of any room and any bed. He had the whole floor, but Nan had us and that's where we felt safe.

I loved going to her house. There were two reasons. First, she lived on the same street as my best friend. So if I was going to see Nan, I could make excuses to go and see my friend too, helped by the fact that my nan and my best friend's mum were also really good friends. Second, it was also the only place that no one really visited apart from us, so her house was always quiet. As much as I loved the mayhem of living in a terraced house with seven other people, on the tip of the Asian high street, with a train track at the back of the garden that rumbled the house every fifteen minutes, as much as I loved living amongst all of that . . . sometimes, just sometimes I longed for quiet. Nan's house had a calm about it. She had a television that she didn't know how to turn on and whenever she did she just railed against the nakedness she saw on there and turned it off anyway. She always had freshly cooked food. She never shouted and she was always in a state of prayer; she was either finishing prayer or just about to start or midway through, making up for the ones she missed as a kid. She was in credit. She didn't need to pray for a few years, at least! So apart from looking for an excuse to see my best friend, I longed for the calm of her house.

One day I walked to her house with my rucksack on my back – my excuse to see my friend. Maybe, but probably not, we would do some homework together then I would spend the evening with Nan. I walked the straight road: today felt different. Not in my head. In my body. I felt different. As I walked the straight road that led to her house, deep in my thoughts, I reminded myself to cross over before the house with the mad dogs.

The dogs were contained behind a steel gate higher than the second floor of the house. I always ran too fast to count how many dogs there were. The barks suggested about five but I think I counted three from a distance. Absorbed in some unnecessary thought, I was abruptly brought back to my surroundings by the sound of barking.

'Damn it.' My heart raced as I hurtled across the road. A car screeched to a halt right in front of me. A small man furiously wound his window down and peered out from the driver's side.

'Get out of the road, you dickhead!' Flustered, I ran back

to the side of the road where the mad dogs lived and as they started barking again, I ran some more till I was out of breath. I realised that I had never walked on this side of the road, ever! And all because of those mad dogs. I hoped for their death; they terrorised anyone passing. I hated those dogs. If they were not going to die I prayed that they would move, at least.

'Dickhead.' The word stayed with me all the way to the end of my road. I had never been called a dickhead before. It felt a very grown-up insult and I was not grown up. Black bitch, nigger, Phoolan Devi, fish, smelly Bengali, midget – these were the words I was used to. But never dickhead. As the word stuck in my head it was paired with a twinge in my lower stomach, but not like the kind in my tummy; this was from somewhere else. I walked past the corner where my nana had died. I remembered him vaguely. Sometimes I couldn't picture him at all and I felt bad; his memory was fading and I knew it. Not that I had a memory of him really, just stories, and they were on the wane. As the stories I heard from my family got shorter and more infrequent, so did my pauses on the corner where he died. On this day I sped past the spot as the pain in my stomach got worse. I knocked on my nan's door furiously and pushed past her when she opened it, throwing the bag across her wide hallway and running up the stairs to the toilet.

I needed to go to the loo; I wasn't sure what for but that was the urge and there it was. The one thing, the finishing line that all girls want to reach, especially when you go to an all-girls secondary school. If you started too early then you were an outcast, strange, weird – desperate, some of them would call it. Desperate for what? As if starting your period meant you were ready to have sex or procreate? A mentality that should have been left behind in the villages where it began seemed to permeate our supposedly modern school. I was not that girl, thank God! I was overweight and brown enough to have my own niche attributes ripped into by my peers; I didn't need to add another string to my bow. I was always happy that I was not that girl.

When you have sisters, you watch as they enter that world, as you wait in the queue to walk through the door. I had done just that. I walked through my nan's toilet door and was met with Mother Nature in my pants. There it was. Disappointing and underwhelming, I must add. I expected fireworks the way some girls described it at school. I was thirteen, nearly fourteen. It was the summer and I was so pleased that I was not at home when it started. I watched the change when my sisters told my mum. They were now women, which meant they were watched like hawks, their clothes washed separately, no mixing with male cousins – even affection with Dad was brought down to a minimum. They had to be ladies. I was not ready to be a lady. I loved my cousins and with all of them being boys, that made it tricky. I would miss my dad's beard rubs and as for washing my clothes separately, well I didn't care about that. Who cares?

What was this practice? It felt medieval. But my mum was doing what her mum did with her and what her mother did before her. As I sat with my pants at my knees, I wondered how I should deal with this situation. A year ago, a lady had done a school assembly and left us all packs of goodies – deodorant, sanitary towels, tampons and a leaflet that I had read a dozen times, for this exact moment. It would have helped if my bag were in the bathroom with me. The leaflet made no mention of what to do if you started your period in your nan's house, with the pack on the hallway floor in your school bag. Should I just pull up my pants and make a run for it? Is it a river or rapids situation? I didn't know what my flow was. With tissue not a regular thing in our family homes, I pulled up and ran. Embarrassed, my face red with shame, I ran down the stairs and felt a gush. What the hell was that? A foreign feeling. I grabbed my bag and ran straight back up. I did exactly what I had been shown in the assembly and walked out coyly from the bathroom. Gently placing my bag on the passage floor upstairs. My heart pounded.

I wanted to be one of those girls who just didn't start their period, ever. How would I tell Nan? How would I tell Mum? Maybe I could just keep it a secret so that nobody would ever know. I paced around upstairs. Do I have enough pads? How many do I use? What if I don't have enough? I wanted the world to open up and swallow me whole. It shouldn't be this hard, yet it was. I quite literally wanted to die right there. In my nan's passageway outside her loo.

'Come down and eat,' she shouted from the bottom of the stairs.

I walked down and sat there. She placed the plate in front

of me. I could not bear to look at it. For the first time, her food made me feel sick. I had to do it. Telling her would be easier than telling my mum; it had to be.

'Nan, I'm ill.' In my mind, 'ill' was code for either pregnant or on my period. I hoped she didn't think the former.

She touched my forehead to test my heat and reassured me that I was perfectly well and ushered me to eat, because if I didn't eat rice then I would certainly become ill. After about a dozen attempts to tell her, when I had considered giving up, she finally twigged my meaning as she washed her hands at the sink. She stopped and said, 'You need to call your mum,' and ushered me to the phone.

'I will tell her when I go home,' I said. I tried to convince her. But she was not having any of it; she handed me the receiver and left. I could hear the drawn-out ring and, panicked; I put it down. I was not ready to tell my mother. What would she say? What if she were angry with me?

I took a deep breath and tried again. My heart pounded as I dialled our home number and waited for it to ring. Please don't be home, I told myself. Hopeful that she had taken the next flight to Bangladesh and I could be rid of this feeling for a few weeks and revisit it at the same time next month. 'Hello,' she answered. Oh man, my heart sank. I hesitated, but she was in a rush; I could hear it in her voice.

'My illness has started.' Dear God, there, I said it, it's out there.

There was a pause. I knew she was sad, disappointed – another grown-up daughter. If I could have stopped it I would.

I would much rather not have blood pouring out of my bajiji every single month. I would have loved to keep everything as it was. I wanted nothing to change.

'Do you have what you need?'

'I do.'

'Okay.' Another pause. 'Are you staying at your nan's?'

'Yes.' Absolutely one million per cent yes! I did not want to go home. Not today.

As I popped the receiver down, I watched Nan peer out from behind the door. She handed me my bag. 'You're going home?' she asked.

'No, Mum said I could stay.'

'You can go home if you want.'

'Can I go to my friend's house?' I could go there and I could tell her that I was now a part of the period posse.

'Are her brothers home?'

'I don't know. Can I go?'

'No, she has brothers, it's not right for you to go.'

What in the actual world?! How can my entire existence have suddenly changed with a few drops of blood? Nan asked me several times that evening if I wanted to go home. Maybe she was just worried about me. Or maybe she didn't want to acknowledge the fact that I was having a period in her house, sitting on her furniture. Contaminating her spiritual surroundings.

That night she made a space on the floor. I slept on the floor and she slept on the bed. I never shared a bed with her again. I walked home the next morning, my sheets from the night before already soaking in the bath tub, the smell of washing powder staying in my nose till I got home. Scared to face anyone. I walked up the stairs to find my sisters as my dad shouted, 'I hear you're a big girl now.' No beard rub, no hug.

That's me, a big, big girl in an even bigger world.

Nan was our mother when our mum could not be there. She was the replacement, the fill-in. She did all the things that Mum did, but without any of the discipline. She raised us when no one else could. She loved us, when that love wasn't there. When the love was miles away in an overheated hospital ward. She gave us comfort. Even when she was late picking us up, she was there. Come hell or high water, despite the looks and insults of people in power, she stood and she did it with strength. She never wavered, she never wobbled. She just did it. Because that is all she knew. Orphaned and married within a decade she became a woman long before she was ready and she was a grandmother long before her time. All she ever knew was to be there when someone needed her, and someone always needed her. Be it duty or love. She never said no. It was never an option. She only knew yes. Yes to having no parents, yes to being a wife, yes to being a mum to dead children, yes to being a mother of her living children, yes to being a mum again to her grandchildren. She didn't know how to say no. She said 'sorry', 'thank you' and 'yes'.

If a tin can had a picture on it she could identify its contents, but if it didn't have a picture she didn't buy it. She only knew how to sign her name. She knew where our school was, and she learned that Fairy Liquid is for dishes only. She could read Arabic, but did not understand a word. She had an inbuilt fear of women. She feared what we would become if we didn't have the same restrictions as her. With no education or love to call her own she is a lioness even now, protective and honest but still deathly afraid of menstruating women. She is everything I don't want to be. She is everything I want to see changed in society, in communities. But I long to be like her too.

'If God made me a man, I would have been the best man, but he made me a woman so I can be tamed.'

I am the change she dreaded her whole life. I can be a lion and still be slowed down by a cramp every month. It is our world and I chew up the bit she never got a chance to take a bite out of.

THE BEST CHAPATIS

This is the recipe for my nan's chapatis. They are soft and delicious and she used to make loads and stick them in the fridge and somehow they never got dry. They were always so soft – which might be due to the huge amounts of oil. But who cares? That's what makes them delicious. She would never measure anything out; she just eyeballed it and got it bang on every time. I, however, enjoy using scales so I have done the measuring part for you.

This makes about 13 chapatis

You will need:

450g plain flour
2 tsp salt
2 tsp caster sugar
100ml sunflower or vegetable oil
300ml boiling water

How to make it:

Put the flour in a bowl with the salt and sugar and mix well.

Pour in the oil and mix together. It will appear lumpy.

Make a well in the centre and add the boiling water. Mix it thoroughly using a spatula. Once the mixture is cool enough to touch, tip it out and knead. It will feel sticky but if you keep kneading it, it will come together. Don't flour the worksurface.

When the dough is smooth, pop it back into the bowl and leave for 15 minutes.

To cook the chapatis, all you need is a pancake pan or a non-stick frying pan.

Divide the dough up into smooth balls, roughly the size of golf balls. Roll out each chapati to a thickness of about 3mm. Place the pan on the heat – no oil – and cook the chapatis one at a time for 3 minutes on each side.

These keep really well for about a week in the fridge.

―᠈ノ۱〜―

WIFE

The trim to my wobble.
The pale to my golden.
The smirk to my grin.
The sun to my blue.
The calm to my storm.
The spreadsheet to my notes.
The stomach to my cake.
The fire to my earth.
The saver to my spending.
The white chocolate to my milk.
The light to my dark.
The satnav to my A to Z.
The order to my jumble.
The hero to my zero.
The other half to my half.
You are the Abdal to my Nadiya.

*

The message was, if I remember correctly . . . Actually I can't remember the entire SMS because it was fourteen years ago, and a lot has happened since then. My goodness, I still can't believe we made the fourteen-year mark! I always count down the years of my marriage. Every year gets closer to the number of years I lived at home, and if and hopefully when I reach that twenty-year mark, I'm going to do a toss-up of which two decades I preferred.

My sister is nearly there in her marriage.

'Which did you prefer? Eighteen years at home or eighteen years being married?'

'Neither!' I think that calls for eighteen years on her own just to balance it all out.

Which would I prefer? The twenty years at home? Or the twenty as a married woman? Still not sure. Some may say I am indecisive or spoilt for choice. A bit of both. Definitely the latter.

So many memories have been formed over the years, some stored in the back of my brain that doubles up as a storage unit-slash-office space, others going straight into the trash. Everything is organised; it just needs to be alphabetised and given a light dusting – might even open a window at some point and let some air in.

So, where were we? The memory of that first SMS I sent. The first bit of real contact. It was so long ago, I don't think kids these days would have an inkling of what an SMS was. SMS: Short Message Service. I think, if I remember correctly, you could initially only use something like 128 characters.

Why 128? Why not 130? Or just round it up and go straight for 150? Those characters mattered, kids. Now we have WhatsApp, social media platforms, imo, Viber, I could go on and on . . . the number of apps is endless and all free! Oh, the world would have been a different place if I had had all those characters. Can you imagine the things I could have said? I would have been like a kid accidentally locked in a sweet shop. Only to be left with a rumbling belly and a sore head. Sugar and social media seem to have the same effect on the body. Amusing, that.

Oh, the good old days when you had to have money to contact someone. We relied on funds to be able to connect to another human. I relied on myself to top up my Motorola V195s metallic blue flip phone. It was all the rage and I saved hard to get that phone. So, if you got an SMS you knew you were easily in the top ten of people important enough for someone to spend money on. If you got two, well, you were up there in the top three for sure! When I spent that 25p on a text message, it would be full to the brim with words, numbers that made up words, single alphabet letters that stood for whole words and a distinct lack of use of the space bar. Because a space bar meant a character and a character meant a space and a space with no actual message was impractical and expensive. So if you had decided that this person was worth the single 25-pence transaction, you would have to make sure you said everything you wanted to say in that one SMS.

I had not decided if my future husband was worth even one SMS. Maybe he was, maybe he wasn't. How would I know if I didn't dare to spend 25 pence? I have never been attracted to saving money, but suddenly I was. Eventually I decided I was going to use all the characters just that one time and that would be that. Let's face it, he had no chance. I had already made up my mind. It wasn't going to happen, but I was willing to spend just 25 pence and only once. See what transpires when you give me all these characters? Like a kid locked in a sweet shop, I already had a rumbly belly and a sore head!

The message I sent was: 'I know this is an obscene time to text, let's just get this over with . . .' And that was me giving it a chance. Poor guy.

Why was I texting at an obscene time, and if I was, why was I admitting it, pointing it out? Surely if I were aware of it enough to mention it, then I shouldn't have been doing it in the first place, right? Apparently not. As for the 'get it over with', talk about deciding it was a no-go before it was even a no-go. Yikes.

Recalling this is like looking back at pictures of my over-plucked eyebrows, thinking, 'Why did I think that was a good idea?' It seemed like a good idea then. SMS, eyebrows and all. Put the phone and the tweezers down, girl, and get some sleep. You have two jobs; you don't have time for this!

I had hesitated all day before I'd finally sent that text. In fact, I'd had his number for close to a week before I'd done anything. I'd looked at it every day as I sat at my call centre desk. I took down patients' information and had one eye on the screen and the other on my phone. Occasionally batting both eyes to my cheese and stem ginger sandwich. Keyboard, screen, phone, sandwich, repeat. Should I text him or not? I always look back now and ask myself hypothetical questions. If someone had told me he was 'the one', that I would marry this guy and have children with him, would I have sent him that message? No way! Or maybe I would have? Thank goodness we can't determine our future, thank God there is no way of knowing for sure, because who doesn't enjoy the thrill of the chase?

For a week, I had never had to scroll very far – there he was at the top of my phone list. With the unfortunate name of Abdal. I think it's a nice name actually, uncommon. He was like Walliams to Williams. Distinguishable enough, if you look at the vowels properly. But when an A is followed by a B, it means he is on the top of everyone's call list. I have spent thirteen years seeing him looking at his phone for about three seconds, muttering 'pocket call' and carefully placing his phone back in his pocket as it buzzes away. Knowing full well that some unassuming parent has handed over their phone to a trigger-happy child.

There's that, but then there's also the other unfortunate thing about being called Abdal. Everyone, and I mean everyone, calls you Abdul. Emails, text messages, letters and suchlike, signed off Abdal, always come back with replies addressed to Abdul.

'Hi, I'm Abdal.'

'Do you mean Abdul?' Yes of course, I have been saying my name all wrong till you corrected me, says nobody ever, unless you're Abdal. I know when his eyes roll – even when they stay perfectly still in his head, I know those eyes are rolling in his metaphorical mind's eye.

He never corrects them. Not ever. Not anyone. If the communication is in written form, he has a passive-aggressive, bold capital-lettered ABDAL sign-off, evident in his brash keyboard tap, tap, tapping. In the hope they will notice. But in person he lets it go. It makes me cackle (on the inside, a lot), as I know that all the while he is keen to say something but is far too gracious to correct anyone.

So, I sent the SMS. There was no blue tick to confirm it. He didn't respond. All I had to do was wait. 'I will feel better, once I have sent it, then it's done,' I told myself. He did not respond – 2 a.m: nothing; 4 a.m: nothing. I woke up way ahead of my 6 a.m. alarm. Still nothing. I wished I had never sent the damn thing in the first place. The alarm went off and of course in true hysterical, marginally desperate fashion I mistook the first few beeps for a message. It wasn't my message tone, I knew that, but my eager, imprecise, intense mind had mistaken it and I leapt for my phone. Still nothing. I rolled over onto my back. I could have flung the phone out of the window. The one window that never shut, faulty like the dripping tap in the loo, which never got fixed. Nothing really ever got fixed. The window remained ajar all year round, whatever the weather. That was the purpose for this window, for this precise instance. For me to overarm my phone directly out of that three-centimetre slit in the UPVC window, so that it would bounce melodramatically on the edge of the wall and fall onto the winter tarmac below, hardened in the unfriendly seasonal air. I wanted to throw that phone out, along with my dignity or lack of. But, last to be picked for any ball sports, or any sport in fact, I had no chance. Even if that whole wall had been taken out, I would have missed. Throwing is not my thing.

'Why the hell did I send that text?' So many elements of my personality have unfolded over the years, some surfacing and then rapidly waning. Others perpetual in their presence. I should add 'foolish' to that ever-increasing list. I was beating myself up at 7 a.m. about a message I sent after midnight. Most normal humans are in deep slumber, shooting z's at that hour, and I expected a response when the world and the sun were barely waking up. There I was, pacing, licking my injuries, feeling unbelievably sorry for myself. Kicking myself. Beating myself up.

Waiting for the clock to turn, minute by minute, hour by hour, I looked but I didn't look. I pretended not to care but I did care. I brushed my teeth and kept my hand on my phone in case it vibrated. I got dressed, making sure to double check that the phone had been transferred from one pocket to another. Taking a peek. I ate my cereal, eyes fixed on the phone, vibration turned off, ringer off, but it would light up if I left it alone and kept my beady eyes on it. Still nothing. It sat on the passenger's seat out of the bag as I drove to the bank that morning. Still nothing. I had a love story in mind that day, a flutter, a stolen smile. None of that for me, just banking.

'It's okay, I will pretend I never sent it in the first place.' Click and delete!

Phone in my pocket, hurrying towards my parked car on my way back from the bank. I paced, perspired a little, held onto my chest. Conscious of my ill-fitting bra, making my boobs look like a pair of buoys, bobbing in the rough sea, uncoordinated and entirely unnecessary. Not the buoys, my boobs!

My beads of sweat got heavier, dripping down the nape of my neck, down my spine and saturating themselves into the top of my underpants. I saw what looked like a man in the distance. He looked like he might be a traffic warden in the blur of the slowly developing high street. I didn't have my glasses on. He got closer and I ran a little faster and sweated a little harder, squinted a little more. Turns out it was a woman, wearing a hat with a bumbag around her shoulder. I got that really, I mean really, wrong. I never did wear my glasses. I never seemed to learn either. I only used them for driving in the dark, when I had to drive through country roads to pick up my dad, really late at night. When he didn't feel like driving and I fancied being fed.

'Baba, I'm coming to pick you up, but it will cost you a king prawn butterfly.'

'Already in the fryer.'

'Can I have . . . ?'

'No.'

My glasses stay coverless and scratched inside my glove compartment, alongside a tube of sour cream and chive Pringles, some Johnson's baby wipes and a packet of Sainsbury's own-brand mint humbugs. Pringles for when I was peckish (I was always peckish), wipes for when my nephew's fingers and my dashboard needed wiping (I hate dust and I hate sticky fingers), mint humbugs because humbugs satisfy the elderly lady in me.

'Mint humbug, anyone?' I would say as people stepped into my burgundy Renault Clio, fully modified with debadged bootlid and bonnet, limousine tints, 16-inch alloys, flared rear arches, straight-through exhaust (with a Japanese-style back box with a 5-inch exit), lowered 35mm fronts with PI springs, lowered 55mm adjusting rear torsion bar, facelift bumpers, interior LED blue lights, full under neon kit, flamer kit, aftermarket head unit, subwoofer system and a KN filter.

'Don't go over the bumps in the car or the skirts will fall off.' That's what happens when you car-share with your brother. At least I had minty fresh breath as I navigated myself around Luton, avoiding speed bumps in a boy racer.

Reaching the car, I sat down and leant right in, making my clothes meet my back, meet my seat to soak up any residual moisture, leaving an unwelcome dampness on the fabric. I rolled down the window; the cool air as I drove would dry off my back in no time. I emptied my pockets into the central console – keys, spare change, phone. I wouldn't look. Or so I told myself, but I kind of did. There it was: a tiny unopened envelope in the corner of the display. Now you cannot get a message without being pestered mindless till you open it. Not this message – it sat quietly in the corner of my screen, waiting patiently. An inaudible, uncomplaining, pending, unopened envelope. If anyone were to be described as an inanimate techy object, this was the personification of Abdal.

I opened it. It had to be Mum, wondering where I was at the crack of dawn. Either I had left the gas on the hob alight or I had left the front door unlocked, or perhaps the kitchen tap running. All of which I was sometimes guilty of. 'Did I leave the water running?' I thought to myself. 'Someone will be up by now, surely.'

It wasn't Mum. It was Abdal. Or Ab, as I had saved him on my phone. A name I had never heard before. In the indecisive week leading up to my text I had typed his name into a search engine at work, with my chips and curry sauce steaming up the office windows and a can of Coke next to me on my desk. I pulled the metal ring towards me, droplets of cold water landing on the ends of my fingers. 'A,' I said to myself. Fat chance, the ring was never going to detach itself from its base on 'A'.

Millennials, this may not have been your thing, but there was a fortune-telling game when I was growing up that predicted the first letter of the name of the person you will marry. I know there are more modern ways of finding love. But everyone was doing it and everyone has a name, everyone has a first letter! So what if it actually worked? You flip a can ring and repeat the alphabet with each flip, as if to open it. When the ring detaches itself from the can, whatever letter you are on is the first letter of the name of the person you will spend the rest of your life with. It was the nineties, guys: we had to busy ourselves with things make-believe; we didn't have phones or tablets or very much else for that matter.

'A' was right at the beginning of the alphabet and there was no way I was getting that ring off with one pull. Just no way!

Does that mean no girl is ever destined to marry a guy with a name beginning with the letter A? I wondered. And vice versa of course, if boys were bold enough to play this game.

B, C, D, E, F, G, H, I . . .

'Who will it be?'

J, K, L, M, N . . .

'It's nearly coming off . . .'

O, P, Q . . .

'No way.'

R! I was hoping it would go full circle and end up back on A, but no, it was R. That was the first letter of the name of the cousin that my parents, amongst others, hoped I would marry. If it had landed on A, I would have been all for this Nostradamus Coke can. But seeing as it landed on R, it was a load of bollocks. It had to be.

Abdal's name meant a substitute, a good religious man, a saint, a religious devotee. As first impressions go, I was impressed, though even I knew at the tender age of twenty that despite his name he could be a total git. I knew a guy called Gabriel and he was certainly no angel. He used his wings to fly high and not in an angelic way. So if names are anything to go by, I had nothing. He could be horrible. Oh my goodness, what if he was repulsively ugly?

In my phone his name was pixelated amongst familiar names, like Jak and Sadi and Pink. I felt like they could see him as I saw their names in a list together. Why did I feel so guilty? Perhaps because I had never done anything like this before.

Why did I want a husband?

I'm twenty for God's sake.

Everyone I know is at university.

Why am I here?

I wanted to go to university but that was never going to happen; it wasn't allowed. I wanted freedom but the curfew was so extensive, freedom seemed pointless, untouchable. I wanted a way out because it was the only way I could be me. Or so I thought. Even though I didn't know who I was, I wanted to learn. But I wasn't allowed to do that alone. I had to have a guardian. A husband could be my way out. Or my way in. To where, I don't know, but it was never going to happen here in the confines of family, law, traditions, community and the whispers . . . oh, the whispers. Of aunties sitting around, as they quietly judged one another's daughters. On what merit? Who was the snowiest of skin? Who had the most pointed, Caucasian nose? Who was the slightest? Who spoke with the stillest of voices?

I had none of those things.

I was brown and not an even kind of brown. I was the kind of brown that suffered hyper-pigmentation, leaving me with dark patches on my mouth and light ones around my cheeks. So I was brown and a patchy brown at that.

My nose was small, short, button and flat – not a single point, not one angle to be seen, no matter how much I was told to knead it with the heat of warm hands. Still blunt!

I was not skinny, oh no – I had thick arms, thighs that rubbed raw, a belly that rolled and rolled and rolled and butt cheeks that protruded.

I was loud, opinionated and didn't take shit from anyone. If you told me I couldn't do something I demanded an explanation. But when I never got one I *had* to do it anyway.

The name of the man who could be my way out. My freedom. Abdal. I read the text message. I don't remember what it said, but we exchanged texts and before I knew it I had run out of credit. So in a rush to top up my phone for later, I put the keys in the ignition, neutral, turned the key and looked up to notice my eyeline was obstructed by a yellow and black bit of paper dangling down, firmly secured to my wipers. I curled my arm out and pulled the public penalty notice from under the rubbery wiper. It was my first ticket. I felt surprisingly proud of myself. First of many. I folded it and tucked it in the glove box under the baby wipes, slammed the door shut and drove off.

'Perhaps we could talk.'

It was his last message to me. But I had run out of credit. So this time he had to do the waiting.

Playing it cool did not suit me. With no credit, the last of my monthly wage spent on a food shop and Scoobies for my brother and a penalty notice to pay, I couldn't afford to text him back. 'I hope he remembers that I'm working till eleven tonight,' I thought. I fretted about whether I had remembered to tell him that information. There was so much to say; he was a whole unexplored person. Why would I have told him my working hours? Maybe I had. Presenting to him my fierce independent woman act. He called at exactly eleven. I was still at work, not yet finished properly.

Should I answer?

Should I let it ring out?

I can't speak to him for the first time and tell him I haven't logged off yet.

I answered quickly, in haste, palms sweating, throat dry and heart racing. What the heck was this feeling? And why did it feel like I was about to die? It felt like an amalgamation of low blood pressure and a sugar high, doing a loop the loop inside of me.

'Hello.' He had a kind voice.

'I can't talk, I'm logging off. Call back in five minutes!'

I slammed that phone down, pressing the red button, clicking it several times for assurance, click, click, click. He had officially been hung up on. That was a hung-up phone if ever I saw one. If first impressions were anything to go by I had made mine. It wasn't looking good. I had no reason to care but I did, a little too much. I cleared away, wiped down, binned and unplugged faster than usual. When I was done taking calls, I was out of there sharpish most days. I had a second job and if I wasn't in college, I was at my other job, and if I wasn't at my job I was at home. I was always somewhere but I never stayed for long because I always had somewhere else to be. Every so often I had to fight to break myself away from my colleagues' endless chats. They got really juicy.

'I was drunk and kissed him.'

'I think I might be pregnant.'

'I cheated on my diet and ate a whole bucket of chicken.'

'I'm cheating on my husband with someone in here.'

I was never a contributor but what they didn't know was that I was an avid listener. They were like *The Archers*, quietly playing in the background. It was like a soap opera playing in my ear and transforming itself in my imagination. All while taking patients' calls. That was when I always missed the best bits, the juiciest bits. My colleagues consisted of middle-aged women who did this job as an extra earner on the side and locum doctors who drove the gaudiest cars, parking badly in two spaces so no one would scratch their ego accidentally. I was from neither of those worlds. So I had no reason to stay for longer than I needed to.

'Where's the fire, Nadiya? You off on a hot date?' Not quite. What it felt like was the start of a severe panic attack, like dangling by a pinky finger on the edge of a precipice, with nothing but a peregrine falcon to witness my demise. I walked down the stairs and my phone buzzed in my pocket. I had never been on a date. I knew what a date was. But I was never going to go on one. Though the thought of being seated at a candlelit dinner, being non-alcoholically wined and dined, did appeal.

'Are you free now?'

I made myself free for six months. My green card. The land of promise. Prospect awaited. He might just be my way out.

I didn't want my parents to know we were talking. Nobody did. You didn't talk to boys and when you did, you hid their names under pseudonyms, ingeniously fictitious names that suited your acquaintance circle like Shabnam or Aminah. 'Ab' felt like a safe bet at first; it looked like an accidental contact entry that I was too busy or lazy to delete. I didn't want to copy everyone else. But if my parents got hold of my phone and saw messages or long conversations from someone other than the few friends they knew, they would know. So I called him Aminah for a while. 'Abs' was edited, 'Aminah' typed in and saved. I was scared they would become suspicious.

Aminah became my confidant. When I was tired and weary, Aminah heard it in my voice. Aminah knew. When I was frustrated I could vent all of my anger and there was silence, simply the sound of someone listening. I could tell Aminah things that I had never revealed to anyone, ever. Aminah was faceless, but Aminah was a voice, an ear, a shoulder. Aminah was companionship unlike anything I had ever had.

Not like a brother, with whom I shared history. I had no history with Aminah, just a back catalogue of answered questions and pitch-perfect answers.

Not like a sister, with whom I could share clothes. But could I share a whole life with this guy?

Not like parents. They loved us, but there was a fine line between nurturing and dictatorship and I felt like I was walking that line. Perhaps we could erase that line altogether?

We had never met in person. Tempted.

'What if we met up?'

'We can't.'

'I know.'

'So how was your day?'

Eventually, we told our parents instead.

They knew. Or at least I think they did. Were they surprised? I don't think so. Were they annoyed that they didn't get a say? Definitely. Were they happy? Not sure, but they had no choice but to be.

They just didn't know we had decided, without them. That we wanted to get married.

We exchanged photos. We saw each other at last. But so did they.

'She has good teeth.' Was that all I had?

'He is very handsome, but will a boy like him stay with a girl like you?'

He might, maybe.

A few weeks later, there we were. It had moved faster than I had imagined. But from the moment everyone knew about us, I lost control again. Within weeks we were on a plane and off to Bangladesh. We were married.

Abdal and I sat in the back of a blisteringly hot car. My tears dried on my face, midway through their downward tour of my cheek. The heat was concentrated, far more robust than I remembered it ever being in Bangladesh before. We had been to Bangladesh (or back home as my parents like to call it) every other summer as a family, but this was a different kind of trip. I was dressed in a triple layer of burgundy and gold. The ugliest thing I had ever seen.

'Can I pick my dress?'

'You picked the man, what else do you want?'

Let's see, to pick my own dress perhaps? Never mind. My life felt like a series of questions in my head to myself and a lot of never minds.

I was weighed down by intricately interlaced golden wire work, which felt like it doubled as an anchor. I never knew my butt cheeks could sweat: turns out, under extreme pressure, they do. My eyes heavy with tears, my heart heavy with fears. I was trapped in the back of a car and I didn't recognise a single face. Not one familiar face. I had left everything that was mine in a dusty road in the distance or in a terraced house on the other side of the world. I longed for my brothers' hands, my sisters' voices and the comfort of a pair of jeans and a loose-fitting T-shirt.

Abs, Aminah, Abdal, my husband, sat beside me. I fought the urge to cry; I didn't want him to think I didn't want to be there. I did, but I didn't. My eyes stung from the airborne dust, as the car raced and laced through roads I no longer recognised. Tired, jetlagged, my symptoms included the inability to stay awake when I was a passenger and not the driver. I wanted to kick the scrawny twelve-year-old driver off his cushion-propped seat and drive myself. Drying my back in my uninviting Renault suddenly felt a world away. All these thoughts were jumbled with the worry that, if and when I finally got up from this seat, I would present my very fresh new-fangled husband with an arse-shaped sweat mark as a reminder of the day we got married. I had longed so hard for a way out but now where I came from didn't feel so bad.

What the hell have I done? I am so scared.

We sat beside each other. He mopped his sweat up with a small rag. Perhaps he was equally nervous, but he was in a lot fewer layers than me, so I had zero sympathy. He might have been nervous but at least he wasn't dressed in forty layers in forty degrees of heat. The side of his knee touched mine. I flinched. I wanted to speak to Abdal, the kind, sweet voice that reassured me when I was a million miles away from sure. He wasn't here. I wanted to pick up my phone and call him. But his phone was stuck in a bag somewhere in the footwell of the car.

I had seen him twice before this day. Once for ten minutes, with my brothers and sister acting as chaperones. Very few words exchanged, perspiration and beaming smiles from under the cover of the draped sari on my head. The second was when we had our religious ceremony, the Nikah, where we sat alone in my parents' bedroom. We ate Indian sweets that lasted for no longer than a few minutes, and exchanged very few words. 'You look beautiful,' he said. I had nothing to say in response, except 'The wooden bead fell out of your sherwani scarf' (traditional attire at weddings such as these). That was my reply. The first time I felt his skin was when my fingertips touched the palm of his hands as I handed him his stray wooden bead. I still have that bead. I still have his hand. The third time I met him was when my dad gave me away in Bangladesh. That was the third time.

'I need to ring him.' He was right here, right next to me. But I didn't see him. All I saw was this awfully beautiful man, sitting beside me. The closest I had ever sat next to a man that wasn't my dad, or my brother. His eyes oriental, his thighs strong and a smile that could melt the polar ice caps. A smile that could outrun global warming. He pulled his long, shoulder-length hair out of his face and over his head, and from the corner of my eye I could see strands of hair tumble back down with every jolt of the car. I kept coyly glancing at him. I didn't want to look, but I wanted to look so desperately. He was handsome and I was attracted to him like a moth to a flame.

'Why does it feel like I'm cheating on Abdal?'

All those seedy conversations I had eavesdropped on at work were now my life. I had never been more confused. I knew that the Abdal on the phone and the Abdal sitting next to me were the same person. Or were they? Why didn't I believe it? What if the person I was talking to had misplaced his phone? Never returned, his phone unlocked by a stranger. Reading through the history, this astute stranger had hatched a plan to become Abdal and take over his life! So my Abdal was pining, somewhere in the midst of Leeds, mourning the loss of a love he only had one contact number for. While this stranger sat here, smugly taking over another man's life. I could have hated him, if only he wasn't so easy on the eyes.

I longed to hear his voice and he was not here. I wished he were here. Our day had been filled with rituals and etiquette. I felt like a circus act and not the main event at that. He was the other act, but he was the headline one. I sat, on display, with words from the crowd ringing in my ears.

'Why would you let your son marry such a black girl?'

'He's too good-looking for her.'

'She must be pregnant otherwise why would he be marrying her?'

'Maybe she's just fat.'

'She must have done black magic on the poor boy.'

'It will never last.'

'I could have found him a bride that really suited him.'

This had to be over soon. Surely they would have to stop the celebrations? They did, eventually. But they stayed so long, they managed to turn tomorrow into today. One by one they all left. The stranger from the car walked in and shut the door behind him.

'I thought they would never leave,' he said as he pulled his hair back from his face.

There he was. My voice, my comfort and all wrapped up in that beautiful stranger who had ridden that bumpy, unfamiliar road with me.

What I should have done was not get distracted by a

smooth voice that came through my phone's speaker. What I should have done was looked at the distance between Leeds and Luton. I'm not that daft; of course I looked at it on the map. They were only six inches away from each other. Luton was there at the bottom, where I lived, and Abdal was up there in Leeds. If I zoomed out it was even closer. If only life was as progressive as technology! I hadn't even heard of Leeds when I met him. Apart from our trips to Bangladesh, I had never really left Luton, so the world outside of me and my family was enormous, uncharted territory.

What was I thinking? For a girl who had a routine like clockwork. Back and forth. Work and home. Work and home. Work and home. Occasionally breaking up the monotony with a weekly trip to the supermarket, and a detour midway to deliver bread and milk to my nan. The engine still running, car door wide open, I would race to her door. As I sprinted up, I always looked just to my right. It had become a rite of passage in my own head. There was a small cluster of daffodils planted in her garden. 'Your nana planted those,' she would always say to me. So I always looked and remembered that my grandad planted those. I always looked for them, whatever the time of year, while I waited for her to open the door.

'I don't need any more bread and milk, I still have some left over from the shopping last week,' she would call from her wide open door, as I greeted her nose with mine and then made a dash for it in my getaway car. I wish I had turned that engine off more and just walked in. Always in a rush to be somewhere. The stained-glass-window peacock would shine an overcast tinted light through the door and reflect itself onto her withered, cotton, widow-white sari. 'Are you not staying?' she always asked. She always asked and I never really stayed, not often enough anyway. 'Don't bring me any more milk and bread if you go shopping next week.' We both knew I was going to go shopping next week and we were going to do this all over again.

What was I thinking? I wasn't. The exact distance between Leeds and Luton is 163.7 miles. That used to be a two-hour-and-fifteen-minute drive. Now with the intermittent roadworks splayed across the M1 it was a total of two hours and fifty-six minutes from my new home to any normal I had ever known. Normal didn't seem pitiful any more. Normal was what I craved and with the cost of petrol, time and judgement, it was a bitter pill I was having to swallow. But I had Abdal.

We settled down together in our house. Well, it wasn't ours. It was my father-in-law's and we were renting a room. We shared with two of Abdal's brothers, which already felt like a great idea. Some movement about the house would make it feel like home. My family seemed disruptive or just unbelievably loud, compared to living with these twenty-something-year-old men, who didn't walk around the house much, or use the kitchen much, or knock on your door for a chat before work, or clean the toilet much! Who cares? A quick first trip to Wilko's was in order. Spending what little we had on cleaning products was worth every penny as I cleaned a toilet that had never drunk bleach or had a scrub. I am quite literally gagging at the memory to this day!

First order of business within the first few days of moving in was that bathroom and I had already asserted my authority there. Now onto some more pressing matters: my clothes. I could clean anyone's toilet, but cleaning a toilet didn't make it a home. Putting my clothes in a wardrobe, however, did. I put it off for a few days, happy to live out of my cases, not accepting the distance or the new title. But I knew it had to be done, so I could move forward.

'So, where am I going to put my stuff?'

By stuff, I mean a total of two suitcases. With all of my life crammed and packed into them. I looked at them from the edge of the bed, unopened and dusty from the brief trip to Bangladesh. They had probably been thrown around in transit, without anyone caring that my WHOLE life was in those two cases. I lay in the dark, looking at the silhouette of the buckle, gleaming in the shadows with every passing car. 'I will open it tomorrow,' I told myself. I was using up all my resources, washing my underpants and drying them on the edge of the headboard. I needed to open it, to be reunited with my own things. But I was flat-out busy, between rationing underwear and early calls to help cook for the family of eighteen – my parents-in-law, my brothers-in-law, the grand-children. I had help in the form of my sister-in-law, but it was still harder than I had ever imagined. I was running between houses and quietly having panic attacks. One of the many things I failed to tell him about.

'He won't love me if he knows I'm damaged,' I thought. He deserved to know the truth, to hear it from me. But I kept it from him and now I had to suffer alone.

'There is only one cupboard; there's your space.'

I would not have even called it a space. It was more of a slit, a sliver, a gap. That shouted to me loud and clear: 'You have no space here.' Mortified, I stayed silent as I could feel my monster getting bigger. Abdal slammed the first suitcase onto its side, ripping open the zip in one long, clean sweep. I held back my tears, my jaws beginning to ache as I swiftly wiped an escapee that had made its way out of my eye. We were not married long enough for him to know, to feel my sadness. Mainly because he was too busy emptying out my case. As he threw a pile of clothes onto the bed beside me, I got a waft. A waft of home. The smell, the tiny hint of Daz, that darted up my nose and stayed there. The aroma of my mum's cooking that clung fiercely onto the fabric as it brawled with the Daz and won the fight, aromas colliding. Then the picture of my baby brother, hugging a gangly-armed stuffed monkey called George. I weaved through the piles and ran downstairs, picture in tow, and spent the remainder of the dark autumn morning crying on the unfurnished floor of the living room. I laid the photo on my lap and sobbed into my scarf, till it was salty and damp with tears of regret and failure.

I ignored the aroma of home and allowed myself to be consumed by the smell of new paint and new beginnings. 'It's okay to miss home, this is a normal feeling,' I told myself, as

I rifled through clothes that my sisters and I had bought together – same style, different colours. The odd socks that had made it in, the clothes that I should have got rid of years ago and the beautiful suit that my mum had made. Occasionally running my hands through the stitching that her hands had once touched.

'Get a grip, they are not dead,' I told myself. It still hurt. Even more so when later that day Abdal picked out some of my shoes, a pair of cork-soled sandals. 'Surely you don't like wearing these?'

'I kind of love those shoes and I have an outfit that goes with them,' I said in my head. Then with a gulp of air, out loud: 'No, I hate them, you can get rid if them if you like.'

Straight into the pits of a black bin liner, never to be seen again. We dragged the bags down the stairs, containing the little that made up my life, and they landed on the empty floor of the echoing living room. I realised that whatever I had left, the little I had left, was going, going and one day it would all be gone.

'Are you going to leave me?' he said softly. Nothing, I had nothing. The sadness consumed me and it consumed us. The sadness left nothing but silence and tears in its wake. I had no answer. I loved him so much but I was quietly spiralling into a plughole of darkness, getting more and more tangled as I fell further.

A flurry of words, sentences, just fell out of my mouth.

'I have a panic disorder.'

'I will never leave you.'

'But I don't love you enough to not want to die.'

'I want to be dead.'

'I don't want to be sad any more.'

Puzzled. He didn't get it and why should he? I'd never told him. I wasn't honest with him from the start. Perhaps I was afraid that my fear of never being good enough would permeate into the one relationship, the only relationship that was still pure, still totally unsoiled and unshaken. How could a man love a woman who came with all this baggage? How could he love me, when *I* didn't love me? He had the look of a man who had just been asked a question in Japanese and had no way of responding. He didn't understand the words that spluttered out of my mouth, through tears and snot. I had not understood the severity of not telling him the truth to begin with. I had to live with this but now he had to do the sentence with me. So he did what he did best. He sat on his computer. He crouched over the laptop as it got darker outside, the artificial light of the laptop illuminating his tense face. His eyebrows, his eyes, his nose all met in the middle, scrunched into his spectacles. Occasionally muttering or sighing. I couldn't watch him.

Despite the sadness I felt on admitting to this weakness, I felt a huge sense of relief. I was finally able to put down the stone that I had been carrying around with me for months. The evidence of its strain was still there, in my aching shoulders and rigid, curved back. But I finally got to put it down. I finally got to stand up straight. I walked out, afraid of judgement, as he let out an irregular sound from his vocal cords.

'Will he hate me for this?' Of course he does.

'Does he regret marrying me?' Absolutely.

'Does this change anything?' Everything.

Head throbbing from crying, my eyes stung as I squinted into the bright lights of the open fridge downstairs. Questions played on a loop in my head as I tried to work out the blasted microwave. I popped in the containers of chicken curry I had made the day before and finally worked out the metal contraption. I had not yet experienced the density of his love for me. For humankind. He was my husband. I was not honest. He didn't have a clue. I was lonely. He had a life here. He was my life here.

'Ping.'

I carried up a tray with a single tub of food, a glass of water and a plate. We ate in our bedroom. It was the only place we had to sit. Carefully balancing the tray as I climbed the stairs, slowly pacing myself, not prepared for what I was about to meet. I was afraid; relieved but really afraid. 'Concentrate on your breathing,' I chanted to myself as I used my back to swing open the door, walking in backwards. He took the tray out of my hands and placed it on the bed.

'I think I get it, I do. I get it.'

'I cooked for you.' The first curry I had ever cooked for him. A peace offering. My way of saying something without saying anything at all.

His eyes rolled back into his head as he swallowed his first bite. 'This is delicious.' He crammed in another mouthful, kissed me with his mildly greasy turmeric-stained lips. 'You are delicious. Would you like to see your family this week-end?'

'I would like that a lot.'

The start of our marriage: sadness, too many questions, not enough answers, but always followed by something delicious. Who knew? I didn't, but I'm glad we stuck it out to find out.

They say 'my other half' – that's how some people address their significant others, their wives, husbands, partners, soul-mates, best friends. Which suggests that they were never whole to begin with. I know, like many, what that feels like, to be looking to be completed because I was not enough for anyone, least of all myself. But my Abdal makes me feel whole. Not because he is the other half or because he com-pletes me or is the missing part to a thousand-piece puzzle, but because I am whole – wholeheartedly his wife, his com-panion, his best friend. Wholly his. There will always be questions and not enough answers, but we will work it out along the way, like we always do.

Also, as a side note, now I have four times more wardrobe space than him. Karma, baby!

—⁊ɪ↖—

ABDAL'S SWEET AND SOUR CHICKEN CURRY

This is his curry, but not because he cooks it. That wasn't the case over a decade ago and it certainly isn't to date. This is the recipe for that first curry I ever made him. It has bittersweet memories but mainly sweet chicken goodness. This curry can serve about five but if you have an Abdal it might just be for one, in two sittings of course! He's greedy, always wanting large portions and a second helping.

Feeds 4–5

You will need:

1 whole chicken, portioned into pieces, with the skin removed
100ml olive oil
1 large cinnamon stick or cassius bark
6 cardamom pods
3 dried bay leaves
6 dried long red chillies
2 tsp mustard seeds

15 cloves garlic (you read right!), peeled and crushed
6 inches of ginger, peeled and crushed
2 very large onions, peeled and diced finely
   (or 4 medium onions)
2 tsp fine salt
6 tomatoes, peeled and seeds removed, finely diced
1 heaped tbsp tomato puree
1 tsp chilli powder
1 tsp ground turmeric
2 tsp ground cumin
3 tsp curry powder
3 tsp tamarind paste
Large handful of fresh coriander, chopped
Lastly, a humble smile, for when your recipient gives
   you so much praise you won't know what to do
   with yourself

How to make it:

Take the chicken and, using a sharp knife, score the flesh and make three slits down to the bone. This will help all the delicious sauce penetrate deep into the meat. Set aside.

Add the oil to a large, non-stick pan big enough to fit in all that chicken and sauce – the bigger the better.

When the oil is hot, add the cinnamon, cardamom, bay, chillies and mustard seeds. As soon as the mustard seeds start to pop and the dried chillies begin to swell, add the garlic and ginger. Stir continuously, making sure it doesn't burn. I'm always on edge. I distract easily.

When the garlic and ginger are a light brown, add the onions. This will seem like a lot of onions but this is what makes this curry sweet. Once these onions are shown some love they will taste incredible.

Add the salt to the onion straight away and this will start to draw out the moisture. Cook on a medium heat for at least 30 minutes till the onions are soft, translucent and just slightly brown. Seems like a lot of time, but this really is the key to an epic curry. The onions will have reduced a lot too, leaving room for other stuff. If the onions do start to stick, add a splash of water and give it another stir.

Add the tomatoes, tomato puree and chilli powder and cook for 10 minutes. Now add the turmeric, cumin and curry powder, stir and cook for another 10 minutes. Add a small splash of water and stir if it sticks again.

Whack in the tamarind paste and the chicken, stir to coat it all and cook on a high heat for 5 minutes. Lower the heat, pop the lid on and cook for another 30–40 minutes. This seems a long time for a meal but spare a thought for me. When I was first married I would be cooking this while five or six other pots were on the stove at my in-laws' house. In the hierarchy of curry cooking, mine never took priority.

The curry should be drier by now, the sauce clinging to the chicken. Add the coriander and stir through. Serve with steaming hot rice. It tastes even better a few hours later, microwaved after a tense discussion!

―✦―

DAUGHTER-IN-LAW

Dear in-laws,
Everyone tells me to fear you.
To be afraid.
I don't know you.
Just as you don't know me.
I love your son.
As you love him too.
I may not know you,
I may fear what I don't know.
But we all love HIM.
We don't know each other.
But we love him.
That is what we know.

I stayed with my grandma, any opportunity I got. My nana left her a big house when he died. A lovely roomy hall, an excessive living room, a large, mismatched kitchen and the most unusual garden. She had the kind of house I would want to own as an adult now. But her garden looked like it was designed by three different drunk men wearing stilettos. It had the tallest apple tree, perfect to ward off eager little hands wanting to pick the apples too early. There was an angled patio area that always made my head go a bit funny – three steps and the third one was always broken. Never repaired, just always broken. The more we visited, the more broken that step became. A triangular vegetable patch, lined with strawberry plants, which we were never allowed to eat. There were never enough strawberries and only the special adults got those. Didn't stop me stealing them when she wasn't looking, quickly washing them down with some hose water. It was like I never saw them in the first place. Strawberry! What strawberry? I don't have a clue as to what you're talking about. There was another patch of land that was desolate, mainly used as a site for a fire, for burning old furniture. The ashes would sit there year after year, annual fire after annual fire.

A garden path led to the back fence. If I climbed it and held myself up against that fence for long enough, I could see faces I recognised. Faces I went to school with. I could never hold myself up, propped against my belly folds, for more than a few seconds. I would come scrambling down, dress dragged north, a splintered graze heading south. But at the end of her garden, a shed sat quietly, in front of the plum tree. We never picked those plums. They were in arm's reach. But not those plums. Any plums but those plums. You had to get past that shed to get to them. No plum was worth encountering the dark spirit that resided in the shed. Its thin glass window, muddy from the rain, would whistle in the wind. The lace curtains hung still and grey. I willed them to move to give us a sign that someone or something was there. They never moved.

We would all pile into her house. A common sight would be my mum, aunts and older cousins toiling away in the kitchen, through laughter and plentiful cups of tea, to help feed the brood they brought along with them. My nan lived alone but she never seemed alone. We were always there, in twos, threes and eights. She was alone, though; I just never realised till I grew up how lonely she really was. As a child her house always felt far away on foot in the summer. In the car it's a three-minute rally down the road and sharp left. But on foot it was another matter. Mum would entrust us with striped corner-shop carrier bags packed precariously full to the top with a tiny barely-there knot right at the very end. Piled with liquid curries, still dangerously hot from the pot. The hope was that they were cooled – I would give the pots a speedy swipe to check; they never were. When the stewed-down curries were cooled, they had the added benefit of being partially set from the gelatine bone brothy bits, making them much easier and less stressful to transport. But never! That ten-minute walk to her house was like a traps workout that would be the envy of any gym bunny.

'Don't spill a drop,' Mum would say. 'That one at the top doesn't have a lid so I've wrapped some foil around that.'

Every step calculated, every step stressful, one foot in front of the other. Mum was sending love to her mum in the form of molten-hot curries in unstable packaging and I for one would not be the first in our family to spill that love all over the chewing-gum-speckled tarmac. I wanted nothing but to turn that corner because as soon as I could see her road name I knew I was seconds away. Passing the street sign, I was reminded of the spot where my grandad died, right there on the ground. I would always stop for a second, both selfishly for sweet relief and to say hello to my dead grandad. It was a mixture of habit and much-needed relief for my straining arms. I would put the bags down just for a second then carefully lift them and off I went again.

Nan always knew someone was coming, not because she had a sixth sense, special wisdom or a connection strong enough to distinguish our every move. Mum would call her. She would know, and she would wait. Not for the last two minutes of my journey, no – she was the kind of nan who waited the whole ten minutes. She would start with the door ajar, panic would set in two minutes in, then – wedging the door with a sandal so it wouldn't slam shut on her – she would tiptoe sandal-less onto the first two steps to look over the hedge. Eventually she would make her way down the worn, cemented drive and wait there till she would see me make my way round the corner. I was always happy to see her, but happier still as she would raise her arms as if to gesture, 'I'll take those heavy bags.' Sweet relief. Leaving her behind to make her way up the front path, I would bound into her hallway, running aimlessly around her empty house and her bedraggled garden.

I would look at the shed at the bottom of the garden and pretend not to look at it. I didn't want to look at it, but I couldn't help it. 'Stop it!' I would tell myself and still I did it. Eventually I would just give in to whatever compelled me to look and just stare. Straight into the window with the netted curtain, in the hope that I might be proven right. There was someone in there and he would wave back if I stared hard enough.

'Come in and have some rice.'

She always startled me. She never crept up on me. I knew she was always there pottering away behind me in the house; I could hear her clattering around her minimal kitchen, heating up my mother's love in a pan that used to be nana's – lidless, handleless but his. Making the curry even more delicious. A light muttering of Arabic prayers would travel through the sliver of her open window. I knew she was there. But that shed had me entranced when no one was around. Just me and the shed and whoever or whatever was in it.

'Come in and have some rice, stop talking to the ghost in the shed.' I can't even write this without feeling a shudder. Breathlessly I would dash in and slam the door behind me. I would eat my rice, plate balanced on my knee, peering through the window. This time I had the wall to protect me but as I mindlessly shovelled in my food I was entranced by the shed again. Blankness broken once more by her soft, fragmented voice.

'I need you to come to the shops with me after you've eaten.'

This was a given. Nan was like clockwork: dinner then shops. Having an English-speaking grandchild who could read and write made her an entirely functioning person for just a few hours. She waited for our visits so she could do her shopping. She knew what bread, milk and baked beans looked like. She never dawdled when she shopped alone. It was in and out, head down, with an occasional, hesitant, ever-so-slightly awkward smile. Oh, but when she had an English-speaking child with her she was a changed Nani entirely. She even walked in a different way. She had questions and lots of them. Dialogue, with shopkeepers and neighbours alike. Sneaky giggles about jokes I don't think she really understood. If they giggled so did she; she giggled with all her mouth and from somewhere deep. If they thought it was funny, it was funny to her. We were her bridge to friendships, to community, to belonging. She was my bridge to ten fried-egg sweeties and if I was a lucky a lolly too. The kind of lolly too big to put in your mouth because some genius thought it would be a good idea to stick a gumball in the centre. Whoever you are, wherever you are, I love you! You made many a little kid of the nineties happy and their dentists less so.

We walked back from the shop and we came to the cross-roads like we did every week. We needed to go left, but Nan always stopped first and looked up the road as it went higher and higher and vanished into the distance, lines of cars and houses turning into a blur. She would even stand on her toes.

I don't know what that achieved apart from a few inches. But those inches were important to her; they mattered. Life on this road filled her with sadness. For the son she no longer prepared evening meals for when he got back from the gym. For the grandchildren she would always recognise, but never really know. She had me for now.

We went to the left, walking past houses of friends I went to school with. We saw a tall figure in the background, majestic. She walked towards us, carrying bags of her own. As our eyes met hers, she turned furiously and crossed over to the other side, her aura cold and unfriendly as she walked past us. I knew her; I called out to her. 'Perhaps she didn't see it was us,' I thought to myself. Nan walked and looked and kept looking till her neck could no longer rotate. She faced forward again.

'Stop calling her, she won't speak to us.'

The tall woman was Nan's daughter-in-law, a title marred with negativity and sadness. Who would ever want to be one of those? Not me.

There was an air of mystery about them, this woman and her family who didn't speak to my nan. Who didn't speak to my mum, or to us. What had happened? I would sit and listen to 'who did what' as my relatives, distant and close, would gather on the floor around the gas fire with their steaming cups of tea. I was enthralled by their gathering. It was an occasion. Something had happened and they needed to touch base.

'What are you talking about?'

'Nothing, this is grown-up talk, go and play with your cousins.'

I didn't want to play. I wanted to listen. The room felt stifling, choking my breath. Their stories felt scary as they leaned in and whispered to one another, the light of the fire on their faces, the women getting louder and louder as they gossiped and waited for their husbands to return from their late-night shifts at the restaurant. I never understood what they spoke about. I wished I did. I longed to be a grown-up, so I too could drink hot tea and have a secret group all of my own.

Till I became a daughter-in-law myself, I never truly appreciated or understood the relationship, or lack of, that my nani had with her only daughter-in-law. But it filled me with horror. When you are a kid, no one really thinks about how these broken relationships, crossed words and torn ties of kinship affect the children growing up. I was told I would be getting married from the earliest age. But to me marriage was as much about being a daughter-in-law as being a wife, and the only one I had grown up with was the one that my nan had. Their relationship was hardly inspirational: who would want to have that much hatred and disdain for someone in your family that you cannot even speak to them? Not me. If that was what being a daughter-in-law meant, I for one didn't want to take on that role.

My friends would jest, 'Let's just marry guys who have no mother!' Mean, I thought, but a natural course of life, so not entirely impossible. But that wasn't a prerequisite in the kind of marriage I was looking for, or at least not one I was willing to admit. As I got older it seemed that daughters-in-law were always at fault, and as cousins and uncles married, the stories continued. The mother-in-law was always the victim and the daughter-in-law the son-stealing monster. Two sides to every story and all that, but I was still not convinced that I wanted to partake in a game that I was sure to lose.

It's one of those things, like when you fall off a bike, choke on a sweet, announce a pregnancy, buy a new car or have a urine infection. Someone always has a horror story.

Did you fall off your bike? I know this guy who fell off his bike and proceeded to get run over by every car that came past for the next half-hour.

Choked on a sweet, you say? I watched a guy swallow a snooker ball on the telly and he died, so they buried him with the ball in his throat.

Congratulations, you're having a baby? Let me tell you about my fourth-degree tear, not to mention the thirty-five stiches and the blood transfusion.

Nice car. But I could have got the exact same car thousands of pounds cheaper; you should have called me first before buying.

You have a urine infection? You need to drink more water; you don't drink enough water; you need to drink up to two litres of water a day.

Not helping.

So, the big one. I'm getting married. Now for the uninvited advice.

Always wake up before your in-laws. You don't want to appear lazy. Set the alarm early and wake up.

Ask their permission before going anywhere, especially long trips.

If you plan on staying over anywhere, let them know in advance, so they can see if it works for them.

Call them Mum and Dad.

Never address your husband by his name.

Always feed your husband as soon as he gets home.

Dress modestly; keep your chest covered.

When guests come to the house, it is your job to be host and look after them.

Never go to bed before your in-laws. Go to bed after they have gone to bed.

If their son is home late from work, no matter how late, you wait, feed him and then go to bed.

You never eat before everyone else: men and children eat first and then the women.

Do not talk back.

Do not argue.

Then, as if that was not enough to scare a soul, the horror stories.

They will make you cook all day.

They won't let you get a job.

Once you are married you will never see your family ever again.

You won't be able to go out without their permission.

You will never be allowed to live in your own house.

You have to give them all your money.

They will hate you because all in-laws hate their daughters-in-law.

You cannot take their son away from them ever. He is theirs.

Gulp.

Then I did the worst thing anyone can ever do. I googled it. 'How to be a good daughter-in-law.'

Don't talk negatively about your husband's childhood.

Never restrict access to grandchildren.

Don't ignore the fact that your husband was raised by this woman.

Don't look for trouble that isn't there.

Never badmouth grandparents in front of the children.

What was this advice? Surely it couldn't be as bad as everyone made out? How bad could it be?

It was a long drive to my new 'home'. On paper, 163.7 miles didn't feel that far away. 'I can do that distance,' I told myself. This coming from a twenty-year-old who as a child had only ever been as far south as east London and as far north as Birmingham in the UK with my much older cousin. As an adult I had driven on winding A roads to pick up my dad from his late shifts working at the restaurant. Both of us too tired to drive, I always drew the short straw. 'Younger and fitter, you should have no problem staying awake.' Problem is I had been staying awake for days while running between jobs, so staying awake wasn't as easy as it appeared, though it was nothing an icy Coke and spicy onion bhaji couldn't fix before our drive home. That was as far as I had ever got. That was my world and it felt big enough to me.

The long drive came to an abrupt halt. Between intermittent tears, my eyes had become hazy and sleep-heavy. My husband put a hand on my knee; under the watchful eyes of elders, that was about all the comfort I was going to get that evening. I woke up to be ushered out onto a pathway. I turned and looked down at a line of houses, uniform and proud, as they faded into the haze of the street lights.

'Here's another one of my brothers.' I knew he had a lot of brothers. Part of me didn't believe it was real, but there they were in all their glory, five in total. Some smilier than others, some shy, others small. Just like the ten-year-old brother I had left behind. Hugs from all directions, making me dizzy, unbalanced and wary. Here was a sister-in-law who I had only met once and briefly. She hugged me. I closed my eyes tightly; I wanted it so badly to feel like a sister's body that felt familiar, but nothing about her shape fitted with mine. She felt foreign. I hugged his sister, the only one he had. I nuzzled my face into the scarf that was pinned tightly to her head and even her scarf didn't caress me the way my baby sister's would when I embraced her.

I felt like a stranger. I was a stranger. I walked up the steep steps into the terraced house. Every step unfamiliar.

I walked into the dark passageway to be met by a brightly lit kitchen filled with happy faces. Hugs being exchanged all round as they embraced one another. Brothers hugging brothers. Children hugging their parents. Daughters-in-law hugging their in-laws. They all knew each other. I didn't know any of them. I stood and watched them, enthralled by each other's presence. They talked over one another, laughing about how hot our travels had been and listing what they had brought back, and reciprocating by telling each other about the bills that needed paying and the things my husband had missed out on whilst we had been away getting married in Bangladesh. His family was now my family. I didn't know them, but it dawned on me at that very moment that I didn't know him either. He was not mine. He was mine when he was a voice on a phone. When I sought him for comfort. But in the real world he was now ours to share. With all the unwelcome horror stories still whirling round my head, I smiled politely and sat down to have dinner, but my heart raced as I sat near a husband who I didn't know and a family that were not mine. What had I done?

We sat in the kitchen, at an overcrowded table. Large pots all vying for space. I sat on my chair, sweating, heart racing. My feet wanting to run, my hands stone cold, my face smiling. I pinched the overhang of the plastic sheet that covered the table as I toyed with the idea of just laying my hand gently on his knee, to let him know I was scared. But he didn't know my face, as much as I didn't know his. How would he know what I was trying to tell him? We all knew that displays of affection were not allowed and I was not about to start breaking the big rules on day one. Start small, I say.

'Do I help myself to the food?' I asked myself. At home I would go straight in, pile up the plate, serve anyone below elbow height and that was no one! Hands washed, I would plonk myself in front of the telly, *Pokémon* with my brother, followed by *EastEnders* with my sister and a National Geographic re-run about seahorses with Dad and maybe even a bit of Bollywood with Mum for when the younger ones went off to bed.

I was served. Not something I was used to. Who said being a daughter-in-law was bad? I was being served, for goodness' sake. Heaps of rice and curry piled high; I refused to refuse, because I didn't want to appear rude. But I didn't want it either. When was a good time, the right time – is there a right time? – a polite time to say, 'I can't eat any more'? Someone had cooked with what felt like love and excitement to feed a new member of the family. I knew this feeling well. This is what my mum would do, go above and beyond to show she cares through cooking a monumental amount of food, and for a second I felt that tiny bit of home descend upon my ever-racing heart, giving it respite from all that beat, beat, beating.

The night was long; we were alone. I heard kids talking through open windows. My departure from home was so raw that I still heard my baby brother's voice in my ears. It gave me comfort, but the comfort was short-lived; the reality was there in front of my very eyes as I lay in bed looking at the

Artex-decorated points on the ceilings. I wished they had polystyrene squares I could count; at least then I would have something to occupy my wandering mind and my empty heart. My husband slept peacefully as I watched his chest rise and fall with every breath. I wondered, if he died would I miss him? If he died, did I love him enough to feel pain so unbearable that I would ask to sleep in his grave with him? Would I mourn him? Or would I simply move back to my home, 163.7 miles away, and slip back into the comfort of my slippers and the warmth of my single bed? No, I wouldn't have mourned him. Not then. I wouldn't feel much loss for a life I barely knew. Maybe for a brief period, but not forever. It doesn't bear thinking about now! It would kill me.

The night was long and drawn out. Forcing my eyes shut to sleep, I imagined my mum's face, smiling, with my nephew on her hip. I imagined I was lying in my single bed at home and throwing bits of the peeling wallpaper on my little sister's head as she tried to sleep. I opened my eyes. I was still awake. She was still fast asleep in my mind, decorated with a scattering of salmon-coloured wallpaper, with bits of plaster thrown in for good measure.

'Go to sleep,' I told myself. 'Another day down,' I told myself. 'Then another day tomorrow to get done,' I told myself. 'Another day of the rest of my life,' I repeated. 'That's for ever,' I reminded myself. 'A whole entire lifetime.' Panic setting in.

The next morning, my husband and I walked across from our rental room to our father-in-law's house, which was just a few doors and a few hundred yards down the same road. The air was cold here. It was different to the air at home. Crisper. It got your lungs; it felt harsh. It woke me up. In my attempt to appear soft, gracious, ladylike even, none of which I was before marriage, I walked across in a dress my mum had bought for me, in hues of pink and mint green printed on white cotton. With the grey Yorkshire sky and the towering terraced miners' houses as my backdrop.

'I can't do this, I'm cold, why on earth is it so cold here?'

He laughed. 'Come on then.' He ushered me back to the house.

I didn't have anything, not one thing that would go well with this outfit. If I was at home I would whack on a hoodie, or my brother's jumper or my mum's cardigan or even my dad's cigarette-infused forty-a-day-habit triple-layered coat. Just like me, Dad hated being cold. I rummaged through my cases, looking for a jumper I knew I didn't have. Stalling. 'It's here somewhere,' I said in the hope I would sound like I had a clue what it was like to be a wedded woman. When all I wanted was a pair of jeans, a hoodie, and to huddle under soft bedding in front of the telly, with my brother at my toes, cradling an entire three-foot baguette and a tub of Anchor butter. 'I know it's here somewhere, I did pack it.'

Such a liar. A fraud. Total and complete phony. All the while I was trying to hide my panic disorder, it bubbled away in the background. As it bubbled I knew it would surface; I just didn't know when or how. I found a shawl I had packed to replace all the tatty hoodies I had left behind. I wondered what my in-laws would make of my Tupac-emblazoned hoodie if they saw it. Married ladies wore shawls, not hoodies. The shawl was thick enough to hide the chill and the regret as we continued our journey down the street. Met by a house brimming with people, a warmth hitting my face from the breakfast being made in the kitchen. 'I wonder what they eat for breakfast here?' It was comforting warmth. I didn't need my shawl any more.

They milled around. Familiar with drawers and dishes. They knew where to go and where to find things. I wasn't quite sure where to put my hands or where to place my feet. I smiled. Because right now that was all I could do. My face hurt. I was handed a hot cup of tea. I looked down at the cup as the steam rose to the tip of my nose. I inhaled the bittersweet aroma. I didn't drink tea. I never had. At least four times a day, my dad would push his half-drunk mug of tepid, sweet tea that he could never finish towards me. 'Baba,' he would call me fondly, as a reciprocation of what we called him.

'Have the rest of my tea, Baba,' he would say, sliding his cup across the pound-a-yard plastic-covered dining table.

'No, I don't want it.'

'Go on, just have it. Just once just say yes, drink it.'

'You know I don't drink tea, I don't want it,' I would scorn. Picking the cup up, I would walk away. 'Why do you always ask me the same question?'

I would make a detour to the sink to pour it down the drain. Walking away. I wish I had just once, just once drunk the tea my father had offered me.

I sipped at this tea and tried to maintain my smile, but it tasted as unfamiliar as my presence in this room lit with bright white skin and tapered eyes. I felt browner than I had ever done in my life. At least at home we were like the shades of a teeth-whitening chart. Here they were the result of three weeks' intense teeth-bleaching treatment. I was way down the other end, off the chart.

'I don't drink tea,' I said, as someone reminded me that my tea was getting cold.

'Everyone drinks tea.' I guess so did I now. That was my introduction to the world of caffeine. For which I am forever grateful. I was quickly handed a bowl of Bran Flakes floating in a bowl of hot boiled milk. I always made my own breakfast. I had not had my breakfast made for me since I could see over the counters. This was weird; I could get used to it, but I had a gut feeling that it would not be forever.

Ushered into the living room, I sat down. The room was warm with the gas heater blaring in the corner. My face red hot. From the combination of the heat of the furnace, the hot milk and my nerves I found myself sweating profusely. I didn't know whether I wanted to cry or to vomit. Every second that passed I felt less and less in control of my bodily functions. But either way something was going to happen, and it wasn't going to be pretty or ladylike. Unless of course there is a Marilyn Monroe-esque way of barfing, crying and screaming at the same time. An art I don't think anyone but my two-year-old nephew had mastered.

I had not drunk milk since I was five years old. I just

thought I hated milk all my life. On advice from our family GP, I was not allowed milk. My mum was told I was over-weight so it was restricted to control my blubber. I would watch my brother and sisters drink their milk every night, envious of this white gold that they drank. 'What did it taste like?' I wondered. 'I wish I wasn't fat, then I could drink it too. Maybe I could have some water perhaps?' Even that was off the list of liquids before bed because I was a serial bed wetter. But the more they drank their hot steaming milk before bed and the less I drank it, the more the look and just a tiny whiff of the stuff made me want to run for the hills, gagging.

Here I was faced with this bowl of Bran Flakes, which I had never tasted. I was not a cereal kind of girl; I preferred no breakfast and then a binge on a packet of McCoy's and a Boost bar at 11 a.m. If I was going to have cereal it was only ever Frosties with ice-cold water! It sounded normal to me and my family never batted an eyelid, but I was not about to refuse the first-ever breakfast at my in-laws' – how would that look?

'So anyway, I don't drink tea, never have, and I never have breakfast and if I do I don't eat Bran Flakes, my choice of cereal would be Frosties, with ice-cold water poured on top.'

May as well walk around with 'weird southerner' written across my back. I chatted intermittently and pretended to eat the cereal, turning it on my spoon occasionally. The more the flakes sat in the steaming hot milk the more they increased in size. Giving away my cunning plan to make out that I had eaten something I couldn't even bring myself to look at. As it cooled, the smell subsided. I could hear whispers in the hallway.

'Maybe she doesn't like cereal.'

'Maybe she's not hungry.'

Their voices disappeared into the kitchen. Maybe she misses home.

My sister-in-law walked into the living room and took the bowl of brown wallpaper paste out of my hand. I sat quietly, listening to the others, trying to acquaint myself with an accent that was endearing and confusing all the same. It had a friendly twang that elevated itself at the end. It made me smile a little. Bowl no longer in my hand, thank the Lord! The weight of the sludge in the bowl and my guilt as it grew had become harder and harder to bear. It was swiftly replaced with a small plate, chipped, decorated with a print that reminded me of the plates at my auntie's house. On the plate, a piece of brown bread, toasted, smothered in what looked like tar from a distance, but on closer inspection turned out to be Marmite. I love Marmite! How did she know? I had only ever spoken to her once and even then, she was rounding up her kids to feed them and we barely spoke more than four badly stringed-together sentences. Either that was a very auspicious guess, or she was psychic. Perhaps I look like the kind of girl who likes Marmite. Is there a look?

'Yuck, I don't know how you eat that stuff,' she said with a grimace. 'Is that enough Marmite for you?' It was layered on so thick, the texture of the toasted bread underneath it was unrecognisable. As it dripped over the edges slowly and onto my thumb, I gave it a tiny lick. Mmmmmmm! The only thing that would tempt me to have breakfast was when I could hear my brother rattle around in the kitchen. He would layer it on; he liked it bitter and salty and lots of it.

'That is how my brother would eat it,' I said coyly.

'Tell you what, let's get that one in the bin and you can come in and make your own breakfast.' I wanted nothing more than to make my own breakfast. I was shown around.

'The fridge is in this room down here.' I was led down some steep steps to a cold room housing a fridge, a tumble dryer, a broom, a mop and his bucket for a friend.

'The bread is here with the teabags. Tomorrow I will show you where the onions, ginger and garlic are. Tomorrow your real work begins, be here at 8 a.m.'

Daunted. Frightened. Did I get just one day before the real work began? Who cares? For that moment, just that single moment, I had a slice of well-done toast, with lashings of butter and just a smearing, with a gentle wrist, of Marmite. I wasn't at home, but my senses transported me right to my mum's draughty kitchen at home at 7 a.m., tiptoeing on the cold lino. My brother and I would wrestle for the Marmite jar.

'Shall I drop you off to college today?'

'Yes please.'

'But shall we have another piece of Marmite on toast before we go?'

'Always.'

My husband and I walked home after a blur of new faces to greet, more hugs to give and lots of names to remember. I was new today. The spectacle. Tomorrow, I would be old. I had a job to do. But I was making my own breakfast, I knew where they kept the bread and that was a start.

I held my shawl tight, smelled it in the hope of getting a whiff of home, just anything. It was gone. It had a smell, familiar: spices, oil, house. But not one that made me feel safe. I tried not to feel the chill. My husband walked beside me in a brown T-shirt. I could tell he was a fast walker as he raced past me every few yards then slowed down, so as to keep up with my pace. That was nice. He seemed nice. He could have walked right past me and walked into the house. But he waited. Our steps now in sync. Slow but synced. He said he wasn't cold. His nipples said otherwise. He was lying.

'How do they know I like Marmite?'

'I told them you like Marmite.'

'You actually like me, admit it!'

'I really, really like you.'

He liked me; I had Marmite. In that moment the world felt okay.

I arrived 8 a.m. On the dot. I was given a key to let myself in. The smell of onions escaped through the crack in the door as I opened it. The thick wooden door felt heavy after the four steep steps leading up to it. Either I was lazy, or I was just an amateur climber. If I was living in the north I would have to get used to steep steps, the peaked terrain and life slightly on the edge.

'Have some breakfast and then you can get started on these onions.' My in-laws pottered around, I made my breakfast, attempted to make other people's breakfasts too. All too aware that I had onions to attend to. I tried to enjoy my toast. Eventually I gave up and gave it to the cat, JoJo. He reminded me of my kitty, Hira. I had given her away so I could move. I missed her. With everyone else that I missed, I forgot about how much I longed for her, too. I stroked him, he purred. Maybe JoJo could be my solace, my shoulder to cry on as Hira had once been my agony aunt. I fed him scraps of my bread as he sat beside me.

'Don't stroke him, he's nasty.' He was lovely, and I think he knew I was sad. I began my onions. Peel, slice, repeat. There felt like hundreds of onions. In fact there may have been that many. My eyes bled with tears.

There were rules. Someone did the cooking, but it wasn't me. I did everything else.

'When can I cook a curry?'

'Not yet.' I could cook a mean curry and I wanted to show off my wares, if not to my family but to my new husband. That's what would capture his heart. I just knew it would. Even when my parents went hell for leather arguing, even when we overheard them flinging the most imaginative curses at each other, the break in their duel would come in the form of a mealtime.

'I have to cook,' Mum would say. Dad silent. Because he

had to eat. Everyone needs to eat. Even an angry man, with a battle to fight. Especially an angry man with a battle to fight.

She would lay out the table. Slamming bowl after bowl onto it. It came in droves, curry after curry after curry. Silence.

'What have you cooked?'

Silence.

'This is delicious, the best you've ever cooked.'

'Do you really think so?'

'What did you do differently?'

Pacified.

So, I waited patiently for my turn to be upgraded from kitchen hand to cook. It was going to be my pacifier. My peace-making power. In the meantime, I carried on chopping. We had six curries to cook and that was every day. Every morning at 8 a.m., I chopped like I had never chopped before. The boards unfamiliar, the knives blunt. My father-in-law stood beside the table that I was hunched over. I could barely make eye contact. But I tried. I could just about see him through the streaming tears and the hazy vision.

'I know you must miss your family.'

I was taken by surprise. I did miss them a lot, more than anything. My heart physically ached. How did he know? Was it that obvious? Had I done something wrong? I stopped for a moment. Elbow-deep in onions, this was actually the first time in days I didn't miss them. It was a brief respite, but I had a job to do. I didn't have time to cry over my family, because I was crying over five kilos of very spicy onions from hell.

'Yes, I do.'

'We're your family now, you have to stop thinking about them.'

Taken aback, I had nothing but silence to offer in response.

'You have to love them a little less and love us now.'

A lump in my throat. Nothing, I had nothing. I couldn't say 'okay'. Because that would be the wrong thing to say. Was that what he wanted me to say? Because I couldn't.

I smiled. Maybe it wasn't a smile, it was a purse of my lips that curved enough to disguise itself as one. I looked down and chopped my onions. This was the perfect time to tell a girl to deplete the only love she has ever known, to hand it over to strangers. I had all this love to give, more than I knew what to do with. My love was firmly placed in the hands of my family. That was not for anyone else to take. I had lots more to give. Would that not be enough?

I carried on with my onions: peel, slice and repeat. The cold tears from the sting of the vapour poured down my face, mingling with the warm tears that came from a sad place inside. Together they ran down my face, under my chin, and nestled themselves into my scarf. Where they would dry eventually when the morning cooking shift was done.

Lunch was thoughtful and eaten in silence that day. I walked back to our rental room at the end of the road slowly. Locked the door behind me. Inside, I rushed to open the window. I took off the heavily curry-scented layers of fabric. Placed them on the clothes drying rack and sprayed them furiously with a cocktail of cheap perfumes. I sat in my underpants and bra on the edge of the bed. The smell had permeated as far as my underwear and with no more clean underwear and no machine to wash it in, I sobbed. With not another soul in the house. I shut the window and sobbed a little more. Then I crawled into bed and sobbed till my eyes were too tired to stay open. I fought to keep them open, so I could wallow in what felt like a death sentence. I stopped fighting it. I slept.

I heard that when a person falls asleep and they dream, their soul is meeting with the person they are dreaming of. I hoped that my soul would go home. Sleep was the closest thing to death. In that moment, death felt like my only option. If I didn't die, then I hoped that maybe my soul would go and make sure my family were okay, wherever they were, whatever they were doing. Because I was here and I had no way of knowing, 163.7 miles away from home. Nothing but strangers for family. The credit balance on my phone read 89p. I had just enough for the texts and nowhere near enough for a call. When that 89p was finished, I would have no connection. No way of knowing how they were. And they had no way of knowing how I was. With no money in my pockets and too much pride to ask, all I had were my dreams and pride that chipped away by the day.

My days as always began in my father-in-law's house; as soon as my eyes opened and I was awake enough I started with breakfast and cooking soon after, chatting while I worked with my sister-in-law.

We would break for prayer. My mother-in-law would announce, 'Drop everything and pray.' That's what we did. I did it for solace, for a moment to myself, to gather my thoughts, to have a few words with God and often a little cry.

'I am going to pray,' I would announce, before taking myself carefully up to the top floor and manoeuvring myself up the two flights of very steep stairs. My mother-in-law, a God-fearing woman, would always reply, 'Go, leave everything and go, nothing is more important.' Not something I was used to. Growing up in a family that was not particularly religious, this was different. We did the basics at home, but I never grew up watching my parents pray. All my mother-in-law does is pray; that is all her family remember her ever doing. She encouraged it, she praised it, she welcomed it. To her, nothing else was important. I enjoyed it more than I ever imagined. She was more like me than I had imagined.

One day I stood as usual on the decorated prayer mat. It was worn from the back and forth of hands as they, whoever they were, used it to submit. A distinct mark of feet where my feet were firmly placed. I was on the top floor of the house, in an attic room with no dormer. I was not tall enough to be affected by the ceiling slant. My feet stood uneasy. I was not used to being this high; before I was married I had never been inside a house that had been built so high up. I wondered how many prayers had been spoken silently to Allah on this mat. It was worn almost paper thin, used, utilised. How many prayers had He granted? How many did He ignore? How many were pending? I sat on the floor, my feet behind me, propping me up. My hands nestled together. I concentrated on my breathing, trying not to be distracted by the faint scent of fresh prawns that I had de-shelled and de-veined. Coming up to this room, to this prayer mat, was the only time I really felt at peace.

As I sat in the silence of my teenage sister-in-law's attic room, I could hear the occasional car fly past. Nobody was home. Or maybe some were. The men were at work, the cooking was done, and everyone had retreated to their bedrooms that acted as their very own private abodes. That was their space; there was nothing communal about those rooms.

'Allah, I didn't know it was going to be this hard. I did not know who I was at home. I don't know who I am here. Why can't I belong somewhere? He has his family, mine are so far away. I have nothing here. Allah, please let me have a child, so I can have something of my own, so that child can give me belonging. Ameen.'

It never ended there.

'Oh, and Allah, I am so far away from home. I can't protect them, but you are the greatest of protectors, look after them for me, for the universe. The universe needs them and so do I. Please make sure my mum doesn't cry too much for me. Please make my dad take his tablets. Please make sure my sisters fill the gap I left. Please make sure my brothers do not detour from their path and always come home. Please let my nan live a long life, for ever even. Keep my nephew smiling. Now I am done. Ameen.'

I folded up my mat and left it at the end of my sister-in-law's tidy, slight bed. Tiptoeing to look through the attic window, through a layer of dust and sand from the evening's rain, I could make out the skyline, the lofty houses and the irregular terrain. Waves of chimney pots and roofs rolled into the distance for miles. Sunsets were meant to be beautiful. I had seen many in Bangladesh. But this was a beauty all of its own. An image of industry, ingenuity, hard work and community.

I was distracted by the sound of pounding. It was consistent and strong. It came from the bottom floor. If I could hear it all the way up here, it was so loud. I rushed downstairs, although the steep stairs had a way of making you go faster than your own ability. I peered into the kitchen and saw my mother-in-law. Let me set the scene. Standing at four foot ten, she pounded what looked like something white in a large bowl using the end of a rolling pin. What an earth was she doing? We rarely saw her in the kitchen. If she wasn't with God, she would come down occasionally to help us deal with an awkward fish we didn't know how to prepare. Or at least that is what I thought.

'What are you doing?'
'I'm pounding rice.'
'What for?'

'To make handesh.' She paused to fix her headscarf. I had lived with her for weeks now and still never seen a strand of hair on her head. Maybe it was straight, or curly, white, black, maybe salt and pepper, it could be down to her knees or short in a pixie-cut. Maybe I could ask her? No way, that would be weird! So, what's your hair like under there? What if she were bald?

'You like handesh, right?'

I do not like handesh. 'I love handesh,' I smiled. I was getting good at this daughter-in-law stuff. Perfect smile, tick. Right answer, tick. Look busy, tick.

Handesh are these beautifully crisp and slightly dense rice fritters sweetened with date molasses. Sweet yet slightly bitter, they are the traditional accompaniment to a hot sweet cup of chai in all Bangladeshi homes. As kids, when we visited homes of relatives on a weekend, we would get a cup of tea and a plate of these dark brown fritters. I hated them, I didn't want them. I craved a Kit-Kat, a packet of crisps, anything but those. Grown-ups ate them so they had to be boring. The first time I tasted one I was convinced it was made of chocolate. Chocolate it was not. Desperate to get rid of our half-eaten fritters, we handed them back to Mum. If we were lucky we might be given a clementine in replacement or an open garden door. 'Go and play.'

My mum would make them the way her mum taught her. When they came with her to England in the seventies, an exotic ingredient like date molasses was hard to find. So she substituted it with good old granulated sugar. Making her fritter the anaemic version of the original: sickly sweet, pale and slightly less crisp. My nan's ones were nice. I liked those. She made handesh that didn't disguise itself as chocolate in any form. It is what it is. A little bit like her. Best of all, it was eye-wateringly sweet. My mum is the most amazing cook; she can nail eight curries in an hour. Ask her to make anything else, not so good.

I wanted to feel nostalgic, even sentimental. Even a tiny bit homesick, as my mother-in-law made the batter. I felt nothing. I hated the ones my mum made, and I was not about to be converted by the deceptive non-chocolate variety. She made up the batter using her hands only. Feeling for the consistency the whole time, her fingers rubbing in the batter as she poured it from her fingers from a height. I wondered what she was looking, feeling for.

'What are you doing?'

'I don't know. This is just how I do it.'

I never watched my mum cook, not really, not intently. She is a furious cook: she would zip through the kitchen and you would be lucky if she stopped to make eye contact. Not my mother-in-law. She had a way about her. She was graceful, slow, and I mean slow. She had nowhere to be. I didn't really want to watch her. But I was compelled to. I had never seen anyone do anything this gently in my life. She ushered me towards the cooker. I watched her carefully pour in the batter close to the oil and up puffed her very first fritter. We didn't say much. I asked her a few questions. In response I got a few quiet words. She fried, and I watched in silence. With only the bubbling of the oil and the gas on the hob for music. We made a large bowlful, piled right up to the top.

'Try one, while they're hot.' She passed one over quickly, ushering me with the other hand to be swift. It was piping hot. I ripped it open. I could fake this one. At least it wasn't hot, smelly milk. I ate it. She watched. As if waiting for approval. She waited, observing my face. I don't think I had ever stopped and looked at her before then. I don't think she had stopped to look at my face either. Abdal looked nothing like her. She has a slight nose, pouted lips and slits for eyes. Her face is small and her stature peaceful. All wrapped up in six yards of cotton. It was the first time in my life I had ever towered over anyone. It felt good. I should have felt nerves, but I didn't. She wasn't scary. She was my husband's mum and I saw him in her. Even though his face wasn't there, his heart was.

'Is it as good as your mum's?' She swayed her head, waiting for a response.

'No.' I stuffed the rest of it in my mouth. 'My mum's are horrible, this is the best I have ever eaten.'

Delighted, she handed me a plate and piled them on for me. I made us a cup of tea, still familiarising myself with the flavour. They tasted good with tea. We sat in the living room with our feet up. Gas fire blaring in the back, we listened to the crackle of the local mosque radio reciting the passages of the Quran. She hummed along with the imam, as she always does. That was her sound.

He will never be my baba, but he is my dad. She will never be my mum, but she is my amma. They are not my family, they are his. But what they are, is ours. I may never fully get my feet under the table. Maybe because there is no table big enough for so many hearts. Or even enough chairs to accommodate us. Some firmly tucked in with their elbows erect, others on edges with one cheek hanging on by a thread, some loitering, some in other rooms, some of us assigned to duties. The table may not be big enough, but the house is. Somewhere in there I have a place. Big or small. It is mine. Strained or simple. It is mine. To keep or to discard, it is my choice and I choose to be here.

HANDESH

These are notoriously difficult to make and have broken many a daughter-in-law's heart and bank balance. I have used up so many ingredients trying to perfect these sweet treats. Every family has their own way and their own recipe, and this is the one that I have come up with. They are closer to what my mother-in-law's ones are like and nothing like my mother's. So, for anyone getting married, vying to impress, these are for you. They are for you if you want to show up your very Bengali mother. They are also for you if you like fried sweet stuff with a cup of tea.

This makes about 12 large or 24 small handesh

You will need:

150g rice flour
150g plain flour
100g molasses sugar
320ml boiling water
750ml sunflower or vegetable oil

How to make it:

Start by making that batter. Whack the rice flour and plain flour into a large bowl and whisk till it's all mixed in really well.

Put the sugar in a jug and add the boiling water. Mix till the sugar is dissolved.

Pour into the dry ingredients and mix to a smooth, caramel-coloured, thick batter.

Cover with cling film and leave to one side. You need to leave it for at least 2 hours.

Pour the oil into a small saucepan, making sure the oil reaches just above halfway up the sides.

The heat needs to be a high medium. But you will only really gauge the right temperature when you start frying. Be warned: the first few will be bad. Edible but ugly.

Take a small espresso cup, small ladle or very small bowl. That holds about the amount similar to a tablespoon.

Use it to scoop up some batter, then clean off the edges. Extra dripping will make for wispy, not well-shaped handesh. This is important, my mother-in-law told me. The more I watched her the more confident I became in her technique. If she says that's the way, that's the way!

Bring the ladle or whatever you are using close to the hot oil. No dropping from a great height. Start pouring the batter in gently in one shot without hesitating or moving your hand around too much. As soon as bubbles start coming up, stop pouring and remove the spoon.

Let it bubble away till the handesh comes to the surface; it should start to rise. Take a slotted spoon and slowly pour a little oil over the puffy bits.

The trick to getting this right is to do one at a time. Just one. Too many in one pan creates too many bubbles and that can affect the shape. Nobody wants a distorted, misshapen handesh, especially not your mother-in-law.

Turn over after 2 minutes and give it another 2 minutes on this side.

If it looks bad, keep going, and keep adjusting the temperature. This is the kind of thing that takes mistakes, practice and instinct. My mother-in-law has it, I wanted it, and now I have it. Now you find it too!

Drain on kitchen paper and eat while they're still warm. If you're having these for breakfast, warm them in the microwave, rip them up and pour over hot milk. I hate this, but my Abdal and my babies have it twice a year at my in-laws' and it's all they want. So it can't be all that bad.

—⁊|⸝—

MA

The children themselves are poetry. They are the here and now, the truth tellers, the soothsayers, the comedians and the grim reapers. They are the good, the bad and the ugly of reality. They are the unsung heroes of poetry. I have spent years collecting their comments and I want to share the rhythm that is ours, the words we share on our car journeys, our travels, at our dinner table and best of all the conversations we have through the bathroom door.

Musa:

So, have you ever wondered what your hands taste like?

Home is the only place I can unsuck my belly.

Stinky bottles have no place in this world.

We need to send some of those Pokémon to *The Jeremy Kyle Show*.

You have it easy, Dawud, you're in Year 4, wait till you get to Year 5, that's when life gets tough.

Let's get in a train and see where the wind takes us. Let's go to *The Jeremy Kyle Show* and Buckingham Palace.

I think Donald Trump might start World War III.

Can I have free money, Mum?

Can I have some money to bribe my uncle?

Let's get to know each other better; there is no need to hate anyone.

Hurricanes have names with letters beginning from A to W. They miss out Q, U X, Y and Z. I mean why? Just because they are different and difficult to pronounce, why leave them out?

Let me just have a minute with this cake, Mum. Just a minute.

This cake is so good I'm going to die of satisfaction.

Ma. Just checking you're still alive.

I can't eat knowing so many kids are hungry.

Dawud:

If you had a blood transfusion, do you just lie there in a puddle?

I like benches, they taste good.

Live life to the fullest but don't eat a hamburger every day.

Ma, you have about twenty years being beautiful, I'm not sure about the rest.

I want to watch a newsreader get a frog in their throat, that would be so funny.

Someone should make a *Great British Porridge Off*.

How many kilos do you think teachers bench press on teachers' training day?

Ma, when I get a car, do I need permission to go to the toy shop?

I bet the toilets in Buckingham Palace are big enough to fit a million people in, but the queen wouldn't want a million people watching her poop.

Whoever finished last, wins.

Jigsaw puzzles are for wimps.

Hurricane Doris did a number on us! How many ceilings do you think fell on people's heads?

I've seen plenty of meatballs, Mum, and these are the best balls yet.

Does anyone get a spicy feeling when they poo?

My dreams are messing my hair up.

I am a person. Accept it.

Ma, I'll tie your hair up when you're old, when you can't do it any more.

God and plastic last for ever.

Is it okay to be scared?

How many biscuits do you eat when we go to bed?

Maryam:

If you don't eat ice cream, your life is like a big sack of sadness.

Who wants to look at my crumpled pinky toe close up?

I am going to wear trousers today, so you can all see that I have actual legs.

Baba, warm up your porridge, unless you enjoy crusty porridge.

If something happened to you, at least I know how to cook.

If something happened to you, would we still have to pay rent?

If something happened to you, how would we pay for stuff? Oh, I could just use your wallet, right? You won't need it anyway.

If something happened to you, I would just call Nani to come pick us up.

Why are you going to work, Mummy? I don't feel bad for you, I feel bad for me.

That is such irresponsible parenting.

Ma, you have not been to school for so long, let me re-educate you.

Ma, your prayers are so long, Allah might get bored of listening to you. Shall we shorten them?

I love you more than I love a lamppost, Mum.

I've been jigsaw training.

He trumped. I think he has issues.

Can we have dinner and just get this day over with?

I like electricity, a lot.

Why can't everything be free?

*

She made it look effortless. She never complained. She just got on with it. Rushing around with frazzled hair, her sari anchal tucked into her tightly tied sari top. She mopped her brow as she cooked rice, did laundry and sewed on collars to her pile of shirts. A seamstress by day, she made a few pennies for every shirt she stitched. She would put on a curry to heat and the rice would bubble away furiously. Even then she made it look easy. Like it was what she was born to do: herd children like cats and keep them alive.

That was the dream – that I was going to make it look that easy. Like it was what I was born to do, too. Girls had babies and if my mum had them, then so would I. Till I realised how they got there and how they exited. I solemnly swore to myself as I walked out of that Year 8 Biology class that I for one was not going get a baby in there, let alone allow one to come out. The images burnt into my psyche for ever. As if the female anatomy wasn't bizarre enough. All of that but on the outside of your body in the form of a half-filled tote bag dangling off an elephant's trunk. Just why, God? Where did you get the inspiration for such a monstrosity?

'I am not having a baby, ever,' I said to myself as I pushed past the sea of giggling girls in their bottle-green uniforms. I wanted nothing more than to get away from the excess of oestrogen, excitement and whispers.

'Mum, why did you have kids?' She was sewing a long stretch of facing on a lilac shirt on her trusty Singer sewing machine. The sound ear-splitting with every long stretch as the needle penetrated up and down. She didn't stop to make eye contact. I know now that she was not equipped to answer these questions. Not because she didn't know how, but it was not the done thing. Her mother would not have had that conversation with her, or her grandmother before her. You learned. You found out. You worked it out. In any which way, any way at all, but never through them.

'Because girls have to have babies and God wants us to have babies.' She paused and faffed about with an odd end of fabric, turning it here and pulling it there. 'You ask too many questions.' She carried on. Her machine could be heard in the background as I walked up the stairs, the noise receding as the fifth stair creaked.

'Sorry, God, I'm all for worshipping you,' I thought to myself, 'but I'm not having a baby just because you think it's what I should do.'

Eight years later I found myself sitting on a plastic-wrapped chair. So securely waterproofed, it made me wonder how many accidents had happened on it over the years. If this speckled, salmon-coloured, waterproofed chair could talk, it would cry in horror at all the leaky arses that had sat on it. The catheter that hung beside me weighed me down, like a designer handbag filled with valuables that can never leave your side. No, it was just a bag of my wee. I watched, fascinated, as it filled up beside me. I had no clue how this was working; I didn't have the urge to wee, but my body seemed to be doing its thing, whatever that was. In fact, I didn't even remember being fitted with it. But as the pain relief wore off, I knew exactly where it was. Now I could feel it, I felt everything. The must-have accessory for all new mothers, it hung beside me, warm.

As every minute went by I could feel the reality of what had just happened. It was hitting me. My legs felt bulbous as the anaesthetic wore off. Then there was the fire that raged in between my legs, pulsating from the pain of the stitches used to sew up what was left of the carnage. My breasts as they expanded were irradiated with Hulk-coloured veins, like a road map leading down to my deflated stomach. A sorry-looking stomach that once had a child in it. It now looked like a week-old helium balloon that was losing its air, little by little, leaving behind a saggy, crêpe paper-like creation that looked like it had been thrown together by a pre-school child.

My mum sat in front of me, holding him. She rubbed his tightly clenched fist. 'He's a big boy . . . my poor daughter.' She knew. I knew. I didn't want to talk about it. She didn't want to either. I sat, in agony, and tried to pretend that she couldn't see the blood-stained gown, the red liquid seeping down my thigh and dripping to the floor. The more I moved, the bigger the puddle got. She could see it and so could I. It was pouring off the edge of my seat. Drip. Drip. Drip. I ignored it. He looked so beautiful, bundled in her arms. I tried to ignore how he arrived as my puddle got larger and the pain became more agonising. But he was there and so was my pool of bodily fluid. Neither of which I could ignore.

'I am going to be the worst mum in the world.'

Seventy-two hours from the moment my waters had broken, finally he was here. Musa. We picked his name after the midwife showed us his sketchy black and white tickle-tackle on the screen. She flipped it over.

'There it is, do you see it?' She pointed at the screen.

'Aaaaah, yes, I see it.' I don't see it! I'm a liar. Who actually ever sees it? I was not about to tell her that though. Yeah, I see it, I was going to start this whole being a mum thing by doing what all mums do best and that is to pretend we know what we are doing and fake it. 'That is my baby's willy and I see it!'

We were going to call him Musa, after the Prophet Moses. Strong-willed, determined, a born leader. I would rub my burgeoning belly as we drove down the M1. The baby inside would sleep the whole way, not a flutter, in a trance from the whirring of the wheels. Abdal would reach out and give it an occasional rub. Just reminding himself that our boy was in there, asleep. 'Musa, Musa, Musaaaaaaa!' he would chant with his eyes fixed on the lanes ahead. Like an alien, my stomach would start pulsating as soon as the engine switched off. He was real, he was alive, and he was inside me, safe. I knew that what goes in must come out. I knew the same rule applied to him. But no amount of watching videos or hearing stories would ever fully prepare me for the reality of a child coming out of my body.

'My sister had her babies in a few hours, so I will be the same,' I told myself. We were total opposites. She had quick labours, no pain relief and small babies. I had extensive labours, all the pain relief that medicine had ever created and massive babies. They were not lying in the leaflets when they said: 'No two births are the same.' That was no lie. We could not have been at further ends of the spectrum.

The next day, I was back at home, in my bed. It was less than twelve hours after the birth and I was amongst familiar surroundings that looked the same yet felt totally different. I felt different. You do feel different, when you leave home with your underside intact and come home with it butchered.

There is nothing like the sleep you have after being awake for days and pushing a human out of your body. That is the best kind of sleep. No marathon, no Iron Man, no decathlon, no swimathon, no race, no run, nothing can beat the sleep you get after spending three days trying to expel a small person. Nothing. Abdal was right there. He was all I saw for days: just my knees, his face and the ceiling. Like history repeating itself nine months later! We were not sick of the sight of each other, which is always a winner.

My new son lay beside me. Happy, silent thoughts whirred in our minds. With nothing to share, with so much to share and no words, we lay there side by side, silent. As he slept in the basket beside me, I looked over at him, fixated by this tiny person. My body rigid, for fear of leaking or pulling a stitch or, worse still, both. I stared at him. Watched him breathe, up and down and up and down. He didn't look so big any more. Swaddled, he slept, undisturbed. My mum was also staying with us to look after me when Abdal was at work. I could hear her humming downstairs, as the water ran out of the taps. I slept. I dreamt of a world where today would be over. I would forget the pain. A world where I could sit. Where I wasn't constipated or scared to poo. Too scared to even think about what happened down there. If today was over then tomorrow I would be an actual mum and not be reminded of the agony every time I saw his innocent little unassuming face. Tomorrow, every time he pulled on my nipple for a gush of milk my uterus wouldn't contract. Everything would be as it was a week ago and I would have this baby and everything would be perfect. I slept.

'Can you not hear him cry?'

My eyes blurry. I couldn't move. My body stiff with pain. I looked at the time. It was 1 a.m. and Musa lay crying. Not just any old crying. The kind of crying that curdles your blood. It had escalated to a repeated, siren-like cry with a perfectly timed gasp of breath at the peak of the wail. His face was scrunched up. He didn't look the same any more. How could a thing so small create such a sound?

'What does he want, Mum?'

'He wants feeding.'

I sat up, my nightdress covered in blood, soaked through to the sheets and all the way through to the mattress. The way I was bleeding, it felt like if I looked far enough my blood would have soaked down to the centre of the earth. That was a clean-up operation I was not looking forward to. As my mother handed him, hysterical, over to me, I sat up and looked at this noise-making machine. I had to make it stop. I pulled out a breast, baby in my other arm, but nothing pacified him. Not a breast, nor religious chanting, nor swinging, nor swaddling, nothing. He got louder and louder and louder still. He was at the point of no return. With less than twenty-four hours' experience of looking after a human, I was already beaten. He was not giving up. He wanted something, and with all my offerings depleted I did not have a clue what I needed to do to put this baby on mute. He was not giving up and I was failing.

'Let me have him.' Without hesitation I gave him to her and slumped back down onto my pillow. Why didn't I know what I was doing? My regrets didn't last long, because what my body wanted was to shut down immediately and my mind followed suit.

I woke to an eerily quiet house, with just the sound of the clock ticking on the wall. Had my broken body and confused mind wished my baby boy away? Was it all a dream? It can't have been; every atom in my body ached, right up to the follicles on my head, pulled and strained in pain. Where was my boy? Wherever he was I wanted him now, now that he wasn't crying. I peered into the spare room. My mum lay huddled on the floor like a cold hamster, curled up on a pile of blankets with a few empty bottles beside her. Baby Musa lay in his basket, sound asleep, satisfied. He stirred, as if somehow he knew I was in the room. His lips pursed and opened a little to let out the gentlest of sounds.

How did she do it?

For years as a teenager, I mocked her in my mind. For all

her bad decisions and choice words. The way she did things and the rules she imposed. She never did anything wrong, but she never really seemed to get anything totally right. She was everything I did not want to be. But there she was in front of me. Curled up in a ball on my spare room floor. Sleep-deprived, yet still feeding, cleaning, nurturing her child. I was still her baby and now she was lumbered with mine. For all the things I thought she never got right, she was suddenly my light in the dark, the giver in my time of need. I had never sought her knowledge; I had never delved into her mind for her wisdom; I had never asked her advice. Suddenly that was all I wanted to do.

'Mum, I don't know how to do this.'

She sat up, gently lifting Musa out of his basket to nestle him in her arms, getting him ready for his morning feed. Her movements confident and calm. 'Why does he feel like he's your son?' I said. She didn't move her eyes from him. She was in a bubble of love and I wanted to be a part of that. Scared that if tried I would be the one guilty of popping this fragile connection surrounding the two of them that she had created overnight. 'Why doesn't he feel like mine?'

She glanced at me, a look of worry. Handed him back to me: 'Here, he's yours.' I held him. I loved him so much, but the pain was unbearable. I wanted to feel something other than the stinging, the burning, the throbbing that pierced my body each time I moved. So, I just sat there. My arms the only part of my body still functioning. I held my boy, nestled him into my memory-foam stomach. He left an indent – baby Musa-shaped. I had my arms and I had him.

'You're really good at this, Mum,' I laughed. Nervous about what was about to come out of my mouth. It felt wrong to think it, so to say it felt sinful. 'Maybe you could have him for a few weeks?' There, I'd said it; the words came out and slapped me straight in my face like a verbal boomerang from the pits of hell where all the awful mothers are destined to go. 'Backtrack, backtrack, backtrack, you total idiot,' I told myself. 'Or maybe you could just stay with me?' I said out loud, smiling nervously, trying so hard to hold back the tears. That's all I wanted. I wanted my mum, but my boy wanted his. Neither of us could give our child what they wanted, but we both knew what we needed.

'If I take him, I'll love him too much and then I'll never want to give him back,' she laughed as she stood up and sniffed his womb-scented hair. 'You will be fine.' She kissed my head. My mum, maternal in her own way. Never gave kisses and hugs and when she did they were so limp and lifeless, it defeated the object. Her affection left you wondering rather than being left with the feeling of relief. As she left me with her kiss, I looked down at him. He looked up at me.

'I would never give you away.' Just for a moment, I didn't feel the pain. I didn't look at him and shudder at the thought of the damage he had done. I didn't flinch when a stitch pulled. 'I would never give you away.'

My mother packed her bags into the car. Standing by the

front door, she held him close, sniffing him deeply and kissing his soft cotton ear. She reeled off a list of curries cooked, where they were and in what order we should eat them. Avoiding a gap in her sentence, because she knew and I knew that a gap, whenever it happened, would be filled with tears. Despite trying to hold them back, they rolled down her flushed cheeks anyway. They had come from somewhere deep. She held me close with Musa gently sandwiched between us. Her grip tight, filled with life; it was the first time I had really hugged her and there was a deeper meaning in it than I had ever felt before.

'I don't know if I can do this,' I sobbed in her ear.

'This is what it is to be a mum . . . you will always feel like this.'

What is it to be a mum? To have thoughts so extreme, your craziest moments prior to motherhood seem almost normal. To feel guilt so intense, the emotion becomes your default. To feel love so strong, you think your heart is going to explode. To feel so protective that everyone becomes the enemy. Is that what it is to be a mum? I watched her drive away.

'I'm just off to get some more nappies,' Abdal said as he walked towards the car.

'Don't forget the Ice Pops to extinguish the heat in my lady bits.'

We can do this, right? I watched them all drive away. Reluctant to walk back in. This was the first time we were totally alone. Just me and my baby boy. Behind those closed doors was reality, one that I was avoiding. It was cold, the absence of people leaving a billowy draught in the house. Not helped by the fact that we had no central heating in the house, just a gas fire.

'Let's turn this on, shall we?' I said to him. If he could talk, and I know him fairly well now, he would have said, 'No Mum, you always make the house too hot.' But I didn't know that then. I turned the gas on. I spread out a large, fake mink blanket, like the one my relatives had bought from the market in Luton. I lay it out so there was just enough space for the two of us. As I gently placed him on the floor I lay with him, my back roasting hot from the fire. The heat felt comfortable against my sore body. With my arm propped up I used it as my pillow, nuzzling him under my armpits. As he wriggled he unswaddled himself, letting himself free.

'I don't really know what I'm doing, but I am going to try to be the best mum.' His lip twitched, and he smiled. Actually I think he broke wind, but whatever it was, it was well timed. I think he knew. 'We're going to be fine, just you and me.'

Awoken, abruptly, simultaneously, by a text and a key in the lock. Abdal threw himself through the front door, crunchy carrier bags in tow, a little windswept by the impulsive September weather. I looked over to Musa and the noisy bags, over at Musa and then the bags again.

'Oh, sorry.' He lay them down gently on the runner. 'You two look cosy, any room for me?'

He snuggled beside him, on a sliver of faux mink.

'What if we get all this parenting stuff wrong?' he continued. I had no idea he was scared too. If he was he hadn't
shown it. Or, I'd just failed to see it.

'We're going to be fine,' I said.

'Oh, and his nappy needs changing.'

Is this what it means to be a mum?

I said to myself when my second son was born that I would
not compare him. I would not say it or even think it. Whether
he rolled, turned, crawled or walked, he was to do it in his
own time. His older brother was never going to be the measure of his individual achievement. Musa had his milestones
and Dawud would have his. When I say older brother, I mean
older by just 371 days. Before I had even healed, we had
decided that we didn't want Musa to be an only child. We
wanted him to have a brother or sister. I am one of six and
Abdal one of seven. So, having just one child was never an
option; we always wanted a family and to us that meant the
kind with more than one kid. In fact, growing up I don't
recall ever meeting anyone who was an only child. Everyone
had someone. I had lots of someones. Abdal had lots of someones and I wanted my kids to have their own someones too.
Half-baked idea, someone having someone, but somehow it
felt right.

'Ma,' he says now, 'I don't remember ever meeting Dawud.'
Well, there is no way that he would. Dawud was born just
six days after his brother's first birthday. He called him

'Adhu' because his speaking skills, still quite slight, wouldn't allow the D out first. He knew he was in my belly; he would point at it with his thumb. As his brand-new brother was placed safely on the floor in his car seat, he pointed again with his thumb – motor skills needing some work – straight into his eye! 'Adhu!' he called, turning back to point at my belly. Dawud got the welcome of all welcomes, thumb in the eye and imposter status. Musa was not sure, and neither was Dawud. Little David. An imposter he was not. Dawud was all Musa knew. Where Musa was, so was Dawud. When Musa beckoned, Dawud was there.

One day Dawud didn't feel like answering. Musa sat on the heavily printed pale green settee. It was brand new, but it looked like it could sit comfortably in a horror movie set. My house's furniture had been handpicked by my dad with his impeccably brassy taste. We didn't have much so we were grateful for the gift, no matter how migraine-inducing it was. We had each other and that made us rich. Isn't that what everyone says? We had a home that pushed us to our limits and two small children that strained us at the seams a little more. But we were okay.

The end of the settee. It was Musa's spot, the spot where the draught came in, so he could stay cool. 'Dawud!' he shouted and patted the seat confidently, three times, for his brother to come join him. *Special Agent Oso* was playing on the TV. Impatient, he tapped again on Dawud's side of the settee, right beside his thigh, three times. Ushering him to join him, with his eyes firmly fixed to the screen.

I looked intently at my magazine. The fact that I could do this with two children under the age of two felt miraculous. Mothers at playgroup complained of sleepless nights, wet nappies, waking babies and exhaustion. Not me. My sons ate, slept, played and repeated. So I could read books and magazines. I could have baths and soak my feet. I could eat when I wanted and not have to eat my food like I had just stolen it. So I put my feet up and read my magazine with a steaming cup of tea placed precariously on the radiator to keep it warm.

Musa tapped again, this time a little louder and a little more belligerent. Knowing all too well that there would soon be a dart of hands and knees shuffling across the laminate, in response to the tap, tap, tapping. Bringing with him dust and crumbs. He tapped again and nothing. I removed the pages of the magazine from my eyeline and peered down at them. Dawud lay on the floor with his protruding, nappy-filled babygro bottom raised in the air, his arms splayed out, palms flat on the floor, and his little face to the side. His eyes peered up at me. Unsure. He breathed rapidly. I had never seen him this slow. He never stopped. If he wasn't following then he was being chased. I had never seen him stationary. Or this far away from his brother.

'What's wrong, little man?' I threw my magazine on the couch and found myself, head down, face to face with him on the floor. Our ears listening to the sound of the humming radiator pipes below us. His breath hot and rapid against mine. His face pale, his cheeks crimson. His blink delayed, eyes opening slowly.

'Something's wrong,' I told myself. 'Is something wrong?' I asked him. Hoping his eyes would answer because at seven months old I was unlikely to get an actual reply. Although I secretly hoped for one. Half of being a parent is guessing and the worst time to do it is in a moment like this. Tap, tap, tap. 'Come on, Dawud!' his brother shouted, irritated. When he called, Dawud came and today Dawud just wasn't coming.

He did try. His brother called so he was going to attempt to come. He knew nothing else. His brother was his world, his confidant; they were the epitome of 'partners in crime'. Little people, partners in tiny little baby crime, which mostly consisted of laughing at me, spilling things and running away from me at bath time, nappiless, opened, exposed and free of confinement. I watched Dawud prop himself up and shuffle a little further. But he was too exhausted and out of breath. He stopped again and lay his head down. This time closing his eyes a little longer than the time before.

'He can't breathe.'

My world came to a standstill. It wanted to stop, but instead everything from that point on moved in slow motion. I moved from spot to spot, frantic, but couldn't remember how I got there.

'He's dying, he's dying, he's dying.' I had never used that word in front of my kids and if I had they would not have known what it meant. I chanted as I called the ambulance. His brother still sat there watching *Oso*. He peered over, oblivious, and carried on. To him, Dawud could just be sleeping. In the eyes of a nearly two-year-old he looked like he was falling asleep. But I knew. I scooped up my boy, his arms and legs limp, almost lifeless in my hands. His lips looked a pale shade of purple. His eyes no longer open. I called him – 'Dawud!' – as I prised his eyes open. Tricking myself into believing he was fine. It's a joke, he's messing around, he's playing peek-a-boo – surely?

Is this what it feels like to watch your child die? All those stories and images of lifeless children in war-torn countries being carried to their shallow graves. Here I am. How will I tell Musa? How will I call Abdal and tell him our son is dead? How will I bury him? 'Please God, don't let my baby die.'

I held him close and prayed. So hard and loud that surely God could hear me. 'God, if you're up there and I know you are, you can't take my child, I'm pleading with you, God, don't take my child, you can have anything but don't take my child.' I prayed like I had never prayed before. I threatened God; I pleaded with him. I negotiated.

'Dawud? Nap time?' I cried, harder and louder. Musa looked at me, suddenly terrified at this unfamiliar sound that came from my mouth. He had never seen me cry, or at least not like this. The tears streamed and collected in a puddle on Dawud's tiny chest as it rose and fell with every shallow breath. I watched it. Expecting it to just slow down and eventually stop. I needed to watch him stay alive, and till then I did not want to look at his face.

The same face that was bruised and battered from the most serene entry into the world. Slow and steady won that race. When he did arrive via an episiotomy and the assault of a gas and air tube, after a long forty-eight hours, he looked right up at me. Nuzzled under my nightie. Not a peep. Just calm. He had come into the world, but he was not about to make a song and dance about it. So he lay inert in my arms; he demanded no fuss now either.

Soon we were seated in the back of an ambulance, Dawud still on my lap, propped up by the steady hand of a young paramedic whose presence commanded respect with his green attire and intermittent radio. He felt important.

'Is he going to stop breathing?'

He never answered my questions. He only asked me questions of his own. It all felt like a blur as we drove through the winding inner-city streets of Leeds. My tears crusted over in the chill of the ambulance. How many people had died on that very stretcher? Did they know that this is the way they would go? An emergency, a 999 call, unexpected. Doesn't everyone want to die in their own bed, warm, unpanicked?

Dawud breathed – this time it was different, his breaths were longer and his arm was up, holding his oversized mask as it nuzzled his little button nose. Musa was buckled up tightly into the chair next to the man. He looked afraid. He didn't cry. He just looked afraid. Always sure of himself, now he looked petrified. Too scared to say anything but using just enough strength with whatever slack the belt allowed to stretch out his hands to me. I reached back to stroke him. Dawud was gripping my other hand. 'Ma is here.'

Dawud held me tight, and every time a spot of the nebuliser fluid fell into his eyes he squeezed his eyelids shut. He wasn't dead. He was alive, and he was holding me. He knew I was with him and he was letting me know that he knew that too. As my seven-month-old baby lay on me, all I wanted from him was reassurance. I was his mother and I had nothing but panic to offer. But I wanted him to tell me he was going to be okay and so were we. 'Ma, you're overreacting, lady. I am fine.'

As we came to a halt, we could hear bolts and brakes go off, echoing inside the ambulance. The doors opened wide, letting in a flood of light. With it the cool air of the evening rushed in. Nature's Red Bull. I could function for a few more hours as I breathed in the fresh air. Dawud opened his eyes wearily. He was awake. Not half awake. But fully awake and breathing as he always had. He used his strength to sit up. He was looking for someone. His eyes looked right through me. 'Never mind me then.' He tried to use his arms to pull himself up but he couldn't do it. He tried and failed again. 'Let me turn you around.' As he swivelled, his eyes widened with complete delight at the sight of Musa, and he splayed his arms out towards him. I handed him over and he held his brother tight and nuzzled into his neck. Musa was all the medicine Dawud needed.

Outside, Abdal stood in the distance, worried, fearful, in front of a bright sign reading 'Accident & Emergency'. His eyes looked drawn in; his face looked how my mind felt. He ran to the ambulance, scooped up the shoeless Musa and held me tight. 'Are you okay?' he asked as he kissed Dawud. 'You have to stop scaring us like this.'

As soon as we entered the hospital, Dawud was his old self again. Needless to say, we saw the inside of an ambulance again and made many a hospital trip after that. As a child I had watched my parents ferry their poorly children back and forth to hospital and never thought it would happen to me. But it did. I never appreciated the pain they felt. But I did now. I always wondered why they had no time for anything else. Now I knew.

Is this what it means to be a mum?

What does it mean to be a mum? Being a mum is like any relationship but it is the one we invest in most. Why? Because we invested in it the moment it was a thought, from the moment we decided that we would use our bodies as a vessel to carry what is essentially a parasite – and I mean that in the nicest, most maternal way possible. If that is even possible. I don't think it is. Which leads me nicely into the other part of being a mother, which involves a lot of digging yourself out of holes that you never intended on digging. Being a mum is unconditional love, which you find yourself questioning every time you get a hint, even a tiny smatter of back chat.

Child or freedom? Being a mum is giving up your own sanity. Aiming to sleep when the baby sleeps but in reality staying awake to watch them breathe to make sure they are not dead, because your overactive imagination tells you that is exactly what will happen if you don't watch them. Being a mum is being permanently tired. Tired of clearing up, tired of vomit, tired of stepping on Lego, tired of being ignored, tired of being tired.

I tapped on the touchscreen keys in the doctor's reception. I tapped, pressed and then minorly abused it with my pointing finger. It never worked. What I wanted to do was just hand in my name, like we did in the good old days. To not appear a technophobe or useless, or not willing to 'get with the times'. I persisted. It got there in the end. Like we all did. I felt the lag that day. My body in the crowded surgery, marred with the breath of dozens of patients, filled with an orchestra of coughs and sneezes. Stifling yet safe in the knowledge that here was a place of help for the sick.

'For God's sake, use a tissue,' I muttered lightly, under my breath. It felt like I was brave enough to say those words. But not me. Only ever in my head. Along with all my other thoughts. It wouldn't be fair anyway. We were all here for a reason. Unwell. I didn't have a dressing, a cut, bump or sneeze. But I felt so deeply poorly.

The electronic receptionist was placed right in the path of the wind tunnel created every time the electric door swung open. The speeding cars outside would give you a clue that you were right on the outskirts of inner-city Leeds. In its windy path there were three seats that no one ever sat on, unless you were having hot flushes, had a soaring temperature and/or were frankly mad. It was always cold in that spot. The surgery was always full, and those seats were always empty. I sat there, watching the large blue screen intently, waiting for my name to appear. 'I could look away,' I told myself, 'but what if I didn't hear it ping?' I would miss it. So I had to look. My eyes glued, waiting to read my name. The wind smashed me in the face, occasionally blowing in a few amber ombre leaves that gathered around my well-insulated feet. A sign of the summer gone and the autumn to come.

A small baby, not much younger than Maryam, maybe two. Wanting to be unleashed from the security of his push-chair straps, he cried relentlessly till he was let out. The mother bedraggled, windswept, a slight woman, no doubt anchored by the six bags of shopping hanging from the push-chair. It wasn't one of those fancy, streamlined things that felt like they were made of suede. It wasn't held together with chrome so shiny it would blind you in the autumn sun. No. Just a buggy. Just like the one I had. It did the job; it got you from A to B. But who didn't want one of those fancy ones? I wanted to look like I knew what I was doing and surely a buggy that costs more than my monthly mortgage would do that?

I wouldn't know; we had one and it did the job and it kept my daughter safe. That was the main thing. She lay sound asleep in my arms, exhausted from a session of tears in the car. Still hiccupping with anger as she slept. She was peaceful now, but my ears were still ringing from the sound of her shrill cries. My throat sore from the scream at the traffic lights that brought to an end the mother of all mothers of three-year-old tantrums.

The little boy had just discovered that the surgery door opened every time he walked past it. A big moment in any two-year-old's world of discovery. Amused. He walked past. The straps of that pushchair were his mother's key to sanity; free of them now, he giggled wildly as he made the doors open and close repeatedly. This was his moment. With each chuckle, a gust of welcome cold air would cool my ever-heating face. The panic was rising. 'Should I just leave?' I asked myself. I sweated, my back wet, my elbow giving way. Despite the draught from the door, I was somehow generating heat. My daughter fell deeper into her sleep, her sweaty head leaving a damp patch on my polyester top. So peaceful, her little pigtail curls stuck to her head and her cheeks were flushed red. Exasperated by her, I loved her so much.

How could I want to wrap us both around a tree some days and love her with my whole heart at the same time? Why not one or the other? Because if I didn't love her, it would mean I would have to H-word her and I didn't H-word her. I H the H-word.

As his mother neared him, the little boy tried to make a beeline for the automatic door, which unfortunately for him had just closed. Had it been ajar, just a tiny sliver open, he might have made a run for it, giving him a fighting chance to not be strapped back in and confined again to the baby-wrangling pushchair. But she got to him in time. He fought her and she fought him back. His back arched and his legs lifted. That was a core workout the likes of which I had never seen on anyone but my own child. So that's what Maryam looked like when she was resisting. It wasn't a good look, no matter what angle.

The little brat.

Does he not see his mother's anguish?

Does he not sense her embarrassment?

Does he not know that for every second he resists, another second of judgement is being placed on her head?

Does he not know that she has a million things to do, and the last thing she needs is this?

Of course he didn't know, but he still looked like a brat from this angle. As he did from his mother's, no doubt. She won that fight eventually. Well, she kind of won, because nothing stopped the glares as he then proceeded to wail, louder and louder – so loud, she resorted to threats. 'Just shut up, for God's sake,' she said through gritted teeth. She pushed down on him, not hard enough to deflate his protruding belly, but with just enough force that it didn't look like abuse. Just enough to appear like she knew what she was doing.

Maryam was now wide awake. Hair glued to her head with sweat, making her look not too dissimilar to a Lego piece. Her face flushed, with one side distinctly pinker than the other. Creases on her face, a symbol of her slumber. She wiped her drool from her face and let out a sudden shudder. She looked at the boy intently, her eyebrows frowning, her ears scarred by the noise that emitted from his mouth.

'Yes, that is what you sound like, when you're crying,' I mouthed to her.

Unimpressed, she let out a resounding 'No' as she lay her head back down, allowing herself some time to wake up fully. Last time she was awake, she was screaming so hard, I thought she might cough her lungs out onto my windscreen. She had fallen asleep that way, strapped in the car. The only thing that kept her safe and protected my sanity. She cried herself to sleep and now here we were in a waiting room.

'You look like that too,' I jeered. Because all I could do was laugh. I was that mother and she was me. I got it. I felt her embarrassment. But Maryam knew her mind and she was sure she didn't look or sound like that.

The lady with the screaming little boy suddenly swung her pushchair towards her, so rapidly she nearly took out an unassuming old lady next to her. She dived into her bags of shopping, elbow deep. Rummaging through them, she pulled out a handful of lollipops, and furiously opened one using the tips of her front teeth. Her son wailed in the background, now resorting to smashing his hands on his knee. This boy was ramping up a gear and even Maryam was traumatised. The child that I thought was the master of tantrums was finally on the receiving end. A spectator.

The mother didn't even wait to hand it to him, allowing him to offer an olive branch in response – a smile, perhaps, or to say, 'Sorry, Mummy.' She just shoved the lollipop straight into his drooling, foaming mouth. Quiet. A battle won. 'Now be quiet,' she said, exhausted. She sat back and looked at that screen. 'Ping.' It was their turn. She let out an enormous sigh as she leant over to unbuckle all her hard work. Scratch that, the kid wins again. As she flung him onto her hip, she offered Maryam a lollipop. 'Would you like one?' she said. Maryam looked at me, unsure. I ushered her to take it, letting out the mousiest of thank yous. The woman smiled. 'You are such a good little girl, I bet you don't do this to your mum.' She staggered away with the child halfway down her leg by now. 'Don't put any bets on it, unless you have money to lose,' I thought to myself.

I couldn't believe that I had taken my eyes off the screen. If my name had been called I would never have known. What was I thinking? So nosy and distracted. What if I had been sitting there all this time and my name had been called? What if I'd missed my appointment? What a waste of time! What an idiot! A tingle up my spine, I could feel something bubbling up inside of me. A feeling, familiar, the only one I really knew. The panic, rising again. It prickled up into my spine and penetrated deep into my chest.

'Ping.' The screen read: 'Nadiya Begum, Room 6'. I popped Maryam on the ground and she curled her body back instantly. Defiant. I wanted her to walk but she had other plans. I had no lollies to deploy and the waiting room, including myself, did not need a repeat performance of Tantrumgate, Maryam-style. I think one tantrum for the waiting-room audience was enough for the day.

Time and again she gives me those 'hmmm' moments, those instances when you tilt your head, squint your eyes, purse your lips and scratch your head. When she was in my belly she ignored her due date, but so did her brothers, nothing new there. She had us frightened throughout my pregnancy as I measured far too small for my gestation; they feared she would be too small, or that my placenta had stopped working. In fact she was the biggest of the lot at eight pounds and fourteen ounces. In my late pregnancy she kept making me think she wanted to come, but as the days passed and my waters remained dry, she came only when she was ready and when she did she was so enormous she dwarfed the weighing scales. She was so loud she bellowed into the echoey room. Then silence. Three a.m. and six pieces of toast later, I had to poke her to wake her as she was due a feed. But she would only wake when she wanted and that was at exactly 6 a.m. when I had just about dropped off, in a ward quarantined due to vomiting and diahorrea. A ward so hot, that even I, the kind of girl who turns up the heat in summer, felt like I was being baked.

'Shall we walk up the stairs? Mummy's back is hurting.' I lifted her up and put her back on the ground and this time she didn't resist, and she put her little feet down. Tippy-toeing, she tried to reach my back in an attempt to soothe the ache. There was an angel in this child somewhere, there had to be. I had no ache; I lied, a lot. Sometimes it seemed the only feasible way to appear like I knew what I was doing. I lied because it made me feel better. Even after having three children, I still felt way out of my depth. But I met women who made the water look like it was only ankle deep and like they were just wading gently in it, while single-handedly running a home, doing a job and raising their children. I, on the other hand, felt like I was in at the deep end, badly treading water, a weak swimmer and only good at the backstroke. I was drowning.

I pretended my back ached as she rubbed it. But as I ushered her up the stairs, she stood still with her arms splayed out. 'Don't give in,' I told myself. So I walked straight down the flight of stairs and picked her right up. There was a time and a place to pick a fight. She seemed to always pick it in public situations. If I was going to pick a fight, it would not be when a doctor was waiting for me. With my five-minute slot running out fast, I scooped her up and stomped up the stairs.

Inside the locum doctor's room I felt guilty as I watched her play in the corner with the box of toys. The toys were mismatched and broken. Shifted from one doctor's office corner to the next. How do I tell the doctor, a trained professional, that I am that box of toys that my little baby girl is playing with? So mismatched, I don't even know who I am any more; I can't even remember who I used to be. Will the two people ever meet again? So broken, that every time I pick the pieces up to fix them, there is another piece missing that will never be found again, a piece lost to the greedy universe that keeps everything in its tight grip.

The most selfish human in the world, my only struggle was me. What didn't I have? We had a roof over our heads, we had each other, we had three beautiful children, who were alive and happy and smiling. We had a we. Something not many people have. We had each other. Yet here I was, selfishly sitting in front of a doctor with all of this! How many people would have sat on these very seats and looked in the doctor's eyes, fearful of what he might say, what test results he might reveal, what he might diagnose? How many? Too many! I was ungrateful, that was my ailment.

'So, what can I do for you?' I looked over at Maryam. I felt so bad saying these words in front of her, although her concentration was fully immersed in the box of well-handled toys, riddled with a fresh cold ready for her to take and gift to her brothers. She played undisturbed, but I couldn't stop the thoughts whirling around my head. What if she hears what I say? What if she remembers and hates me for ever? Even if she doesn't it could sit in her psyche and trigger something at any given point. What am I doing here planting these seeds, placing this ticking time bomb?

'I'm sorry, this was silly. I shouldn't be wasting your time.'

'Okay, if you're sure. But you know you can book another appointment at any time.' The doctor turned away, losing interest.

Of course I wasn't sure. Of course I wanted to be there. That's why I had dragged my three-year-old out of her cot midway through her nap, knowing full well it would wreak havoc on our meticulously timed routine. That's why I had left all the damp laundry in the washing machine, because between getting the boys ready for school, making my husband's lunch and mopping up an impromptu yoghurt spillage,

I had to be there! I had waited over thirty minutes past my allotted appointment time and I hadn't even complained to the receptionist once, even though in my head what I wanted to do was hammer against the receptionist's glass window in protest at being left to wait every time I came for an appointment for which I had already waited four weeks. I wasn't here because this was a holiday camp; I was here because I was ill! None of us were here out of choice; we were here because we needed help, in some way or another.

But you are a doctor, you have chosen to be here, and so now you are going to listen to what I have to say.

'I suffer with panic disorder and I am struggling.'

'Struggling how?'

It all came out in a rush. 'I'm having more attacks, I'm struggling to do normal things, I just want to sleep, I want to love my kids like normal mums, I know I love them, I protect them like a lioness, they are my world, but I want to feel happy, why don't I feel happy?'

I cried as I looked at her, my face streaming with tears. I thought saying it out loud would make me feel better, lighter, like I had shared the burden. I felt worse. How could I be feeling worse? I didn't think I could feel worse then I already did, but I did, and I wasn't sure how; I was going to come back from this. I had said it out loud now; a higher being had heard me, and what if my God tested me as a result? 'Well, if you are so ungrateful with all the beautiful things I have given you, shall I take them all away?'

'God, Allah, no, please don't take them away from me.

I will smile more, I will appreciate them more, but whatever you do, please don't take them away.'

The doctor looked up at the clock while simultaneously typing with two fingers. The printer started whirring and out slipped a prescription. Really? There are pills for this shitty disorder?

'I think you're depressed.'

Depressed? I wasn't depressed; I had a panic disorder. And if I did have depression I couldn't pay for CBT. I just wanted help – anything – as long as it didn't cost the earth. We didn't have the money; we had three small kids. So now I had to add depression to the list?

'How can you determine that in a few minutes? Maybe I should come back another time and talk about it again?'

The doctor ignored me, scribbled something and pushed the pale green sheet across the table to me. 'These are weak, see how you get on.'

Later that afternoon, I sat in the car waiting to pick up the boys. The pills sat on the passenger seat; I looked at them and they looked at me. They wanted to be opened. I was not so sure. Maryam grunted in the back, catching up on her broken sleep. With every grunt I thought back to her tiny fingers rootling through the sticky, germ-ridden toys and then immediately reaching some entry point like a nose, mouth or ear. I opened the box up quickly, like ripping off a plaster, fast and painless. 'May make you feel drowsy, can take up to two weeks to work, don't drink while taking these.' What was the worst that could happen? I hadn't tried anything really; this was worth a shot. There were only so many cakes I could make before the feeling of impending doom and a creeping heart attack would take hold.

I quickly swallowed one of the pills down, then stuffed the box into my bag, like a dirty secret, as if my six- and seven-year-old would even know what it was. I stuffed it away just in case. I think I was hiding it from myself, not them. I couldn't face the reality of depression; it was hard enough having a panic disorder. As I unbuckled Maryam from her seat she gave me the tiniest, sweetest peck on the cheek. She drove me insane most of the time – tears, tantrums, snot and more tears – three years turned into a blur. All I knew was I loved her, somewhere in between the panic and the insanity. I was looking for myself and she was finding herself and somewhere in between we loved each other. I needed her, and she needed me more. As the years go by she still needs me, but I need her more.

We drove the six miles home from the boys' school, always the best part of my day, when we were all reunited. Lost without them, I knew I would feel lost with them all too soon. So I savoured this moment five days a week. It wouldn't last in the gap between post-dinner and pre-bed. The radio gently played in the background after I was done asking the obligatory after-school questions.

'What did you do today, Musa?'

'Nothing.'

Okay. 'What did you do today, Dawud?'

Again: 'Nothing.'

Thank goodness I wasn't paying for their education, or I would be spending all our money on nothing.

'Shall I tell you what we did today?'

'Maybe.' That is resounding, unanimous 'You're all right, love.' These children were meant to be a threesome. Reunited in their car seats, they would happily tell each other about what they did that day and I would listen in, strategically tuning out the radio, trying not to listen to the lyrics I knew from hearing the same station all day.

We were in the car driving along the dual carriageway, everyone sitting silently after their initial clamour, too dazed from the motion of the car to speak now and not late enough in the day to bicker. All we heard was the sound of Dawud eating his snack and the radio, quietly chatting in the background. 'Today we're discussing identity: who are we, what defines us, what is it that makes us who we are?' The silence didn't last long.

'We're from Bangladesh, so I'm Bengali,' said Musa, proud of his culture.

'We pray to Allah, so I'm a Muslim,' Dawud replied, equally proud of his religion.

A short pause. Silence. No one expecting a response from three-year-old Maryam.

'Well, we're all from earth, so we're all humans.'

In that moment I forgot all the knots in my neck, the pounding in my head, the heaviness of my chest and the tingle in my spine. For a second, I felt like 'what panic disorder?' as I yanked up the handbrake and the boys scuttled out of their car, leaving a book bag and a pile of jumpers in their wake. Today I didn't call them back to pick up their things. Maryam stumbled out of her seat, adamant she wasn't going to be picked up; she was going to walk. Sweeping her up nonetheless, I held her close and cried into her cardigan. She was a person under all the waterworks and peeves. She was a human, as she had so boldly claimed to her brothers. She was not going to be stopped, not by anyone and least of all me. Because of all the beautiful things she already was, she was a human. My human.

What does it mean to be a mum? Being a mum is being so afraid of your own child that you don't even know who is in control any more. Being so fearful of your thoughts that you live one life in your head, a dark sad place, and another facing outward, all smiles and rosy, like you know exactly what you are doing.

Mum, Ma, Mummy, whatever it is. The word is too simple to truly define what being a mother is. To me being a mum was my mum. She worked hard, never complained and gave up her whole life. I ask her now, was it worth it? She says yes and no. Yes, because we were always neat, clean and present-able, and we turned out to be okay kids. No because she did nothing with her own life – no real job, no friends, no life outside of us. When we all left, one by one, we took a little of her with us. So she had nothing left. She felt empty.

But that piece I took with me, that little piece of her has

made me the mother I am today. I have faced far fewer obstacles than her and her mum before her. But that doesn't make me any less of a mother. My fears are the same. They are irrational. Every time they are without me I fear they will die; I will get that call and they will be dead. I will always be afraid, every time they wheeze and cough, because when they are ill my world stops, because they are my world. When they stop, I stop.

For a long time I dreamt of a life outside of being just a mother, but looking back I can see I did that title an injustice by using the word 'just' in front of it. I am not *just* a mother; I am a mother, that is my full-time job, with no probationary period and a contract signed to infinity and beyond. I will always worry; I will always be afraid. I will laugh when they trump, laugh harder when they hide it. I will hold them when they cry. I will clean their grazes and wipe their tears. I will blow raspberries till they let me and kiss them on their nose while I still can. I will tell them I love them every day and they may not always respond. I will pick up their wet towels and always complain. I will make them load the dishwasher and unload their burdens. I will smile when they gel their hair or secretly wear nail polish to school. I will do all of that, whilst being riddled with my own foolish fears. One day they will leave, and I know they will take a piece of me with them. Even if I am left as an empty shell like my own mother, at least they will have a piece of me. So that they too can be riddled with the same anxieties and fears of raising actual, real-life human beings.

Being a mum is scary, from the moment you feel that first kick, but I think it is meant to be. I want to always be worried and scared. I want to always feel. My children gave me something that nothing else ever could: with them I belong. I am their human as much as they are mine. All the best kinds of love fill you with dread and motherhood is the same.

World, I cannot wait to give you my children. Because they are the best of me.

—/ı\—

EGGS THEIR WAY

We all eat eggs our way. We all have our own way. I like runny eggs. Abdal hates them. The kids like egg white; I like the yolk. But they love eggs this way, flavoured and runny and cooked well all the same.

Makes enough to feed 3 hungry kids

You will need:

6 eggs
1 clove of garlic, finely crushed
1 tsp salt
1 small onion, very thinly diced
Small handful of fresh coriander, chopped
1 tsp whole cumin seeds
1 tsp chilli flakes
200ml double cream
4 tbsp sunflower oil

How to make it:

In a bowl, add the eggs, along with the garlic, salt, onion, coriander, cumin, chilli and double cream.

Give it all a really good mix, until everything is well combined.

In a small saucepan, add the oil and place on a medium heat.

Lower the heat and pour in the egg. On the lowest heat, mix continuously. The eggs will cook gently and you will know it is ready when you have something that looks like a thick white sauce rather than scrambled eggs.

Take off the heat and pop into a bowl, to stop it cooking.

The kids like to eat this with crisp toasted and buttered bread, topped with loads of the egg. So much so we have had to make a fifteen-egg pot!

⟶⟋⟍⟵

EARNER

My hands.

They may not be withered or worn.
Calloused.
Or dry.

But they work.

Once they worked, to get somewhere.
Now they work to get by.

Still they get somewhere.

Me and my hands my work.

I leisurely strolled around the house. I looked at my watch.
I had forty-five minutes before my shift started. My sandwiches would take me five minutes to make, wrap in foil and

carefully place into the bottom of my large work bag, which in itself contained a pair of heels inside a carrier bag. You never know when you need a few extra inches and in my case a few inches always made a difference in helping me feel less like a child amongst adults. It was hard being the eighteen-year-old amongst middle-aged doctors and women, who did what I did as a second job after coming home from their real jobs. For them this was just a little call-centre job to help pay for that big holiday, the new car, the extension. But for me, this was my full-time job and if I wore heels, I felt less like the sheep amongst wolves. Just having them rustling in my carrier bag gave me a sense of safety. When I transferred my footwear from my comfy Adidas Campus into my towering, nude (for white people) heels, I would feel powerful. Never really worked though, because even if I had changed shoes, had a leg extension, put on a bouffant hijab and stood on a stack of Yellow Pages, none of this would have made a difference. My colleagues towered over me anyway with their dreams and lives and second jobs while I floated – unsure, no direction, and slightly bleary in their sharp focus.

Among my heels, I also carried a four-pack of sugar-free Polos, because being around fortysomethings with coffee breath not only made me gag, but also made me overwhelmed with pity. Did they not know? I would cautiously offer them a mint.

'Would you like a Polo?' There goes Nadiya with her Polos, I would hear, as my packet of mints would travel from one end of the room and back, with just a few remaining at the

end, writhing in their manhandled foil and paper casing.
Polos were on the shopping list of things to buy on Sunday.
But at least my generosity meant the air didn't having a lin-
gering aroma of morning breath, coffee and old carpet.
Because when someone designed call centres they did not
take into account personal space. Elbow to elbow, we could
smell each other's auras, we were so packed. Polo, anyone?

What else was in my work bag? My wallet, so I could buy
a carton of chips and curry sauce if I was working late. Baby
wipes – those were the days when antibacterial gel wasn't a
thing. You always needed wet wipes, be it to clean shoes,
scrub a dashboard or wipe hands. That's a habit that remains.
Pre babies, in the thick of babies, post babies. Two tubes of
Pringles: one pot of sour cream and onion for when I was
hungry and one of salt and vinegar for when I was hungry
and feeling sick. An elastic band, because even under a headscarf, my gargantuan hair had a habit of popping my band
and the last time I used an elastic band from the office supplies, it had to be cut out using a pair of my mother's sewing
scissors, taking a cruel amount of hair with it. Luckily I have
enough hair to go around. Vaseline, because dry lips are an
actual thing, and just seeing a pair of dry lips made me want
to reapply. I liked a glossy lip and if I was feeling fancy, a little
on my eyelids wouldn't go amiss either. I hadn't yet truly
discovered the sorcery of make-up at that age. I didn't really
love my face. Though it's marked by past breakouts, hormone
imbalances, general life and my inability to not pick a spot,
overall I now think it's in pretty good nick. At the ripe old

age of thirty-four I certainly appreciate the benefits of a pore-minimising primer and concealer now. Oh, how I love you, concealer, my friend.

What do I have in my bag now, I hear you ask? Well, the bag has certainly increased in size and altered in type. Now it is a rucksack, so I can be hands-free. In it, a bag filled with medication: Berocca for power, painkillers for tough days, sanitary towels for the painters and decorators, eye drops for when I don't want to appear tired but I am pretty much sleeping on the job, and decongestant, because it turns out being tired and getting older make certain orifices get blocked. Make-up bag: concealer to conceal, powder to blot, lipstick to go from work to 'I really mean business', hand cream for my hands and often my ankles – a brown skin thing! – an eyebrow brush because those are the wobbly things on my face that do not play nice and good old Vaseline. My trusted friend. Alongside the mini pack of wet wipes and of course antibacterial gel.

Oh, I'm not done yet: there is more. There is also the electrical bag, with the portable charger, just in case there is no plug socket available. Except when I'm in a remote village in the middle of nowhere, I haven't found it to be useful. My earphones, which I never use, perhaps because I enjoy them so beautifully wrapped in their packaging it feels a shame to undo them, given all the untangling tantrums that will inevitably follow. Then there are the other things that are in amongst the base and pockets, including the glasses for the short-sightedness I have now come to accept. Glasses make you look smart, right? I have worn glasses since I was eleven. You can deny it all you want as a kid, but as an adult there's a moment when you suddenly realise: 'What the hell? I actually can't see!'

Wine gums, Colin Caterpillars to feed the sugar addiction and a bottle of water for when I come down from my sugar high. Always Polos and gum in emergencies, because fillings and gum are friends and when they meet there is no prising them apart. A pair of flats in a carrier bag, because I don't care about appearing powerful or confident these days. I can't imagine how a grimace followed by a wince in a pair of towering six inches can make anyone appear confident; surely one just looks more unsteady than anything else? So when I've had enough and my feet are screaming 'Hail Mary', I give in to the pain because my feet have feelings too. I may not stand tall at five foot and barely one inch, but the smile on my face as I look up at you from waaaaaay down here is better than the face I make after twelve hours in a pair of heels that I have spent the last six hours cursing.

Lunch was the same every day. Allinson's thick sliced brown bread with Anchor butter – and not the kind that was spreadable. It had to be the block variety; that was the only acceptable type. I would take chunks of butter and spread them carefully on my very soft bread, trying all the while not to create gaping holes in my baked beauty. So when anyone asked me, 'Is that cheese in your sandwich?' I could say, without shame, 'No, it's butter, but the butter was hard out of the fridge, so this will have to do.' It was the only way to eat it;

my waist didn't care back then and my conscience certainly didn't give a damn. Life has since taught me that you can have your butter like slabs of cheese but only after you've done a 5k run and micro-managed every morsel that has passed your lips. I have since grown a huge guilty conscience around food and my waist cares a lot more now. I just wish it was as receptive to more butter and less exercise as it used to be.

I would always make two sandwiches, one without anything apart from butter and the other spread with a thin layer of Marmite and that was it. That was me done. That was me every single day. If I ate bread every day now, even just one slice, I would be a trumpet-blowing, windy, bloated mess.

So five of the forty-five minutes before my shift started had been used up, mostly hacking at the fridge-cold butter and trying to find a motion smooth enough not to create holes in my bread. Unsuccessful every time, I would wrap my mouse-eaten sandwiches in foil, popping them into the top of my bag before hanging it on the bannister so I could make a sharp and efficient exit. The forty minutes remaining gave me plenty of time to get upstairs, moisturise my face, and throw on some clothes – as loose-fitting and black as possible – at which point I would still have about thirty minutes before I needed to be at work.

It took fifteen minutes to get there. Getting to the outskirts of town was easy enough with a flyover that ran proudly above the towns, but I would take the slower route through Bury Park, behind my sister's house. If I drove through this area, I could pass our old house, maybe see a few familiar faces, neighbours of old, relatives disconnected. I would drive with the window down, so I could see the latest in Indian fashion trends to report back to my sisters. The familiar smells – fried chicken and paratha – would waft through the street all the way to our old house. The sound of the trains rattling along the track as I drove by. The mayhem was relaxing, nostalgic. Perhaps it was life's way of saying, 'Take it all in, you won't be here much longer.'

But first I had to get out of the house. I ran downstairs and pulled my bag off the bannister. Sitting on the second stair up from the bottom, I pushed my right foot into my trainer and fought to put the left one on, twisting my foot into the ground like some badly performed Bollywood move. Furiously, I tied my laces on my navy Adidas Campus, then grabbed my bag off the floor.

'Mum, I'm going to work!' I shouted, grabbing my keys and slamming the door shut behind me. We never locked the front door. Gently placing the bag on the passenger's side of the car, I got in and shut the door. Sigh. Looked at the time. Fifteen minutes to get there, fifteen minutes to set up and hand out mints. Like clockwork. As I reversed out of the drive, I saw Mum's arms flailing at me from the front-room window as she precariously wedged the phone between her shoulder and her ear, using the other hand to hold up the net curtains. She signalled for me to come inside as soon as my eyes met hers.

'No, no, I've got to go to work,' I said as I continued to

reverse. She came flying out of the door, by this point furious at my refusal.

'There is a woman on the phone about a job you applied for,' she shouted through my car window. Mum looked puzzled. Why the hell had I given the house number, when I could have given her a mobile? The kind of mistake people make when they work a night shift. I hit the brakes. Left the car exactly where it was with the engine running. Snatched the phone off mum: 'Hello?'

Mum looked at me as I listened intently on the phone, nodding and saying a few words. She was even more confused when I punched the air. She gestured with her hands, saying 'what is it?' with her eyes, as mothers do. But the more I gave her the one-minute sign with my index finger the more infuriated she looked. A look that didn't scare me as much as it had done when I was a teenager.

I clicked the red button, to disconnect. We both stood in the driveway. The evening warm, my back sweating with excitement and anticipation. My mum stood barefoot on the drive as she apologised to passers-by for the Renault Clio, still running its engine in the middle of the footpath.

'Sorry,' she said. 'Who was that?'

'I got the job!' I looked at the phone. I actually got the job. Secretly I had applied at a chauffeur company. Already working a job, in the evening and nights, I wanted a way to fill my hours during the day.

'What job?'

'I applied for another job and I got it.'

I was getting later for work and for the first time I didn't care. But that feeling didn't last very long.

'Must go – I'm going to be late for work!' I ran to the car as a young man walking past shouted, 'What kind of idiot parks a car like that?'

'Your mum!'

What can I say? I was eighteen and feisty and I was going to be late for work.

'*What* did you say?' He came towards me. A face I recognised from college. Not a friend, not an acquaintance, just a face I recognised. I don't forget a face. I didn't have a clue why he was approaching me – for a fight perhaps? Or a telling off? Or maybe he was going to show me how to park my car?

'Don't start a fight with this boy please, Nadiya. What is this job?' Mum said. 'Why do you need two jobs? She didn't mean it,' she added to the gobshite, trying to make him leave.

I turned to him myself. 'Listen, I've seen you in college, with that girl that you go with behind the prayer rooms.'

Funny how he stopped walking towards me. Halted in his tracks.

'And you know I know your sister. I could tell her if you like.'

'Bitch!' he shouted as he walked away. Muslim boy with a secret girlfriend. The best kind of ammunition, in a world where a nineteen-year-old with a girlfriend should not make anyone bat an eyelid. Not in our circle. Although I'm not the blackmailing type, it was always fun to watch them squirm a little. I didn't care who people got off with behind the prayer rooms, who got pregnant, who had an abortion, or who secretly got tattoos. But sometimes, just sometimes, it came in handy.

'Why are you getting another job?'

I got into the car. Angry with my mum and happy at the prospect of another job. Another job, more money, less time at home.

'If I can't go to university, I want to work all the time.' I got in the car, reversed straight out and didn't stop to look at my mum once. I cried my way up the main road, avoiding my regular haunts behind my sister's house, late for the first time.

I didn't want a second job; what I wanted was to go to university. But as with most things, there were conditions. The university had to be in Luton and I had to be living at home. I didn't want to live at home and I had my heart set on a university outside of Luton. I knew it would take some convincing. In the end I lost. So I worked every hour I could fill. Eating on the go and sleeping where I could, I spent only a few hours at home a day. An act of defiance, in the only way I could. I was doing my own thing, but under the guise of guardianship. I was flourishing in the world of work, but always under the guise of guardianship. I had financial independence, but only under the guise of guardianship.

For years I coldly rationed this anger towards my parents for not allowing me to go to university. Enraged to begin with, I met them openly and only with hostility. As the years passed I felt a bitter taste in my mouth, so bitter I could never hide the disdain on my face. Now imagine how that flared like a seafood rash when my brother went to university? But he lived at home and that gave them the security and reassurance that they needed. I didn't want to live at home and I was not shy about expressing that.

'Everyone else moves out to go to university.'

'Well, you are not everyone else.'

I wasn't. I was the first girl in this family to get into university. I had a plan and there was no Plan B. So when it didn't happen, when I didn't get to pack and leave and study psychology with strangers and live with people I didn't know, I was suddenly in No Man's Land. Focused, however; I have always been focused. So I focused on making my parents remember for as long as I could physically keep it up that they didn't let me go to university.

But why didn't they? Were they afraid that I was going to take drugs? Get a boyfriend? Have sex? Stay out late? Party all night? Drink alcohol? Everything that they thought society encouraged. Well, no, that's not what I wanted to do. I wanted to study psychology, that was all. Perhaps through that I would have a richer experience that I hadn't thought about at the time. But really, all I wanted to do was go to university. Just like I had proclaimed when I'd made a green felt Roman bulla on which I'd written 'One day I want to go to university' and placed it round my neck. Stupid bulla, did not work. Nor did pleading, begging and crying.

Looking back, I understand more and judge less. If I were

an immigrant in a brand-new country, isolated by a language I didn't speak or understand, surrounded by faces that were not familiar, food that was mysterious, customs that were misunderstood with a culture so far from what I was raised with . . . how would I feel if my child said, 'Can I just go off out into this scary unknown world on my own?' I may as well have said, 'Can I get in a rocket and be blasted into space?' It was that alien to them. What would I have said if I were them? I was not scared, because the world that they were so afraid of was the world I was raised in. Alien and unresponsive to them, it was mine and I felt alive in it. It was mine to discover and mine to get lost in, but it never really did become my world. My path was going to lead me somewhere eventually, but at the time, the sat nav was set to Rage Street, in Angryshire, just off Grudge Grove. That is a destination that has been taken off my list of favourite places to go.

The anger subsided when my drive and determination to succeed resulted in two jobs, which meant two wages, which meant more money than I knew what to do with. Slight exaggeration: after doing a food shop, putting petroleum in the car and paying for my insurance and road tax, I often didn't have much left. But it did give me freedom to do mischievous stuff and who better to do it with than my unassuming younger siblings?

'Shak, shall we go out?' I said to my brother. He looked at the clock.

'But it's bedtime.'

'So what?'

Mum was away in Bangladesh and Dad was working. It was just us two at home.

'Come on, let's go,' I urged. I kicked his bottom off the floor where he sat perched like a bird with his packet of cheese and onion crisps.

'But where will we go?' he enquired. What do I say to a nine-year-old boy to get him to peel his corneas off the *Pokémon* splashed across the screen?

'Toys R Us?' No sooner did I finish saying those words than his little butt had come off the ground. Switching the TV off, he was into the hallway in an instant and already slipping on his shoes.

'Come on then, let's go!' he yelled from the front door, my keys in his little hands. We were off.

'Shall we get chicken and chips on the way?' I asked.

'With leftover chips, so we can cook them later?' he said.

'For sure!'

We walked through the aisles of Toys R Us. He knew where everything was. As he walked a few paces ahead of me, pointing and pausing and pointing some more, eventually he came to a halt.

'Please can I buy these Scoobies?' He picked up a packet of the coloured strings that were all the rage when woven into friendship bracelets and key chains, looking at me for approval. A muted silver collection, classy to say the least.

'Why don't you pick one in every colour?'

He looked at me with an expression of horror mixed with

a drop of excitement. His face read, 'She's kidding, right? What's the trick here? Is this a joke?'

'One of each?' he enquired.

'Yup, one of each.'

He hurtled towards me, giving me a squeeze so hard, my lungs got wind. Then he ran right past me, dodging the passers-by so fast it felt like he feared I would change my mind if he didn't get a basket in record time. He emerged from the corner, basket in tow. He started grabbing packets one by one and looked at me after every few packs he laid inside the basket.

'Are you sure?' he asked.

'Would you like me to change my mind?'

'No way.' He carried on filling his basket.

The tannoy announced: 'The store will be closing in five minutes.' So we hurried past the stationery, the board games, the cuddly toys, picking up a Kinder Surprise on our way. We paid for his mammoth pile of Scoobies; he had to use both hands to carry them out and fling them over his shoulder for extra stability. His excitement shone as the setting sun reflected off his multicoloured Scoobie loot and bounced off his glowing face. Never had I seen a nine-year-old so happy. He carried them on his lap the whole way home. Stopping off to pick up his chicken and chips – and extra chips, of course – he sat with the mountain of food and plastic string on his lap till the steaming chicken began to scorch his little thighs. When we got home, he sat on the floor and I sat behind him, his plastic bits of string all over the floor while he attempted to weave his most complicated pattern and his chicken got cold.

'Can I eat my chicken now and maybe you can make me your special chips tomorrow?'

That sounded like a plan. Money can't buy you love, but it can buy smiles, even if temporary, even if brief. In that moment, every penny was well spent.

Thirteen years later, here I am. I started to work because that is what everyone did. If you were a summer baby you had to wait in the wings while everyone got their National Insurance numbers. Thank goodness for being born on the right side of the academic year.

'I've got a part-time job in a coffee shop', 'I'm working at the chemist', 'I'm working in town', 'I'm doing a paper round'. Post work experience, working for experience and not getting paid well and truly sucked. Why work and not get paid? I see what they did there! It wet our whistle; we wanted to work, to get out there, and I was no different to everyone else. Little did I know that life was going to thrust me into a world of work unlike anything I had ever imagined. It certainly wasn't the dream or the hope compared to what I am doing today.

After working two jobs, days as an assistant at a chauffeur company and nights at a medical dispatching centre, my life changed dramatically, what with marriage and moving 163.7 miles from my family – that's a big leap for a girl who had only been to London and Birmingham a handful of times. The world closed for me when my dream of university died, and with it a few of my own aspirations to see anything outside of Luton. But there I was, 163.7 miles from home. My job was now to be a mother and wife, yet I never stopped yearning for a life where I worked and earned and spent without question.

'Shall I go back to work, once the baby is born?'

'Let's have a look at what childcare costs are like.' Having never had a child before, we were not expecting to see the numbers that we were about to be presented with.

'So I'll be earning to send the baby to nursery? And adding more on top to cover the cost? And actually bring nothing home? So I'm working just to pay someone to look after my kid so I can never see him?'

Scratch that. Made no sense. But secretly, I always looked, just to see what was out there. I considered becoming an Avon representative, a driving instructor, dinner lady, packing envelopes, paper round. Anything to satisfy the need to feel useful. To feel like I was contributing.

My neighbour came round for tea like she often did in the early evening. The kids playing around us, we sat at the dining table, feet crossed. We were neighbours long enough to be on repeat chats: same stories, different angles.

'I really need a cleaner.'

'I'll do it!' The words could not leave my mouth any quicker; she had barely completed her statement. Was it a statement? Had I seemed so desperate for job? Was she doing me a favour? Had I mentioned my absolute desire to earn anything, even just a few quid?

'I'll do it, I can do it when the kids are in school!' I may as well have begged. She could not have said no, even if she tried. A week later she showed me the ropes, how to get in, how to do the alarm and most importantly what needed doing. I take no joy in cleaning other people's houses – I don't even enjoy cleaning my own – but I was being paid. The first time in years I was going to earn a few quid.

'You're not embarrassed that I clean the neighbour's house, are you?'

'No way, do what makes you happy.'

Happy is a strong word. But secretly I was embarrassed for my husband. Would he say with pride and puffed chest, 'That's my wife, she puts her hands down bogs to earn some cash?' Probably not. It didn't make me happy; it made me feel needed. It wasn't something that I told anyone else, not something that I advertised. Even to this day I'm not quite sure why I never said anything out loud. Maybe I was embarrassed? Who knows. It was better to do a job I didn't love than to sit at home feeling worthless and empty. At least it made me feel fulfilled. I saved enough money after a few months to take the kids out on the first cinema trip that I had paid for in years.

There was that girl again, the one I kept losing. The same girl who didn't go to university and used her anger to fuel her desire to work. The same girl who could do the weekly shop without hesitation, pay her road tax, take her brother on an impromptu Toys R Us trip, buy an Xbox that wasn't even in the sale, skip college to take her sister on a shopping spree. She was the same girl who cleaned someone else's toilet and felt nothing but utter pride. I had thought for so long she was gone and there she was all over again. She had gone nowhere. Life just hid her away for a little while. Little did I know she was here to stay.

Now if anyone asks me what I do, what my job title is, I haven't a clue how to respond. There are so many hats I wear these days that often I can't answer that question myself. Something about saying 'Well, I'm a published author, cook, writer, columnist and presenter' sounds a little bit . . . I don't know, big-headed, egotistical – pompous too. But why not say it? That is what I am and I should be proud of the path I have walked to get here.

Because the one thing I won't be called is a reality TV star; that I am not. I only mention it, of course, because that is exactly how I have been introduced in the past. The definition of reality television is a 'genre of television pro-gramming that documents supposedly unscripted real-life situations and often features an otherwise unknown cast of individuals who are typically not professional actors'. Not me! I entered a baking show, I had to know how to bake to get onto that, there was no acting or making it up as we went along and never once did anyone see me in a bikini. The most you saw was a saucy wrist, when I feared my sleeves would be soiled with my warm crème pâtissiere.

About three years ago someone asked my son, what does

your mum do for a living? This question was much to his shock because at this point in his life he figured everyone knew who I was. Poor kid, not everyone watches *Bake Off* – most people do but there are a few (just a few) who don't. The question came out of the blue, like those ones that teachers used to suddenly ask you in class to see if you were listening. 'What did you have for breakfast? What did you do over the holidays? What are your parents' jobs?' Random spot quizzes to keep the kids on their toes. Oh yes, still alive and kicking – I remember them from my own childhood.

'What did you have for breakfast . . . Nadiya?' my teacher asked me one time. You had to answer fast: no thinking meant no lying. I totally judged the kid before me who said he had cherry soda. What a dick, who says that out loud?

So now it was my turn to reply. 'Rice and curry.' I hid my head in shame. Who's the dick now? The teacher looked at me with disgust and her head angled, unsure, wondering if perhaps I had made a mistake. But I couldn't take it back.

'Rice and curry?' They all laughed, loud – it didn't stop for what felt like an age.

'Yes, Miss, I had rice with fish and pumpkin and it was really tasty.' It was out there now; I may as well make them salivate with jealousy. She nodded, still unsure, then asked the same question of her next victim. 'Peas,' came the response. A gasp filled the room.

'Did you just say peas?'

'Yes, Miss,' the girl answered.

'With butter and salt?' she enquired, as if somehow that

would have made peas more appealing before 8 a.m. No, just boiled peas! Life can be cruel when you're seven.

Anyway, there was my boy, faced with a similar type of situation. What does his mum do? What does a kid say when he has no clue what his mum's job title is? His reply: 'She lives her dreams.' Technically not an answer, but what an answer. Vague, obscure, fantastical, I could be a unicorn for all they knew, but whatever I was doing he saw me live my dreams. All my children do.

Living the dream, being a cook. Cooking was something I had watched every woman in my family do my whole life. It wasn't a dream. It was a thing that you did. People needed to eat, so someone needed to cook. That's what cooks did. Right? When we're kids our mum cooks and we eat and then life goes full circle and we cook and our kids eat and so on. My mum, like everyone says about their own mum, is the best cook I have ever met. But she knew what she knew. Curries were her thing, because that is what everyone ate and that's what she cooked. She never deviated, and when she did, it didn't always work out. She attempted to make traditional snacks but someone always made them better. However, her curries always tasted like they had been touched by an angel. Melodiously delicious, her food sings tunes in my head when it touches my taste buds. She was consistent. Dad, the mad hatter at the dinner table, always found new ways of not wasting and cooking. If it was poisonous you were only going to find out afterwards. Thank goodness for the internet because at least now he can look things up before serving it up to his 'never quite sure what they're going to get' guinea-pig offspring.

One night, my parents giggled and laughed, which was a strange sound. They didn't often have private jokes. They served up dinner on the table – new curries in large pans, older curries in small bowls and some food still in foil containers from the restaurant. A normal occurrence; the only things that weren't normal were the quiet cackles and signals to one another.

'Are we having another baby?' I shouted. They were annoying when they fought but they were worse when they were happy.

'No!' Mum said. Dad just looked at Mum and smiled as they ushered us to the table to eat our dinner.

'Try that one in the foil container.' He picked it up and dunked a spoon in. Dishing out a helping onto our plates.

'What is it?' my sister asked. Mum laughed and walked into the kitchen. Dad tried and failed to hide his smirk, which resulted in him spluttering all over our dinner. As if their giddiness wasn't vomit-inducing enough, he had to spit all over our food. Like anyone was going to eat that now, I thought, though by the time the words had formed in my head my brother had already tucked in and gone for some more. 'This is good,' he proclaimed as he went in for another heapful.

'Tell me what it is or I won't eat it!' I said.

'Eat it or I won't tell you!'

Stand off. It didn't last long. I was hungry and they were

getting annoying. I mean, how bad could it actually be? It couldn't be anything we hadn't eaten before. After the foil container was well and truly empty – and may I add it was pretty damn delicious – Dad said, 'Do you know what you just ate?'

Pause. What the hell did we just eat?

'Lambs' balls!' Dad spluttered, laughing so hard he fell to his knees.

'Okay.'

Our reaction was unexpected. Not one gagging sound, no pretend vomiting, no fingers down throats, no storming off, no red faces, no anger. For a man who had fed us grape pulp for breakfast, tripe for lunch and cows' hooves for dinner, why did he think that lambs' bollocks would surprise us? Shame on him for even trying it.

To grow up with two confident cooks makes me nervous in their presence. But what it has given me is resilience and creativity and the innate need to try the things that everyone else retches at the thought of. That may have come from the lambs' balls. At school, it was burgers, chips and beans followed by cake and custard. At home it was rice and curry with a large helping of lychees. One you ate precariously with a knife and fork and the other you got your fingers in. One you sat at a table and used chairs, the other you sat on the floor cross-legged. One you ate what you were given and that was that. The other you were cheered on for going back for more. So when I think up recipes like mango and parsley Pavlova, crisp (actual crisps, not the texture) chocolate tart and carrot cake pakoras, I see a little bit of what I was given, from my parents, from my life, from the two worlds that never really collided till I learned to find my own feet in my own kitchen. That is when I became that hybrid cook that lives in all of us. With little respect for convention, be it Bangladeshi or British, I am a firm believer that traditions were made to be mixed. If we can do that in life, then imagine the magic when you do it with food. I believe in that magic; I embrace it, I am it.

We're all writers from the moment we awkwardly pick up a pen and scribble our first few letters. Framed by some parents with pride, they mean nothing, they say nothing. But they do mean something. We're all writers. Some of us write because it soothes us to create; some of us write poetry in order to express ourselves; some of us write because we like lists; some of us don't write and prefer to type. Some of us doodle; some of us sketch. We all create.

Me, I started writing when I was seven. I remember the moment I decided to become a writer. I was sitting on the shiny herringbone floor of the gym for an assembly. I looked up and extended my neck, as it was always my luck that a huge kid with the widest back and the longest neck would be sitting in front of me. Either that or I was destined to be incredibly short. Don't even think it! I know it's the latter. I wriggled to see as the winner of the poetry competition was handed his gold envelope. Nothing bad ever came out of a glittery gold envelope.

'Nadiya, do you need a wee?' loud-whispered the teacher as she tapped the top of my head.

Startled, I stopped fidgeting. 'No, Miss.' I fixed my dress as I felt the blood rushing up to my face.

'Well, sit still! And you – read it out then!' the teacher urged the beanpole boy standing in front of us.

He opened the envelope, his eyes widening as he read the contents. 'I get to meet the queen!'

He shrieked and jumped into the air, his feet landing without a sound. He can't have been that excited, I mean who only jumps once at the thought of meeting the queen? I would have jumped at least a dozen times. He was ushered away as they carried on giving out prizes. 'We'll hear all about it when you get back from your visit.'

I was filled with jealousy. I told myself there and then that I was going to enter that competition next year, that I was going to write the best poem and I was going to win it.

I was as good as my word. I entered, I won and I too got a prize. My prize did not come in the form of a golden envelope. Mine was thicker, just a little bit thicker. I stood, touching it, inspecting its hidden contents. Perhaps my poem was so good it came with a prize *and* an invite to meet Her Majesty? 'Go on then, open it up, we don't have all day.' I ripped off the tape and unveiled a set of pencils in different colours, the best kind, Crayola in fact. I looked and felt for anything else, in the corner of the envelope, but no invite. No queen.

That didn't put me off. I just kept writing. I filled every empty page of every notebook I ever owned with words. End-of-year textbooks that never got filled with schoolwork got embellished with words. Napkins at my dad's restaurants. My high-school planner. Then the inside of my ring binder. My notes at work. My children's nappies. The frost on my winter windscreen. The sand in Portugal. The dust on my mantle.

'Find a book that you relate to, read it and write a thousand words on why you relate to a character in the book, or the story in the book,' my GCSE English teacher once said. Class dismissed. I searched library after library, bookshop after bookshop and still nothing. Not one book, not one blurb, not one cover, nothing. That was the only time I went back to my English language lesson empty-handed. 'That is why we need more writers of different backgrounds, ethnicities, religions and culture,' my teacher said. 'You should keep writing.'

So I wrote and I wrote. For peace of mind, for the thought that somewhere in a quiet part of Luton a brown bilingual girl was writing her story. Of love, life, conflict and belonging. Of sadness and scandals. Of joy and grief. A tale of two lives. So that one day someone might read her story, even if it was just her own children. They will know that there is a tale in all of us to tell. Writer or not, we all have a story. That's why I write, because someone will read it and they won't be that girl, like me and many others, who traipsed along the soggy streets of Britain to find a story to belong in. I write because someone will find belonging in my story, whether it's a recipe they read that reminds them of a taste in their memory, a passage to connect them to a particular place or a sentence that gives comfort. I write to soothe my own soul and in doing so it soothes others. So for as long as there are readers, I will have a pen in my hand, or I'll be close to a computer at least.

But all of that has brought me to an unlikely place now, right in front of a camera. They call it being a presenter in this industry. What is a presenter and what am I presenting? Well, myself. What do I have to present? Apart from a scruffy English accent and a face so agile that it won't let me lie. I thought I was going to become a social worker, not a presenter. But here I am. Make-up done, I stand in front of the bright lights. Pulling at my shirt, tugging it, as I suck in my belly and look at my silhouette in the reflection of the glass French doors.

Unfamiliar, this kitchen is not mine. They call it a location kitchen, which is code for someone else's kitchen. I like my kitchen, though. It might be small, but it has beautiful light; as I cook I can see my chickens through my window. My special pots are dotted on top of my units for the sheer lack of space, yet aesthetically somehow they work. One pot for each child when they buy their first house and own their first kitchen. Spice racks on the walls, alongside an original Chris Terry painting of rice fields that reminds me of a distant home. Two coffee machines and a small utility room for chicken mucking-out boots and crap. That's my kitchen; that's where I feel safe.

Not in this kitchen. The wide spaces and high ceiling make the room eerily cold the second the lights are switched off. The light is harsh from the glass roof: too cold on a bad day and a blistering greenhouse on a good day. The hob is unfamiliar, I can't work the sink, I have never seen the insides of the cupboard and the set is dressed to look like a home that I will never have. Too afraid to say that my kitchen would never look like this, I sit quietly while the room is set, the lights are tweaked and my face is dusted again to hide the panic. People mill around, the smell of coffee dances on my nose, people walk in and out, and the air is filled with greetings and goodbyes.

I look at all my little bowls of ingredients in front of me on the kitchen counter, each one individually placed. I hear an order I can't understand and the recipe I thought I knew is suddenly gone. 'What on earth am I doing?' I ask myself. I look up.

'And . . . action!' I can see the red light is on. I had felt safe in the humdrum activity of people organising things: ingredients, lights, spoons. I was a part of all that till the man said, 'Action!' Now I am alone. My mouth is parched with nerves and the words don't come out the way I had practised in the mirror. Cooking is what I love to do. This is my safe place. But actually THIS is not my safe place.

'I need to go for a wee!' I ran upstairs. That was the day I learned that when I say stop everyone stops. A feeling I am not accustomed to; it takes twelve tries to get the kids to brush their teeth, at least three to get my husband to do the ironing and more than a few to get my dad to give me a call. With my mic still on, I heard everyone disperse and someone say, 'Who'd like a cuppa?' I heard a trail of 'me's fade into the background as I ran upstairs. The unfortunate sound man would have had an earful of my sobbing mixed in with a forced trickle of wee. He had probably heard worse, but right now this felt like the worst thing ever. I didn't want everyone to see I'd been crying, so I stuck my head out of the window in the hope that it would express-dry my tears.

I was ready to go down. Well, I wasn't but I pretended anyway. In a room full of people I pretended to be excited and enthusiastic but all I wanted was for it to end. There was nothing natural about what I was doing. How does Nigella make it look so clean and effortless? Maybe I needed a few more fairy lights on set? Or perhaps, just maybe, this isn't my world. I walked out the door after that first recipe and held my arms out wide. Not so I could feel free, or to allow my lungs to take in the crisp air; it was simply to dry my sweaty pits. I sweated less giving birth to my eight-pound-fourteen-ounce behemoth of a child. Yet here I was, cowering in front of a camera, full of the fear of being judged as the girl who doesn't belong in this world.

From the very moment I stepped into the public eye I

heard these words: 'You are a reality TV star, not a chef, you do not belong here.' I cried myself into a stupor as the words seemed to be the only thing that rang in my head on repeat whenever doubt set in. How can I be a writer, when there are so many writers out there who are better than me and have a better story to tell? How can I be a cook if I have no formal training? Can I even call myself a cook? Why did I think I could have a cookery show? What right do I have to be here?

I still find myself crying and turning into that same crumbling wreck often. Every time I walk into a room and find I am the only woman, amongst men twice my size. Every time I walk into a space where I am the only person of colour. I am the awkward cook who doesn't drink alcohol or eat pig in its many forms. I use grape juice instead of red wine and substitute smoked turkey rashers for bacon. I don't know what black pudding tastes like and frankly I don't know that I would eat it if I could. I still hear those words, when I doubt where I stand. But what I have learned and what I remind myself of is that it's not about where I stand, it's about what I stand for.

Earlier I bashfully listed all the jobs that I do. So I am going to list them again. I am a cook, an author and presenter. I love the jobs I do. With these jobs come many challenges, simply because I am also much more than these job titles. I am a devoted mother, which means I won't work every hour God sends; I am a Muslim, so I will stop to pray; I am brown so if you only come with a default shade in your make-up bag perhaps you should rethink *your* job and yes, I do have a vagina – I'm a girl, lady, woman, whatever you want to call it – so I will stop to take painkillers when I struggle to smile through the cramps while grating cheese on camera and profusely perspiring under the lights rented from hell. I want to do my job; I'm not here to take yours.

—✦—

SPECIAL LEFTOVER CHIPS

Remember those special chips I wrote about? Well, even to this day, whenever we are getting a takeaway, we deliberately buy extra chips so we can make our special recipe with the cold leftovers. It's pretty basic. The result will vary depending on how many chips you have to start with.

Enough for about 300g of leftover chips

You will need:

Leftover chips
6 tbsp oil
5 cloves of garlic, thinly sliced
2 medium onions, thinly sliced
Salt to taste
7 tbsp chilli sauce, either left over from the night
    before or out of a bottle
1 green chilli, thinly sliced
Large handful of fresh coriander, chopped
5 tbsp mayonnaise
100g strong Cheddar cheese, grated

How to make it:

Put your chips in a bowl and soak them in cold water for about 5 minutes, then drain.

Add your oil to a large non-stick wok and when it is hot add the garlic. When the garlic is really brown but not black, take it off the heat and add the onions and salt. Cook the onions till they are really soft and brown.

Add the chips to the pan and cook them till they are hot, then mix in the chilli sauce, chilli and coriander.

Take off the heat, add the mayo and mix through. Then sprinkle the cheese on top and serve straight away. We go straight into the wok with forks and all.

᜸᜵ᜢ

COOK

I measure, I cut, I peel, I pour.
It makes me stop, though my feet keep going
And my hands can't keep up.
My eyes scroll as I make sense of the numbers.
It's my head I want out of; I fill it with more.

I mix,
I scrape,
I wipe,
I level.
It makes me stop, takes me away.
Though my feet keep going, they no longer pace.
My hands can't keep up, because of the excitement it brings.
I want out of my head so I fill it with more.
Numbers, lists, weights and mess.

I measure, I cut, I peel, I pour.
I mix,

I scrape,
I wipe,
I level.

It makes me move. But it makes me stop. It takes me away.

'What would you like to be when you're older?' she asked the whole class. We all flailed our arms about.

'Me, Miss, pick me, Miss,' we all shouted over one another. I was one of the shortest, so I had to go the extra mile and get on my knees against that cold, hard, rubbery flooring.

'Me, Miss, please pick me!' I set about on repeat. I knew what I wanted to do and I wanted so desperately to say it out loud. There were a few who looked at me out of the corner of their eyes as they sat there, arms crossed. Too cool to be seen to be eager and too stupid to know what occupation actually meant. I knew deep down that they were destined for an interesting future; turns out at least one of them is in prison now.

'Let it be a lesson to you, kids,' I tell my kids now. 'You don't have to know what you want to do, but at least be bold enough to dream.

'Don't ever think you're too cool to answer that question.

'Don't ever think it's not the "in" thing to think big.

'Always raise your hands in class.

'And for God's sake, please tell me you know what occupation means.'

Back to the classroom. 'Yes, Nadiya.' She picked me; she actually picked me. 'What are you going to be when you're older?'

I held my head up high and swallowed my saliva in one large gulp, ready to say this big word. I knew it was a big word compared to the nurses and teachers that just got listed. I knew no one wanted to be what I wanted to be.

'I want to be an archaeologist, Miss,' I said. Loud and proud and hopeful that I wouldn't hear a single 'me too'.

'What's an archaeologist?' I heard in the room.

But then I heard something else – my teacher's voice. 'You can't become an archaeologist; your parents are not rich enough for you to become an archaeologist.'

Those words stayed with me forever. Since the age of seven. I liked digging in the garden and finding bones of pets deceased and forgotten. I enjoyed identifying objects. Once I dug all day in the hope that I could reach the centre of the earth. Instead I dug up all my mum's coriander that she had planted for the summer. She was not happy; I had unearthed her good work and I was a muddy, soiled mess. So I stood and showered under the cold hose. The first of my 'you can'ts' in a line of many many 'you can'ts' to come. Little did I know.

Several years later, I sat on the living room floor writing an essay for English about a book I had just read, *To Kill a Mockingbird* by Harper Lee, still one of my favourite things to come out of my English GCSE years, a book I now share with my children. My older cousin was sitting on the settee directly in front of me, waited on hand and foot. A flurry of tea and snacks came to him, one after another after another. I watched the television in the gaps where my mind needed a break, but with the football on, the luminous green screen was not the kind of distraction I cared for. He occasionally broke my calm when he screamed and raised his arse off the settee, post-goal. Not that it stayed off there long. Soon he was back on his seat again, being topped up with mugs of tea.

I had no desire to talk to him. We had nothing to talk about. So I avoided all eye contact and fell straight back into my 1930s-set modern American literature. My mind wandered around the streets of Alabama, often being rudely interrupted by modern-day Luton. Our house was never quiet and doing homework in a quiet place or even attempting to create one was near enough impossible. So I stopped trying.

'So what are you going to be when you're older?' he asked casually as he slumped in his seat. There had to be a break, otherwise why would he be talking to me?

I tried to ignore him, pretended I didn't hear him. I'm a bad liar; no doubt he saw right through the façade. I carried on writing on the pieces of paper leant on my thigh, examining each page, as if to busy myself.

'Oi! I'm talking to you, are you deaf?'

'Sorry, Baia, I didn't hear you.'

'Baia' is a term of endearment but mostly respect. As I mentioned earlier, anyone older than you had a title; you didn't use names, which in my book defeats the objective of names – what was the point in giving people names if everyone used a title? As for endearment, what if they were a total prick and you didn't want to grace them with an affectionate title? I for one wanted to say, 'Yo, dick, I'm doing my homework, piss off back to your own house and if you are going to sit here at least turn the volume down and while you're doing that you can get off your lazy, deadbeat, drop-out-of-school backside and make your own tea, rather than grunting every time you need a refill!'

Of course I didn't say that; I just wished my mum would stop giving him tea so he could get the hint and leave.

'Sorry, Baia, I didn't hear you.'

'What are you going to become when you're older?'

'A nurse. I'd like to help people, I think that's what I want to do,' I said, in the hope that my response was to the point and provided enough information to fill the gap of his ad break so he would stop talking to me.

'Is that because you're not clever enough to become a doctor?'

Prick!

'No, it's because that's what I want to be.'

He called my mum over. She came, no doubt excited to replenish his tea, gesturing for him to hand over his mug.

'She wants to become a nurse, that's a nasty job. She will have to clean bums and she will smell of wee when she comes home.'

Double prick!

'I don't think you should become a nurse, that's not a good job,' Mum said, walking back into the kitchen to tend to her steaming pans.

'Yeah, that's a stupid idea,' he muttered and went back to his remote control, flick, flick, flicking. The light of the television enhanced his smug face. Back to Alabama for me with a new plan of action.

Why did I care so much about their opinions? Why didn't I just stick to my own plan and follow through till the job was done, without inviting discussion? Did every decision need to be steered in a direction that led to more money? Reputation? Status? I wanted to have a career, one that required me to go to university, something that no one had ever done in our family. Surely that in itself was a step up.

'I am going to be a chef in the army,' I declared to my mum one evening when we were sitting on the floor, eating our rice.

'First, you are not becoming a chef: girls can't be chefs. And second, you are not joining the army,' she replied.

That's when I found my fight. I was already a soldier battling through the community's expectations of me. I was already on a battlefield, fighting one fight to get to another.

'Yes I am, and I have to study to do it.'

'Will you be cooking like the chefs in your dad's restaurants?'

I supposed so, but not everyone likes curry, so I figured I would learn all sorts of other cuisines too.

'Will you be a part of the army?'

Well yes, an integral part, keeping the troops sustained, fed and happy.

'Will you have to leave home?'

It's not really a work-from-home kind of vocation, so yes, there would be an element of travel.

My mum's verdict was blunt. 'No.'

'Why?'

'You can do anything else, but not that.'

Back to the drawing board. After I finished my GCSEs, I worked two jobs and managed to get through college, mostly sleeping through classes and using my dictaphone to record the lessons so I could make my notes at work later. I was chasing my tail, but I needed to save for a car, for my education. I knew I needed a safety net. So I was slowly toiling, tired but determined that I wouldn't have to ask my forever-struggling parents for handouts. My parents were polar opposites: Mum saved so much it drove her mad and Dad had no concept of not spending what he had in his pocket. I don't know which type I was but I'd like to think I was neither. I was smart enough at seventeen to understand that I needed to help myself, because I was not going to get it anywhere else, but I loved life enough to spend the money on the people I cared about.

After a year of college, I decided I wanted to become a midwife. I needed a goal and I needed to reach it. I wanted to say, 'This is what I want to do,' and to work hard to achieve a vocation. There it was: I wanted to become a midwife.

'I need to change college,' I said. I feared a lot less now. I just kind of said it, allowed it to spill out of my mouth, 100 per cent convinced, certain, of what the response would be.

'Why not stay where you are?'

'Because I want to do midwifery and this college special-ises in it. It would be perfect for me.'

In the face of all of the questions, I laid it out straight:

'It's in Bedford, so I will have to travel every day.

'No, I can't do the same thing at this college.

'Yes, it will cost more money, but I can cover that.

'Yes, it will mean I will have to go to university.

'. . . Which by the way will not be in Luton.'

Then, another question. 'What is midwifery?' I was making headway; nobody had yet asked for a breakdown of this information. This was like giving me a piece of string. I wanted that string. I wanted to touch it and then hold it tight. Wrap it around my palm three times and give it a gentle tug.

'I get to help women through their pregnancies, from start to end, and I get to deliver babies.'

'Actually deliver them?'

Here it is. 'Yes.'

'I think that's inappropriate. What will we tell people?'

'Who cares about people? Who are these people anyway; do they pay your bills? Who cares what people think? Besides, how would you have had your babies without a midwife?'

'I don't think this job is for girls like you. It's a very Eng-lish job.'

Another one bites the dust.

*

I got into university! I was going to study psychology. With an A level under my belt, I figured university would be the place where I would hear yes, and I could start carving out a path that led to somewhere. I still didn't know where that somewhere was. As long as it was a respectable job (whatever that was) and I loved it, I didn't care how much it paid. I wanted nothing more than to feel fulfilled, satisfied in the job that I did. I wanted to quench that thirst and feed that hunger, till it made me sick with joy. So full, so content that I couldn't think about anything else. I used to laugh and say, 'As long as I'm not a prostitute or an exotic dancer my parents will be happy.' Though of course, pulling babies out of distressed women, nursing the elderly, digging up the remains of bones, cooking for soldiers, they were also all up there with jobs that just wouldn't do.

With two weeks to go before I had to pack up and move out, I could see, taste a way out, a future. Away from no and towards yes. The yes that only I could create for myself. I was straining to see through the fog that surrounded me. I was surprised that I still saw a future, but I did, I really did.

However, like archaeology, nursing, cooking in the army and midwifery, it turned out that university was up there in the large list of 'nos'.

'If you leave for university, you are no longer welcome back at home.'

The fog became thicker; it became too dense, it filled my lungs, it enveloped me and held my chest tight. It surrounded every part of me so that even my tears had nowhere to go.

They remained deep inside my head. Now I couldn't see the light any more. Just smog. I didn't see direction. For the first time in my entire life I didn't dream. I had dared to for as long as I could remember but I didn't any more. There was no dream, there was no direction, there was no hope. Without it, who was I? I wanted a suggestion, just anything, even if it immediately got knocked down, but I didn't even have that any more.

My series of 'nos' led me to the path that was expected of me. The same path that was destined for my mum, her peers, her sisters, her mother, my grandmothers and their peers and the generation of women before them. They all had a destiny and that was home-maker/wife. It was on my radar as my cousins got married one at a time; I hoped for one to break the rules, to go to university, to do a job that raised eyebrows. But they all followed each other like ducks in a row. Happy in their lives. I never saw myself entirely content in that scenario. I saw my grandma and my mum. Exhausted from childbirth, tired from raising humans, there was no let-up. They had to be up before the men and waited for them to return so they could be fed and only then could they sleep. There was no taking turns. There were clear roles. Men made money; women made home.

I lay awake at night dreaming of a life where I would travel the world. I wanted to see the Taj Mahal in India and walk along the Great Wall of China. I wanted to go to Scotland and stand on the tip of Great Britain. I wanted to see Machu Picchu, but not before climbing Snowdon. I wanted to sit on the hard rocks in Bournemouth and to tickle my toes in the sand by the Dead Sea. I wanted to drive up the M1 and perhaps even brave the M25 one day. I wanted a job where I could be promoted every year. A job that made me feel fulfilled, one where I could make a difference. I wanted to be the best saleswoman. To wear a sharp suit and killer heels. To be late home from meetings and take trains to regional branches. I wanted a new car with a private number plate. I wanted to buy a house and give money to charity. I wanted them all to look at me and say, 'She broke the mould. She did something extraordinary.' When really all I wanted to do was what everyone else was doing anyway. I was dreaming big, but I was doing what was normal to most. I wanted to be the normal.

I had no means of getting away from destiny. I was a wife and mother before I was twenty-two, though this was late to the game by many's standards. I felt out of my depth. With a husband, a home and children. This was everything I had never hoped for. Yet here I was. It was 2016; I had a family to keep afloat. How was I any different to my mother, who wasn't even twenty-five when she had a home and five children under the age of seven to look after? How was I any different to my nan, who was wed and with child by the time she was thirteen? How was I different?

Difference was I lived in 2016. That was it. Nothing had actually changed. I saw the change, but it wasn't enough to see that change alone. Someone had to push the boundaries, someone had to break the rules. Someone had to *be* the change. I remained angry at myself for years for not being the change that I wanted to be. But the anger and regret subsided slightly with every coo of my child. Nan's words rang in my ear.

'You do what is expected of you.'

So now I have this child, I have this home, I have this life. This is my job. I wear the word mother with pride; if I could have a badge made I would wear it over my vomit-stained, curry-smelling pinny.

With the 'job' came the love of a world I had once, if only briefly, imagined myself in. The kitchen. The kitchen was the central part of our home as a child. Mum was the one who ran the house and she was always in the kitchen and that felt like the heart of the place. It hardly ever stopped. And even when it did, there were signs of the activity to follow. It was evident in the chapati dough resting under the boiler for breakfast puris, the rice soaking in a pan for the pilau the next day and the chicken defrosting in the sink for the curry after school. It was going to come alive again: with the first hum of the pilot flame in the boiler, my mother would be up and at it all over again.

Mum is a soldier. She can cook without pause. The only time she did pause was to take a sip of her tea. Even then she would scald her mouth each time, the need for a caffeine hit interrupting her frantic yet outwardly calm cooking. With no extractor fan to suck up the steam, the windows would be wide open and the side door wedged ajar with a sandal in its hinge. Despite all the effort to get rid of the steam, the windows would become soaked with condensation till the droplets were too heavy to carry their weight and they would drip to the sodden wooden frames. She could hear it in her head, and I could hear it, Dad complaining: 'The house will become damp if you don't clean up that water straight away.'

These were the days of a freestanding cooker, on which all four hobs would be roaring. It was never just one curry, it was always six, seven, maybe eight – and that's not including the small bowls of leftovers that remained on the sides of the worktop. One by one she would finish off each dish with a flourish of coriander and set it aside. The second she had one space free on the hob, the running water of the rice being washed would stop and a pot of rice would be firmly placed on the stove top. She made it look seamless. Dinner was always ready and so beautifully timed that we would finish eating and Dad would immediately walk through the door, ready for his feast. She would clear up around us and around Dad and finally sit down to her own meal after everyone else. With so much cold food to choose from, the microwave was her friend.

I learned to cook like her. I never practised that way at home when I was a child. But life forced me to learn to manage like her. When you marry a man with enough family members to account for all your fingers and thumbs, it was never going to be a walk in the park. They enjoyed their food, they enjoyed the variety, they enjoyed eating it and they enjoyed being fed. I was suddenly my mum: master chopper, mixer extraordinaire, all the while making breakfast for the latecomers and plating up for the early lunchers.

How in the world did she do it? I was exhausted; at least she sat down afterwards to eat. For the fear of having to wash up again, I avoided eating altogether and resorted to snacking on my three-kilo bag of nuts in my bedroom. It filled me up, it did the job and I didn't have to get my hands dirty. Result. But it turned out I did have it in me: whatever she has, I have that too. Cooking up for a total of twenty-four – and that's just immediate family – doesn't scare me in the slightest. Partly because I do a few things differently to her. The whole family eats together. We all clear up and I am not a maid!

'You should always feed the kids and then the men and then we should eat.'

'Not in this lifetime, Mum, not in this lifetime.'

Growing up, she never really allowed me to cook in the kitchen with her and still to this day she only gives me the job of chopping or washing. No actual cooking allowed. Even then the onions are rarely right. 'I said sliced not diced,' or 'When you wash the dishes make sure the bubbles are totally rinsed off or the liquid will poison you.'

What she gave me was the instinct as a cook – the confidence to trust my instincts that were passed from her somehow, but are all my own. When I cook, it feels like I am performing the most effortless dance. I doubt my combinations but never my ability. Sometimes it works, other times it doesn't. But I like to think that I am the same type as my mum who, despite being knackered, cooks with love for the people she loves, because they are the reason she is in that kitchen in the first place. For their full bellies and fuller smiles. I am more like her than I care to admit. Even now I enjoy watching her from the corner of my eye as I cut her onions all wrong, floating around like a wizard. Having a little taste sometimes.

'Mum, that's horrible . . . like, really bad!' I can't lie or keep a straight face but she falls for it all the time. Her face always drops and Apologetic Mum surfaces. She never says sorry normally, but she does if she thinks she's made a minger of a curry.

'I'm only joking, it's delicious.'

With that, after a sweet mouthful of Bengali profanity, she carries on cooking in her condensation-filled kitchen.

Dad is an entirely different cook. Now, if you put the two of them together in a room where food is prepared, it almost always ends in tears – and not the kind induced by stinging onion. It's more like: 'I will slap you if you tell me how to chop an onion again' or 'maybe we should cook another three curries' on top of the existing eight. That is the kind of ruckus it creates. Even now, in their late fifties, they cannot bear to be in the kitchen together. Mum has a system – 'Get out of my way!' – and he just gets under her feet. Dad likes to mix things up – 'Shall we use kale instead of spinach?' – mostly to wind her up.

I was in the kitchen washing the dishes. I must have been about eighteen. It was around lunchtime in early summer and although I was washing the dishes my mind was wandering between what to take to eat on my night shift at the call centre I was working at and when Shak, my youngest brother, the youngest of us all, would be home for lunch through the gap in the fence at the back of the garden. That's the gap he came through, him and the local fox family. I watched him appear out of the distance and run past Dad, out mowing the lawn, who brushed him on his back as he passed by, to the sound of metal cutting through fresh dewy grass. I ran to warn him to leave his freshly-mown-lawn-lathered school shoes outside, but he'd already anticipated me, his shoes placed neatly outside on the crazy-paved patio. He ran past me with a quick kiss on the arm, settled in his favourite spot in front of the television and switched to *Pokémon*.

I pinged the microwave, where his food sat ready prepared by Mum, just needing warming. As it whirred I could hear the faint sound of the *Pokémon* theme tune against the harsh sound of Dad mowing the lawn. The smell of chicken curry, freshly cut grass and Dad's cigarette smoke wafted through the air. I went to close the window. The mower stopped.

'Nadiya!' Dad shouted.

'Yeah?' It was not like him to want to indulge in conversation midway through a job.

'Do you think we can eat grass?'

Well, he had officially hit a midlife crisis early.

'No way, Dad, that's mad, absolutely not. Please tell me you're not thinking it!'

The microwave pinged. I handed my brother's rice to him where he sat on the floor, along with a tall glass of water. He could drink more water than he could eat food. His tiny tummy was like a well; he would move and we could hear the water jiggle like a waterbed.

'Would you eat grass, Shak?'

'Maybe.' He's as mad as Dad. But I knew he was so engrossed in his cartoon that there was no way he had heard a word I said. I watched as he rolled a ball of mixed rice and curry with his fingers, without looking at his plate, not even for a moment. Then I watched him putting a whole cardamom pod in his mouth. That'll teach him. He spat it out.

'Well, cows eat grass!' Dad shouted. His voice faint from the other end of the house.

'We're not cows, Dad. Besides, cows have four stomachs.' He should know that; he was glued to National Geographic almost every evening. With his hand in a plate of jellied cow's feet while watching sea snails mate. I love watching animals and I love eating food, but the combination of these activities makes my spine tingle.

'You always say we have two stomachs: one for dinner and the other for dessert,' he shouted from the back of the shed.

'That's not an actual fact, Dad. Greedy people like me who like dessert just say that.' Surely he had to know that?

It all went very quiet. I could hear the sound of him raking as I ushered Shak back off to school and made my way up the stairs. Our eyes met as I walked up and he carried in a bowl of freshly cut grass.

'You're not.'

'I am.'

That's the kind of cook my dad is. The kind that sees no

bounds. All he sees is another opportunity to create something new. He knew when he said something out loud that it didn't always sound right. But that didn't mean to say it wasn't going to work. Apart from the time he cooked us mussel curry, which was horrific; when we probed about the unopened ones, he said he had prised them open and put them in too. We were not as sick as we'd thought we were going to be. Or the time he made home-made grape juice, unstrained and so concentrated a spoon stood up proud in the glass. So tart it nearly eroded my teeth. Or the time he attempted to make crisps, which he thinly sliced and left to dry on the shed roof all summer, but still managed to convince us were totally edible. I think there is Blu Tack that is more palatable.

He was the kind of cook who featured every generic food item on his anglicised Indian menu, bearing in mind we are neither Indian nor English. However, he also had an Ali special – the one thing on the menu that was so delicious, he sold at least one on every ticket. He was the kind of guy who used his own vegetables he grew on the sliver of land at the back of the restaurant to feed his customers seasonal food, but also could not bear to take off the chicken korma that looked like vomit and tasted average. He was unconfident in his ability; he needed to look after his family and was scared to take risks in his restaurants. Yet he never questioned why the Ali special was the only thing that they ran out of every single night for years, while the korma bubbled in the back, destined for modification Ali-style or the compost bin.

I see my face in his when his eyes light up at the thought of something unusual. I see my face in his when he is so desperate to create whatever it is that is bubbling away in his brain. I see my face in his when he says 'I think it will work' with confidence, only to be shot down with 'I don't think so'. I see how he is desperate to prove people's taste buds wrong. I see my face in his because I am literally a clone of his face. There is no mistaking our genetic tie. He gave me that spark, that glimmer, that shines like neon. 'It's okay to let your mad show, Nadiya.' I am the mad, the daring, the safe and the caring. I can be the cook who fills holes, straight after school, just before swimming and all without breaking a sweat. I can also be the cook who doesn't care what anyone thinks of the veg that nobody has heard of, to cook it, to taste, to feed and to get it wrong. I can be all of those things and without being taught any of it, there it is.

The one thing my parents didn't give me was the ability to bake. We had a freestanding cooker that came with an oven by default. But it was always packed with frying pans, some filled with old oil, others just too greasy and ugly to have on show. It was the part of the kitchen I hated the most. The smell of old oils and oven innards lacked a certain appeal. I never knew what the knobs were for or that this pan storage cupboard was even a vessel in which to prepare food. I watched Delia when I was growing up, perfectly placed against her kitchen island with the green backdrop of her beautifully cultured and trimmed garden. She had an oven, the kind that came out of the wall. The kind you could put your baking in while standing up. That was an oven. Not this dark cesspit of old oil-scented cupboard. I had a relative who stored her tea towels in her oven.

'Why do you have tea towels in there?' I enquired, rolling my eyes at her insanity.

'Because they need to go somewhere.' True that, but she was still mad.

'My mum puts her pans in there, that cupboard is for pans.'

'We put our pans in there too, sometimes.' Okay, so they were not totally insane, just slightly.

It was only when I was in my food studies class and Mrs Marshall mixed up a cake batter that I discovered what ovens were for. I knew what cake batter was; I had seen it being mixed a dozen times. Delia showed me at least once a week. But I had never seen it being made in real life. Mrs Marshall flung open the frying pan cupboard and as we all looked in from a distance a wave of heat hit my calves.

'What are you doing?'

'I'm baking it in the oven,' she exclaimed.

'That's not an oven!' Lady, what is wrong with you?

'Ladies, tell me you have all seen an oven?' Pause. 'Anyone?'

There was a silence in the room, just the sound of the gas flame from the oven cupboard thing.

'Has anyone ever baked a cake?'

An elongated 'noooooo' hummed through the air.

'Has anyone eaten cake?' Every hand shot up.

'Well, this is how it's baked.' She leant over and popped it into the oven, and as we finished off the washing up and wrote the recipe for our next week's lesson, the room filled itself with a smell I had never experienced before. My nostrils could actually taste the cake, the air full of butter and sweetness. There was something golden about this aroma. I knelt over to take a closer look. This was like magic. No stirring, no turning the heat down, no adding water, no checking for seasoning, no taking off the lid. Something was happening in that oven and I was not allowed to interfere in the sorcery.

'Can I open it to have a look?' I said as I went for the handle.

She held my hand back and firmly announced, 'Never.' Okay.

Her timer pinged and we all huddled around her, this time a little further away. She flung open the oven door and the hot air escaped again. I was getting a front row seat at this magic show this time. The heat hit my face and in that one moment of blinking a little longer than normal, Mrs Marshall stood there with this golden cake, perfectly domed. She placed it on a rack to cool as we all waited in anticipation.

She came along the row of girls. A tiny sliver on a piece of green recycled kitchen paper. The butter staining the green into a darker shade. I took a small bite and it was one of the most delicious things I had ever put in my mouth and I had eaten a lot of delicious food in my time. No amount of

Mum's toil or Dad's imagination could have prepared me for this, the single most mouth-watering cake I had ever tasted.

'It's all a lie,' I said to my mum that afternoon as I took all her pans out and piled them on the floor.

'This is an oven, Mum!' I shouted from inside it as it echoed back. 'Did you know you can make cakes in here?'

'Yeah.'

She knew the whole time and didn't think to tell me. 'So why are you not baking cakes in here?'

'We don't bake cakes.'

Yes, we bloody well do! I wanted some of that magic for myself.

With a baby due in just four weeks, I was nesting. We had just moved into our tiny two-bed terrace. The carpet was fresh, the walls unmarked and the cupboards full. A lentil curry bubbled away alongside a chicken curry, while I washed the rice under a cold running tap. I looked out onto the back street and watched the kids throw a football into our yard. They hesitated to walk through. They looked to see if they were being watched, without a clue that I could see them clearly through the thick, netted curtain. I would have moved the curtain to give them the go-ahead, the permission they wanted to retrieve their ball. But my burgeoning belly would not allow it.

I waited eagerly for my husband to come home. I watched

the clock and 6 p.m. was dragging its feet. With a new baby on the way he worked longer hours, the sacrifice meaning that we ate later and slept earlier. It was setting us up perfectly for life as parents.

'I'm going to bake him a cake.'

I stopped the tap, drained my rice. I turned the cooker off and dug out the only recipe book I owned. It was faster than loading the laptop. A Madeira cake recipe. I had always loved Madeira cake, the kind that came in slabs and sliced perfectly. I promptly put on my headscarf and found myself waddling incredibly fast to the car. I tried to manoeuvre myself into the seat; in the last few days of not driving, my steering wheel needed adjusting. I kept getting further and further away from the dash. Eventually I managed to wedge myself in and drive to the supermarket.

Perusing the baking aisle was something I did every week. I looked but I didn't touch. But with my last twenty pounds left from the food budget that had to last me the rest of the week, I tracked down the cheapest scales I could find and a cake tin that had some money off because it was dented. With that I filled my basket with own-brand butter and flour and a six-pack of eggs. I was on my way. I could not contain my excitement; my husband was going to have dinner *and* dessert today and I was going to make it all.

Back home, I mixed the batter in a pan because all my bowls were too small. I couldn't afford the baking paper, so the tin was going to have to be simply greased. Now the cake was ready to go in the oven. I closed all the windows to contain that aroma of butter and sugar that I once smelled. I wanted him to walk in and the sweet air to slam itself into his face and straight through his nose. Signalling to his head and his stomach that tonight he was going to be fed well.

'Can you smell it?' My shoulders hunched, my hands pursed.

'Nope.' He ran upstairs to get changed. Disappointed, oh just a little. How can anyone not be excited by this smell?

'Can you smell *anything* different?' I shouted from the bottom of the stairs.

Nothing. Just silence. He was praying. So I plated up our food and we sat in our spots. His food on his lap, while I stayed propped on the edge of my seat, any other position meaning I wouldn't be able to get up without assistance. My plate propped on the top of my stomach. As the heat penetrated my skin, the baby kicked a little harder. As Abdal helped me take the dirty plates out after our curry I watched his eyes. 'Please don't look left, don't look left,' I muttered in my mind. He looked left, but totally missed the cake in the tin, on top of the microwave.

As he spilled back down in his spot in the living room I remained in the kitchen, sweating, trying to chisel out this cake that had cooled and sat in the tin for hours. I mean I didn't know when to take it out, did I? Although the recipe did say after ten minutes. But I did also have baby brain. This was my first cake. He was going to hate it. Plus I'd spent the rest of the week's money, so this had better taste good, or at least last a week.

I scraped the wedges out, placed them on a large plate and walked into the room as if I were presenting him with his child. No, just wedges of badly cut, uneven chunks of cake. He looked over as he patted the seat next to him, instigating a snuggle.

'What's that?'

'That is cake. I know it's hideous, but I baked it myself.'

'For me?'

'For you and a little bit for me and the baby.'

Before the plate could land on the couch, a slice was already half eaten and swallowed and he was going in for a second bite.

'You are the best wife,' he said, as the words struggled to make their way out through the mounds of sponge.

'That is the most delicious cake,' he continued, as he polished off the last slice.

'I used the last twenty pounds on cake ingredients, I couldn't have twenty quid, could I?' I said, embarrassed but satisfied that he had eaten the lion's share.

'Only if you make more cake.'

He has eaten cake every day of our married life for thirteen years.

Fast forward eight years to another important date.

'I think you should enter *Bake Off*,' he said, holding a plate of chocolate fondant that oozed as he cut through it.

'Don't be silly,' I said.

*

I cooked because when you are the head of a kitchen your job is to feed and I had a job to do. With no other job written in my destiny, this was the one that would find me, regardless of my apprehensions or my desire to change society's thoughts about women in the kitchen.

Despite my defiance, my wish to take a different path to the other women I knew, like my grandmother, like my mother, I became them. Tied and weighed down. The one thing that I had never dreamed of or wished for, I got. I was a doer, a list-making teacher's pet who, if ever I got given a job, however big or small, knew that it was mine and that I was going to be the best at it. Better than anyone. My job was now a home-maker and that's what made me a cook: the desire to feed. I baked to feel happiness, to heal, to fill a sadness. I learned that I had been given the resilience of my mother and the edge of my father and that is something I carry with me, whether I'm cooking for two for date night or twenty-four at Christmas. I take it with me if I'm making banana bread with over-ripe black fruit that the kids won't touch or a wedding cake for my brother's wedding. It's there with me every time I pick up a knife or pull out a spatula.

It's love and a job in the same breath. The best kind of job that produces masses of food.

'Who's got the better job, kids, Ma or Baba?' Who do you think wins that argument? Until information technology can produce plates of deliciousness and pictures don't count.

I'm now in a world, an industry, where there are not that many five-foot, brown, Muslim girls cooking. I don't always feel welcome or wanted. Maybe I'm out of my depth? I often ask myself whether this is a mistake, whether I should stick to cooking at home. I can't compete with all these chefs. I'm just a home cook. As the ego drowns and my own self-doubt pulls me under, I look at what brought me here in the first place: a love of food, a love of sharing and the need to heal through food. However we get there, even though my lack of qualifications and experience highlights me as a misfit, there is one thing that makes us all the same. We love what we do. We love being in the kitchen. We love to feed. We love to make people happy.

I am not out to take anyone's job. I'm here to make new ones. I am doing this for all of those people who were told no: no, you are not rich enough; no, that is not credible; no, you can't; no, you won't; no, you are not allowed; no, that is not appropriate. I was told, 'No, you do not belong in this industry.' Finally I am saying, 'Yes I do.'

—⟩⟨—

MY MADEIRA

This is the first recipe I ever baked. It's one I swear by. Doubled or halved, flavoured how you want, this is the basic recipe for a delicious buttery Madeira cake that will fill your nostrils with the smell of warm butter and sweet sugar.

Serves 8 (or one happy husband in my case)

You will need:

200g unsalted butter, softened
200g caster sugar
4 medium eggs, beaten
200g self-raising flour
1 tsp baking powder
4 tbsp whole milk

To add extra flavour to your cake, you can add the zest of a lemon or lime, a few drops of flavouring extracts of your choice or a teaspoon of vanilla bean paste. If you want you can top the batter with some chocolate chips just before baking or add one over-ripe banana to the mix.

How to make it:

Preheat the oven to 170°C/gas mark 4 and line and lightly grease a 900g loaf tin. You don't want to do it in a 9-inch cake tin like I did all those years ago, or it will be as flat as a pancake, delicious but thin.

Add the butter and sugar to a bowl and whisk till light and very pale. This should take about 6 minutes.

Add the eggs, one at a time, till they are well incorporated.

Now add the sieved flour and baking powder and fold together till the mixture is smooth. Add the milk and mix through.

Pour the batter into the prepped tin and level off. Bake in the oven for 40–45 minutes, till the cake springs back when prodded and a skewer inserted into the centre comes out clean.

Leave in the tin for a maximum of 10 minutes, then turn it out and leave to cool on a wire rack. It is now ready to make someone smile after a hard day's work.

―✦―

USERNAME

'I am getting fed up of being told to go home! For the millionth time I AM HOME!'

'Has anyone spit roasted before? If so, any tips? Any recommendations? Need to get summer ready for a special party! #BBQ #summer 2018'

Who needs poetry when you have all of the above! For anyone who is wondering, I was talking about cooking in the second tweet; I was neither on heat nor in need of extra tips for the bedroom. Who knew the world was a walking, living, breathing, talking, typing, double entendre-filled sphere of filth, oozing innuendo after innuendo? I wanted to barbecue an animal whole, that's all.

I am Nadiya. For a very long time that was my name and now I'm Nadiya Jamir Hussain on Facebook, @BegumNadiya on Twitter and @nadiyajhussain on Instagram. Along with all the other names I go by, including 'Megabitch' if my dad's annoyed yet not really annoyed. He's never *really* annoyed. (You know I'm sorry, Dad.)

As for my mum, she doesn't have to call me anything; she just has a look. (I'll just go now, shall I?)

And I just face a wall of silence if I've irritated my siblings, in which case having a name is neither important nor relevant. (Please can you add me back to the group chat?)

Not one pet name where the old man is involved either. Nadiya it is, and although I quite like my name I wish he had a different name for me when he's feeling silly, or frisky, or jovial, or down. But it's pretty much always Nadiya. In varying accents – his favourites are broad Yorkshire, or Essex-tinged southern, or Nigerian, or more often than not the bilingual side-to-side-head-type south-Indian-slash-English accent or the one where he sounds just like his dad's particular Bangladesh accent.

My kids call me Nadiya Hussain, or mostly just 'Mum', but if they are in the mood to story-tell, which is pretty much all of the time, they like to relay a detailed tale when they know they need a wee and have one foot in the door, squirming. That is the kind of story from school that they like to tell. 'Then she said, "Is Nadiya Hussain your mum?"'

Those conversations often happen across the unlocked toilet door, with a rush of liquid and sigh of relief as background noise. 'I'm Ma to you, Nadiya Hussain to everyone else,' I explain. I think they quite enjoy saying my name out loud. I know of a few people who call techie parents by their first name and not even in a professional setting. They just work on a first-name basis and it makes me squirm a tiny little bit. It's acceptable, I'm sure, but all I'm saying is if my kids start calling me Nadiya, I may have to rethink the inheritance!

So in a world where I have all of these people who love me, who know me, I am Nadiya, albeit said with profanity, a deadly look, silence, varying accents or as my full name. I am that person. The Nadiya who says the wrong thing when really that gap just needed silence: 'I think I ate too much bread today, anyone else feeling gassy?' Or who starts feeling crazy when she's happy: 'I'm so happy I'm having a panic attack. How is that even possible, you stupid brain?'

To them I am Nadiya. But to the other people in the outside world, I am a username. The user ID that sits beside a picture. The face and a name.

This is a relatively new development. A few years ago I was the person who sniggered at my sister's internet addiction.

'Why are you constantly scrolling?' That's what her finger did: flicking up, over and over again, stopping occasionally to pinch and stretch an image. Phone in both hands as she rapidly tapped in the text. There she was, scrolling again, between conversations, interrupting meals as her eyeballs moved up and flicked down in quick succession. 'How can it be so interesting?'

I didn't get it. Facebook was all the rage but I was not the kind of girl who had the time or patience to care about getting in touch with people who I had previously lost touch with, for a good reason no doubt.

'You can talk to your old high-school friends!' my sister said. Why on earth would I want to do that? 'You can look through pictures of people,' she added, 'and you get to see what everyone looks like now.' But again, what was the point when I have ten thousand photos of my own clogging up my memory to look at? 'And it's quite fun,' she finished. But what was fun about it?

I was dead set against it. For the most part, between ironing underpants and cleaning the floor by hand, I had no time to sit and scroll. I had no time to breathe because I filled it with the jobs nobody else wanted to do, like washing the rug by hand when the sun was out, like cleaning behind the radiators and manually pulling out all the weeds from our pebbled drive. Who had time to look up old friends? To see what dress someone was wearing? Or how much someone else weighed? To see who had moved to sunnier climates and who had stayed in the grey of the UK?

'I don't get it!'

'Well, don't get it then.'

Fair play.

So through my less than gentle judgement, I vowed never to enter my details into that world. I was quite comfortable not to be a part of it. My curiosity allowed me to wonder what it might be like but I never voiced this out loud or allowed my curiosity to appear transparent. So I wondered alone in my own head. As my friends and family threw words around like 'status', 'handles' and 'hashtags', I quite enjoyed not being a part of that mysterious alternative universe. Deep down I was desperately curious about it but determined never to cave.

So what did I do but cave?

I didn't just cave either. I went for the dive. Heart racing, poised, I jumped. Counting 'one, two, three', my toes lifted off the board and I spun and dove straight into the clear blue water, streamlined all the way till I was fully immersed. I caved, I dove like an Olympian, a gold medal-worthy dive. Top marks for me.

'Are you just on Facebook? Oh no, you've got to try Instagram and Twitter,' I would encourage others who had not yet seen the light, like a social media pusher. The best kind, the kind that appeared to have class.

Other digital natives urged me further too. 'Are you on Snapchat?' people asked me.

'No way, I would never do Snapchat!'

Never say never. But Snapchat feels like the time I went into New Look and enquired about boyfriend jeans.

'Do you have boyfriend jeans?' I asked a sales assistant who looked like she was fresh out of school. Her porcelain skin and rosy cheeks wouldn't need to meet any blusher for at least another decade. She looked at me, unsure. I had to change my line of questioning. 'Do you have anything else apart from jeggings or skintight jeans?' I asked, squirming at the thought of skintight jeans. It's hard enough being in my skin without adding another layer of tight fabric to make me feel more uncomfortable with its waist-chaffing and bajiji-sweating qualities. 'I'm looking for a more comfortable-fitting jean.'

'You could try the maternity section in Next if you want? They have comfortable trousers,' she said as she moved on to her next rail of clothes.

I mean, I knew I'd had that entire packet of Jaffa Cakes the previous night and I hadn't really exercised much that week. But I didn't think I looked like I was with child. To be fair, I had eaten a monumental amount – I forgot to mention the two plates of pasta and the pasties and the chronic constipation that may have led to me feeling about four months pregnant at the time. But still. Rude! I did find my jeans in Next, of all places. That doesn't mean the shop assistant was right; it just means some of us don't want to wear second skins. Sometimes we do, but not on this occasion.

Anyway, Snapchat is like being in New Look aged thirty-four and knowing very well that you don't belong there. But who knows, my kids might appreciate my presence on their social spaces when they eventually get there themselves. Somehow I very much doubt it, but it could be fun for pure entertainment value.

Fingers, nose, all the way down to my feet, I was in there. I was in that world that I so desperately despised. A world that made no sense and the people in it were like aliens that I failed to communicate with or understand. I felt a bit like how my grandad must have felt in the sixties: the language was different, I didn't understand what anyone was saying, they saw life differently to me, they lived in another world entirely. This was kind of like my grandad and his immigrant's tale, though of course on a much less dramatic scale and far less interesting or life changing.

There I was, inputting data, cautiously, reserved, but I was doing it, I was actually doing it. I texted my sister. 'I'm doing it, I'm actually doing it! I know I said I wouldn't but I am.' I tried to justify my actions. After years of scorning and raising my eyebrows at her, over her shoulder and across the room, I was doing what I'd said I would never do.

'Welcome to a new world. Let me send you a friend request.'

'Wait, a what?' As I flicked and switched between chats and screens, I punched in my details with a tap tap tap, a few swipes and the odd pinch. Profile picture done, basic information. Now input who I am, in just 120 characters. How is that even physically possible? I'm sure nobody wants to read your life events in chronological order, including your medical history and dental records – yeah, I get that. But how do I best describe the person I am in just over 100 characters? That is near impossible. I know I'm a talker and so of course this is an impossible task for that reason but also as a writer I can never go under my word limit. I can hear my English language teacher now: 'This does not look like 2,000 words to me. Did you go over much, again?'

This was like a dating ad, the one chance to sell myself in the best possible light. You can add a picture, yes, but just a picture is surely not enough; I'm not Halle Berry, or Zoë Kravitz, or Demi Lovato – those beautiful faces need no words. I need the words; I need all the words; I need all the help I can get.

So where to begin? But this was so difficult. There are so many thing I love, like my family, my purple settee, my KitchenAid, my offset spatula, my kids, kids' ears, my husband, my husband's calves. There are so many things I enjoy: sunsets, getting delayed on a flight so we can shop some more, chips out of the paper in the freezing cold, crisps in front of the telly under my son's Pokémon duvet, bread and butter and salt. I don't like getting things wrong, I don't like my panic disorder, I don't like my hair, I don't like it when people walk with shoes in the house. I hate taking hairs out of the plughole, I hate rain and wind, especially together, I hate leather sofas, I hate being cold, I hate a cold bed even more. I have a slight obsession for shoes. I really like rainbows, in the sky, on my clothes, on confectionery – anywhere you can put a rainbow, I am for it. I love tea and hate coffee. I want to drink green tea so I appear grown-up but I'll swap that for hot chocolate and marshmallows any day of the week. I can touch-type, I love Zoflora and enjoy collecting buttons, I used to have nine cats and now I have none. I don't like grapes but give me a crisp Braeburn any day of the week.

I'm sure that was way over 120 characters. How was I meant to pick this apart and choose the best bits to appear balanced, or dare I say it, 'normal'? And should I admit I have an obsession with labelling things? It was impossible. So whenever I went to post something I would go back and edit it, rearrange what I'd written or simply not post at all.

There I was, the username, my fears confirmed; I already felt handled by my social media handle. Did it handle me or did I handle it? Of course I had the power in the tips of my fingers, to change, edit and add. I had the power to write the characters that explained who I was. But already I felt sucked into something else that felt much bigger than me. It was a much bigger world than I had anticipated or imagined. From that first picture of me that was posted online after the *GBBO* announcement, I felt the wrath of the internet. As I scrolled through reams and reams of images, as I liked and commented, proofread and deleted, posted and shared, I was pulled into a world that was so big it seemed to have no end.

I joked with my *Bake Off* buddy Tamal about our social media following, even as we competed on screen as the series aired. His following climbed and mine was just behind. Occasionally mine stepped up by a few paces but he soon whizzed past, leaving me in his dust. Eventually I caught up to him, steadying the pace, then I raced ahead with him still on my tail. We laughed and joked about it in the back of a taxi on our way to an event. Grumbling and laughing at the race neither of us really cared about. But maybe we secretly did?

'Look at my following, it's higher than yours!' I jested as I showed him my screen.

'I'll beat you, you little turd.' His names for me are so unique, he knocks my dad straight out of the ballpark and into outer space. He is so inventive that even I'm impressed, despite being the recipient of his love and choice words.

This is what prepubescents and adolescents do. They look at their likes and followings. They watch the numbers rise and fall; they read the comments and add their own. It's a measure of their popularity, something that is important as a teenager. In our day we measured it in a less technical manner: it was all about how many mates you had, what clique you clicked with and how good-looking you were. Not much has changed; it's just a little less in the real world and more in this fictional world of social media. As an adult I found this new environment surreal. Is the amount of followers you have a measure of your success? Does it in fact determine how popular you are? Can something like that be measured and is this really the best way to do it?

Twitter

'Your attitude is the reason why mental health issues are brushed under the carpet. Sickness of the heart, body and mind does not discriminate, it doesn't pick and choose. It can affect anyone. Stop being so ignorant. If you can't be a part of the solution don't add to the problem.'

You can use your imagination to figure out what this comment was in response to. I for one can remember; I always do. Something about how celebrities are always moaning about mental health and how really it's just a fad. I can't quote it because of course it has since been removed. I would watch all these conversations unfold on Twitter. People would leave their comments on articles published about me, interviews that I had done and images of shoots that I had attended. All there for Twittersphere to see, read, dissect and comment on. I would watch the comments spool out, seeing words like 'nobody', 'ungrateful', 'token Muslim'. The words stayed with me as I read them. I resisted the urge to engage and for such a long time I was a spectator – a member of this new world, but a mute one. As conversations ensued and comments piled in, I watched and ached a little every time I was judged. For every few dozen nice comments a nasty one slipped through the cracks. But did I remember the nice comments? Absolutely not. It was the single nasty, badly worded, terribly undescriptive and unoriginal tweet that stayed stuck in my brain. It had a heartbeat of its own. As my own heart raced, the comment thudded in my head.

This had become the pattern of my evenings. As soon as the kids were in bed.

'You won't believe this!' I'd say. 'Listen to this. How stupid is this?' My life revolved around refreshing and scrolling through the comments so I could read them and pile the latest outrage onto my growing heap of insecurities. As my laundry pile grew, so did the mass of unpleasant comments in my head. I spent hours in the evening reading but not responding. Laughing on the outside, mocking the ignorance, sniggering at the insensitivity. But crying a little on the inside.

All we all really want is acceptance, to just be liked – not even loved, but it's nice to be liked. I lived to be liked by people I did not know. That's what gave me comfort: the nice comments, the likes, the retweets made me feel at ease. It gave me the outward approval I wanted. When all I really needed was to be liked by friends and family in the real world, in my world, yet there I was, manically refreshing and absorbing strangers' opinions about me. I ignored my husband's eye roll every time I said the same thing but stringed together in a sentence a little bit differently. 'He doesn't get it,' I would tell myself.

Then one day I actually responded. I spoke back. I didn't just sit and watch. I was no longer a spectator as I watched myself in a bullring with a red hijab on, like a rag to a bull, saying, 'Here I am, come get me.' I responded. I wrote it, spellchecked it and then deleted it. Then I did the same thing over and over again till I plucked up the courage to send it. There it was, gone into that world with the tap of a finger. I walked away, not thinking for a second what I had started.

My phone began to ping on and on and on. I could hear it from the kitchen as it lay on my bed, pinging. I ignored it, resisted. I didn't know it was my Twitter feed making that noise – it was a sound I wasn't familiar with. Eventually I succumbed to curiosity: 'Perhaps it's an emergency, I should check my phone.' There it was, a flurry of messages; they were coming in so thick and fast I felt snowed under. Messages of support versus messages of anger and defiance. I felt the blood rise to my face, burning me as it rose. What the hell had I done? This didn't feel good. But it also kind of did.

If I was on the street, out there in public, would they say the same things to me? Unlikely, really – they might say the same things but they would surely word it differently, sugar-coat it. And would I respond if they did say something in person? Probably not. I don't like confrontation and the last time I confronted someone he threw a can of beer at me, so no, I wouldn't. Yet here we have this public place, open. Where people can say what they like without fear of punishment. Everyone can be bold enough to be honest about what they really feel, about the people they follow. In this same public place I also feel bold and brave enough to respond, whereas in a previous world I would have stayed totally quiet for fear of being attacked.

Whether it's for good or bad, this platform makes us brave. We are faceless. Whether you have a blue tick or not. Whether you are out there for people to see, in movies or on the telly. Whether you are a voice on the radio. A journalist. An admirer. A rebel without a cause. It's there for all of us, giving us the bravery to say what we want and respond if we wish.

But does it make me feel better? No. I don't like confrontation full stop and I have learned that through trial and error. By posting and regretting. By posting and deleting. By following people I admire and unfollowing the ones that I don't. By muting and blocking, I can avoid the confrontation that I dislike, be it in the real world or the make-believe one.

Instagram

With barely a filter on my phone, I snap and post in record time. But when I people-watch, I see the continuous stream of pictures being taken. Swiping and tapping till they have the image that suits them perfectly. Then send.

Someone told me, 'Once it's out there, it's out there for anyone to use, so be careful what you post.' A wise woman, but did I listen? No. Because I just don't. So click and send it is.

I read the comments that have flooded in, in response to a picture in which I posed for a charity to encourage people to cover their nose and mouth in the colder months, to avoid getting seriously ill. A good cause, you ask? Well yeah, with children who have asthma, it's a bit of information that could make all the difference to help a child avoid an attack. I would have loved to have been a part of social media earlier on in my life if it meant finding out more about the things that I was unsure about.

'You really need to think about sorting out your eyebrows.' The comment on Instagram was slightly more elaborate than my recollection of it, but it was something along those lines. I don't actually mind my eyebrows. Although they have been the butt of jokes my whole life.

'Watch out, there's a caterpillar on your face.'

'Pube face.'

'Broom brows.'

The list could go on. Of course in the past these eyebrows have undergone many obligatory overplucks. A fashion must-have for those between the ages of fourteen and twenty-one. By which point you will have accumulated enough pictures to look back on in horror when you come out the other side. I should never have been allowed to be alone with a pair of scissors, brow brush, tweezers and kohl.

I would do it in the morning and I was an early riser. With all the jobs done, samosas made, clothes pressed, bath over, the only thing left was to tackle those brows. Still dark outside, I would pull my sister's duvet over her face. She was like a three-headed dragon before 8 a.m. and it was a long way off eight. I would pull it over her face but before I could even turn the light on she would say, 'Don't you dare put the light on, or I will punch you.' So I would sit in the dark in front of the full-length mirror and pluck whatever was left of the eyebrows that I had. There wasn't much. I would go at my face like a scorpion, with little sharp hairs flying off and hitting the ends of my nose, making me sneeze furiously. I often went too far; it looked like I used a hedge trimmer to landscape my face. I would panic when I saw the result, but thank goodness for eyeliner pencil and its double uses.

So after that I grew them out – not out of choice, but with two pregnancies over two years, somehow grooming the caterpillars was not high on the list of priorities. It was way below, down at the bottom, along with 'wash my hair' and 'do exercise'. I quite liked my brows when they were big; they were a carbon copy of my dad's. I wonder who gave him his eyebrows and whose they were before him. I wouldn't wish them on anyone else but they were mine. Grown back, patchy in places where the roots had been torn from their base, but nothing a small trim, pluck and brush couldn't fix, in excellent lighting this time, of course – that is key.

I thought I was okay with them till I read that Instagram comment. At thirty-three years of age you would think that one comment alone wouldn't have me rushing straight upstairs to inspect my wares. But that is exactly what I did. I brushed them with an eyebrow brush and examined their faults. My anonymous critic was right; they looked untidy and unkept. They could probably do with a closer trim, the odd hair plucked out and maybe even being finished with some brow powder. I looked at the image. I zoomed in. I took screenshots. I was in agreement with her. I shouldn't have been but I was.

Wait, hold on a minute! What the hell is this? I just had to stop. I had posted in the first place simply to help a charity that was raising awareness about an illness close to my heart and someone had taken it upon themselves to comment on my eyebrows. Why was I the one examining my eyebrows, when that person needed their head examining? Why did I care what they thought? But I did. I didn't want to but I did, a lot. I don't want to look ugly – nobody does. So I did what all insecure people like me do: I changed myself to make someone else happy. The things that I'd thought were lovely as they were looked lovely no more. So I had to change them. I was not as heavy-handed with my eyebrow tools these days, so it was less of a renovation and more of a tidy up.

These days I look through some of these perfectly polished photos that people have posted and I wonder how many times that picture was taken before it was given the seal of approval. And as I look down at the images on my screen, crisp and controlled, the sight of the fuzzy faces and mayhem in front of me in real life seems like the better side to be on. So I do what I always do in these situations: I think about my eyebrows while I make rocky road. Because marshmallows and biscuits encased in chocolate make untamed eyebrows feel empowering, natural and goddamn beautiful.

Contrary to my air-punching statement, I still don't just click and send. I click, check, delete, click again, add filter, take off the filter, pose, click, add words, hashtag, delete, reword, delete again, spellcheck and then send!

Facebook

I began on Facebook long after it was established so I feel like I might have missed the boat there. I enjoy seeing my cousins from across the pond, their smiling faces and their poor fashion choices. Messages of love and support often pour in from them and in those moments when I feel disconnected from my extended family, they appear in photos with their warm climate and single layers. I sit reading their messages in my thermals, envious of our home on the other side of the world.

'Are you on Facebook?' I asked my nephew.

'No, that's for old people.'

Am I considered old enough to be on Facebook, in which case I'm insulted, or am I youthful enough to agree casually? I think he knows I'm old and there's no hiding that. No matter how many odd combos I wear with rainbows on them. But this has to be the shortest bit of writing I've done in this entire book. I literally have very little to say about Facebook. It sits on my phone, a little rounded corner square that enables me to enjoy seeing my family from across the way. So even though I slag off technology, I have to admit that just being able to share and see these images warms my heart.

YouTube

I don't really even know if this is social media or if it's just a platform where people post videos. Not sure what category it sits in. It's something we don't allow the kids to roam around on willy nilly (I just like saying willy nilly) but if we restrict or monitor it, it means it's up there somewhere with social media.

'Mum, I want to be a YouTuber when I'm older.'

'No, you don't.'

That's not even from any one single child – all three of mine have said it at some point in their existence, perhaps even more than once, maybe a few dozen times. I'm all for letting kids follow their dreams and in truth if that is what they really, REALLY wanted to do, I would not stop them. But it wouldn't be my first choice for them.

Here I am sounding like the 'me' I never want to be. If that's what they want to be I should be like any good parent and say 'follow your dreams'. In the meantime, I'm going to do what all good parents do and manipulate them – subtly, of course – to remember their dreams of becoming a zoologist, an animator and a geologist. Either that or I will remind them who pays the bills and threaten them with eviction! I wouldn't do that. (Or would I?)

The word 'influencer' gets thrown around a lot where social media and especially YouTube is concerned. The definition is 'someone who affects or changes the way other people behave, for example through their use of social media'.

The people who influenced me were real people. People I could see and smell and touch. My nan: her persistence was inspiring. Her life was like a never-ending storm but she always remembered her umbrella.

'Nan, did Nana look after you when you were ill?'

'I never got ill.'

My parents were inspirational for their graft. Their hands, feet, mind, body and soul were consumed in raising their family the best way they could.

'What choice do we have? We have to carry on.'

My friends influenced me in the way they created a circle of trust, which broke often but was always mended back, differently each time.

'You know you're best friends when you can't remember when you met.'

My brothers and sisters were inspirational for just always being there. Quiet but firm they remain, standing tall. Then there was my maths teacher, Dr Jabbar, who died so suddenly. He made me smile; he was liberal and warm and unusual. He met us with kindness every morning and left a massive hole in our class when he died, allowing no room for anyone else, because nobody, simply no one, could fill his space. My Arabic teacher gave us a love of learning beautifully and would lift his hooded eyelids to makes us smile (we laughed nervously because he was nothing short of horror-movie frightening). Distracted by the way he pinched his eyelids, I spent so much time being curious about how they got that way that it stopped me concentrating on the learning my parents had paid for. My Bengali teacher never mocked me for speaking slang Bengali, but was charmed and perhaps amused by the way we spoke. She taught us how to speak properly and we taught her how to speak, well . . . not properly. I admire the way she overlooked my mischievous antics when I played 'how many Polos can you stuff in your mouth?' because she knew sometimes even we had to laugh and she didn't mind the sound of laughter in her class.

These were the people who influenced me to be better. No matter where I was or how old I was, or where my mind was, these were real people, tangible people, who affected the decisions I made every day. I don't have to find them with the click of a button and I couldn't even if I tried. But they are buried somewhere deep in my memories and in my heart.

I have come to accept that perhaps my children will have influencers of a different variety. I hope and pray they can also find comfort and inspiration from the real people in their lives – people who make mistakes, the people who laugh and cry with them every day. But I know that their influencers span into this world that I am so afraid of. A world I am a part of. And I have to accept that I am now also an influencer in this same frightening world.

'Ma, can I have a chat with you?'

Whenever they say that, any one of them, my heart sinks. It could be anything.

'What is it?'

'I watched a YouTube video . . .'

Of course I interrupted. It was going to be another hack video, or what happens to household items when you put them in a blender, or a bloke making giant BFG-appropriate chocolate bars.

'So what was it about? Because I don't think I need to learn another new way of hulling a strawberry.' We all do it, right? We assume what they will say and say all of the wrong things. Reassure me.

'There was a man on YouTube who made a video about you.'

'Right, go on.' This wasn't going to end well. I knew it

then. The look on my son's face said it all. He looked at his little big feet, using one foot to scratch the top of the other. 'He was talking about how much he hates you and all the reasons why people should hate you.'

What does any parent say to that? Regret, instant regret for ever allowing YouTube, internet and general technology into my children's lives. I didn't know what to say. What do you say? What does anyone say? It was a unique situation. It wasn't like I could ring my sister and say, 'How would you feel if your kid saw a YouTube video listing all the reasons why you should be hated?' I'm sure it's not a scenario she has played out in her head. 'What's the right age to buy my daughter a crop top? Why isn't he walking yet? He said a bad word, how do I deal with that? Should we go to hospital? Do those shoes match those trousers? Aren't these the cutest hair bobbles?' That is the kind of stuff we talk about. Not YouTube, not videos and certainly not about me.

'Where did you find this video, did someone send you a link?'

'No.'

'So where did you get it?'

'I typed in your name.'

Oh jeez.

'And why would you do that?' I had done it before, so I had gone into ultra-hypocrite mode at this point.

'I just wanted to see what comes up.'

Well, that is the exact reason why I'd done it, but I couldn't tell him that – or could I?

'Why would anyone hate you?' He was crying now, not the blubbery, snotty kind of crying, the kind that results in you sounding like a fish out of water and looking like one too. No, these were the silent kind of tears that came from a hurt somewhere deep. So much of my hard work felt undone in that moment.

'You're kind and lovely and they don't even know you,' he reassured me. To be called kind and lovely is a warming feeling, but under these circumstances I wanted to find the video and comment the hell out of it.

'They don't know me, and we can't stop people from being mean,' I tried to reassure him. It's not like he could go to school and say, 'You know what it's like when people post hate videos about your mum on YouTube?' But in that moment he had me and I had him. He always has me, they all do, and I will always have them.

So just when I think I'm winning in life and that I have my s*** together, I realise, I don't really. I never will. But I am my children's biggest influencer. I may also influence many others through social media, but for my children I am their primary influence and if I can do that job to the best of my limited ability then being an influencer to others who see me through airwaves and screens will feel like nothing short of an absolute honour.

'I feel bad for you, Mum.' He hugged me.

'Don't feel bad for me.'

I hugged him back. I was a little sore, a little bruised. Nobody wants to be hated, but to be hated enough for someone to take up their time filming about it is dedication. I'll give the YouTuber that. He is not an influencer, certainly not one that I want playing in my house. Despite temptation I have never looked for that video.

'Shall we not put Mum's name into any search tool? Are we in agreement?'

We have a rule in our house: no googling our names. We know who we are and no pictures or collection of words should take away from that. Because these words, pictures and defamatory articles leave nothing but bruises. Yes, they go away eventually but the pain is instant and that takes a little while to heal. No more googling names. I for one don't do it, especially images: no girl needs to be reminded of her poor fashion choices and fluctuating weight, and why did no one tell me I needed Vaseline?!

We know that the big, wider world is out there, but there is a time and place for bringing it into our homes. So we put that world away into a biscuit tin in the office after seven. Because we quite like the clutter and chaos, the warmth of ourselves, which no big wide world can really truly ever give us. Unless of course I have a chocolate emergency, in which case it's Amazon all the way. Click, stretch, swipe and buy.

Sometimes I like it, I have to – but for the most part, let's pop it back in the biscuit tin and leave it on a high shelf in the office.

EYEBROW ROCKY ROAD

Here is the recipe for my eyebrow-distracting rocky road. It's pretty simple and has that much sugar in it, it can make even the fluffiest or thinnest eyebrows look like a dream.

Makes 12 squares

You will need:

300g biscuits – I like to use digestives – crushed and
   roughly broken
100g mini marshmallows or large marshmallows cut
   into pieces with scissors
100g raisins or any small dried fruit
100g whole toasted hazelnuts
1 tsp ground cinnamon
600g milk chocolate
3 tbsp golden syrup

How to make it:

Crush the biscuits roughly and pop the crumbs into a bowl. Add the marshmallows, raisins and nuts and mix through. Then add the cinnamon and mix to coat everything with the beautiful spice.

Melt the chocolate and the golden syrup together in a heatproof bowl over a pan of simmering water or in bursts in the microwave. As soon as it's liquid, stir it into the biscuit mixture till it is totally coated.

Line a brownie tin with greaseproof paper and pour the mixture in. Use the back of a spoon to push the mixture down till it is compact.

Chill for at least an hour in the fridge and then cut into squares to serve.

—✦—

WOMAN

To the women in my life,
Settle down for just a moment
To answer me this:
I know you're tired,
I know you're worn,
But step back for a moment,
Let the spinning subside,
Ask yourself this,
What makes you proud,
Stop and think, what makes you proud?
Proud to be a woman?

'I am proud to be a woman because I can do everything.'

'I am proud of my arse.'

'Life revolves around us as wives, mothers and daughters.
Take just one element out and it all seems to tumble.'

'No wonder women love shoes – we have one pair
of feet and many shoes that'll fit, many styles, many
functions.'

'I grew two beautiful humans inside of me.'

'Because women are badass.'

'I'm proud to be a woman because we face so much
shizz and we deal with it.'

'We carry on no matter how hard things get.'

'We have fought for our rights and for our voices to
be heard.'

'We are strong, we are capable, we are beautiful.'

I have spent my entire existence wanting to be anything,
anything else – but not a woman. I hated being a girl, and
knowing full well that I had a lifetime ahead of being a
woman filled me with dread.

I had my hair cut short; it was a 'business at the front,
party at the back' kind of vibe. It was the hairstyle you gave
to a girl who had unruly, curly hair like mine. As soon as it
was within centimetres of a brush it turned into an untamed
mop. When it was tied up, it hurt till it came back down. But
to bring it down took an army. I would squirm at every tug
and pull, hearing roots being ripped from my scalp one by
one, in slow motion. It always ended with a pair of scissors

being used to cut me out. There my shorn hair would sit stiff on my head, unrelenting, refusing to move from its upright position. Free at last, I would run my fingers through my haystack: sweet relief.

'Right, let's cut your hair.' Dad was great with a pair of scissors. He would set up shop in the downstairs bathroom, where he always seemed to make us face the avocado toilet, the thought of which still sends shivers up my spine. An overused avocado toilet was the last thing I needed to look at as my point of focus. Especially when I never knew what art my dad was about to create on my hair. I reassured myself that whatever he did would be better than what it was like now.

So I shut my eyes. We talked about things and I occasionally picked out some hair from my mouth. Short, stubbly hairs. How short was he going? I could hear the snipping of his special hair scissors, the blade right across my ear. Something buzzed against my head, not a sensation I had experienced before during my four-times-a-year haircuts.

'Let's have a look!'

I was excited; I loved having my hair cut. Dad handed me the mirror tucked behind the sink.

'Oh my God, I look like a boy.' Unsure, I smiled just a little.

'You look just like me!' Dad was beaming with pride. I looked like my thirtysomething-year-old dad and I wasn't angry, not even slightly.

'It looks like I have another son.'

I was his son. I liked the sound of that. My sister was next;

we formed an orderly queue. She had hair that was just like mine but on crack. Dad snipped it a few times, pacified her need for a 'new do'. Passed her the mirror.

'What, is that it?' Disappointed. She wanted a proper cut.

'Would you like to go as short as your sister?' he asked. She couldn't run out of the seat fast enough.

I ran my fingers through my hair as I waited for Dad to finish in the bathroom so I could wash out the prickly hairs that tickled my back. I was really enjoying this cut; it felt fresh! For fear of shedding hair into the curries in the kitchen and with no room in the bathroom, I was banished to the No Man's Land of the passage that led to the garden. I waited, the air flowing over my ears and through my hair. Was this what it felt like to be a boy? Because if this was what a boy's head felt like, imagine what it would be like to be an actual boy?

Dad prepared to go to the bazaar in Bangladesh – our holiday, you could even call it our home every few years. I could see him getting dressed in the dimly lit room. With only one oil lamp per room, I could barely make out his face, but the silhouette was his. His hair was big and his tummy round, his legs hidden in traditional longi cloth. He pulled a shirt over his head.

'Dad, can I go to the market with you?'

All the men went to the market after dark; it was where all the fishermen and farmers gathered with their wares. Dad would come back every night with a trail of carts behind him.

Each craft pulled by its own man and full of fresh vegetables and fruit. Piled so high you could see them teetering on the edge of the cart, almost over the edge – some wild creature would have a feast if anything fell into the rice paddies.

I always wondered what the markets were like. My brother would return with my dad, excited, brimming with energy – he would talk about the snacks he ate and the dead animals he saw and would relay the contents of the carts to me. His clothes, his hands, his skin gave off an entirely different aroma to the one he had left with. Freshly laundered clothes out of the suitcase we packed back in the UK now smelled of fish and flesh or smoke and oil. It was a good smell.

'Dad, please can I go to the market with you?'

'Girls don't go to the market,' he replied.

'Yeah, but I don't look like a girl!'

He knew I was right. I knew I was right. After that haircut, dresses didn't look quite right on me, not that I had much of a liking for dresses anyway. But after that haircut, the one that made me look like a Bollywood villain, I decided dresses were not for me.

He couldn't argue. There I was, a girl, wearing a pair of jeans, a T-shirt and a waistcoat, yes, a waistcoat, going to the market girls were not allowed in. We sat in the back of a rickshaw, and Dad held me close, as if someone would snatch me from his grasp. He looked a little wary. I for one was having the time of my life as the lights of the market drew near. I could smell it: the fumes from fires and the oil frying the lentil pakoras dragged up my nose with every breath.

We stopped. My uncle insisted we buy some snacks. Grinding to a halt, a street vendor handed newspaper parcels dotted with grease to my uncle and he passed them to me. My not-yet-asbestos hands couldn't cope with the heat of the fresh oil seeping through the headlines. But I held on tight. They were mine and I was going to eat them.

We walked through the market, my uncle warning me about every puddle he thought I might step in and pointing out as many buffalo dungpiles as possible. I hopped, skipped and jumped with my head down, missing everything that was going by. Eventually my uncle swept me up and threw me over his shoulder. It was uncomfortable – my butt was too wide and his shoulder narrow – so I lifted my leg right over his head.

Now I was relatively comfortable. I could see right across the market; it was brimming with activity. There were men visible for miles, walking up and down and across the aisles. The rows and columns as organised as any supermarket I had ever seen. Lanterns set on the tin hatches of each shop. No words or lettering, signs or boards to allow the shopper to identify what kind of shop it was. You had to squint hard and lean forward.

People shouted at one another in a language I understood, but they spoke harshly. They were loud and persuasive.

'Brother, come over here.'

'Brother, look at this fresh fish.'

'This meat, shall I cut it for you now?'

As Dad walked through the crowds, he must have felt like

royalty; people were stepping aside as he walked, giving him a clear path. Now I know why he loved Bangladesh so much. It wasn't just because it was once his home. Or because he missed it so much he had to return twice or maybe even three times a year. It was because here he was king. The burgundy passport was his ticket to royalty.

'If you did not have a Londoni passport where would you be?'

Well, I would probably be in Bangladesh, with my parents if they still lived there, but technically if they hadn't got married I would be nowhere.

'What's your point?'

'You would have been stuck in a village waiting for a man in London to come and take you.'

Well, that was an unlikely dream, if I was me in Bangladesh – brown like a farmer's granddaughter, chubby like a kid who hangs around at dinner time and so mouthy that even her dad worried what she would say next. No, girls like me were not the kind that even made it onto a shelf in the village. Instead you needed to have the type of malnourished physique where your kidneys are visible with the naked eye and your stomach touches your back. Skin so fair that it has to be maintained using formulated bleaches, scrubbed half to death in the dark and never exposed to daylight. Rosy cheeks and small boobs. That was the ideal. But I knew even at age eleven that I was not that girl and I was never going to be her. It was physically impossible, of course; no amount of bleaching moisturiser or dieting would rid me of the skin my dad had given me and the hips my mum's mum had given me. So no, I would not be waiting for Prince Charming. There was an ideal and I was not that ideal, not in any place I called home.

So I was quite content with being a make-believe boy on my uncle's shoulders. He was the one who had saved me. He made me feel safe.

'Pull your pants down,' he said as he yanked my little pants down all the way to my ankles and laid me abruptly onto the hard wooden bed. Not long before he had led me by the hand to a room in a corner of the village, one that people only used when they were passing through, or when other rooms were occupied by their Londoni residents and their piles of suitcases. I knew then at five that this did not feel right. That grown-up woman's instinct was already within me, even at five. Not because I was one. But that adult knowledge was there sooner than I had anticipated. Long before I knew what a woman was. I knew it was wrong.

'Stop it,' I said. I stood up and yanked them straight back up, neatened my pink dress, patting it down. He grew angry and I had never seen his angry face before. He was usually nice. Today he was angry. He pulled them down again, this time faster. He looked around, glancing from side to side. He pushed me onto the bed, this time with force.

'Stop it!' I yelled this time.

'Shhhhhh,' he said loudly, his spit on my face. I wiped it

and struggled to get up. He put one hand on my chest, holding me down firmly. I had never felt this kind of force before and no matter how much I fought it, I couldn't get up. With the other hand he unbuckled his trousers, struggling with his belt.

All I remember is feeling confused. I didn't have a clue what was happening; this was a new situation. This was not playing, I knew that; it wasn't fun, I knew that; so I struggled, because I knew I didn't want to be there, I knew that too. That was certain. I struggled to get up as he shushed me furiously, the shhh getting louder and more ragged each time. He undid his trousers and I was horrified at what he took out. At the sight of it, I cried, 'Please can I go?' I had seen that before but only my baby brother's in the bath. This thing he took out looked different.

I called 'Sasa!' out loud, which means uncle. I was sure I had seen my favourite uncle around that day, the one with no kids, the one who gave us all his attention. In any case I had plenty of sasas so I figured one might come. He held my mouth closed and tried to point his thing straight into the parts that the teachers said were 'private', the parts our parents called 'shorom', which translates as shame.

I squirmed even more, kicking it. He shouted loudly and held me down harder. I didn't stop moving. I wriggled wildly. Was it instinct? Because it wasn't knowledge. I didn't know what he was doing and I didn't know what he needed me for. I closed my eyes tight shut, still furiously trying to get free of this odd human. That is what I thought at the time, but now

I know he was a monster. I tried to free myself from the monster. I opened my eyes and he was touching the thing that came out of his pants, one hand still on me and the other on himself, till there was a stream of white liquid that flowed from it. I watched a small amount land on my dress. That was my favourite dress, you bastard, and you made a mess all over it!

At that moment my nice uncle came in. At once I felt the heavy hand lift from my chest; it ached where his fingers had dug into my ribcage. I stood up immediately, free and saw the monster furiously put away that thing as he tried to make an escape. My uncle slapped him, hard. 'What did you do, you son of a swine? I'll deal with you later,' he said in the angriest, yet most muted voice I had ever heard.

Something happened that day that shouldn't have happened, I knew that even at five. My uncle pulled up my pants and scooped me into his arms. I inhaled his body odour as I nuzzled into his sharp collarbone. He was sweaty from the day's work. He patted my back. I felt safe. He took me to the pond and washed my dress; all it needed was a few seconds in the blistering heat to dry and it was as if it were brand new. He obviously knew something I didn't as he was cursing in Bengali, with tears streaming from his eyes. I wiped his tears. 'Why are you crying?'

'No reason, you won't understand.'

He was right, I didn't understand. But I did after my biology lesson years later in Year 8, when I vomited straight into the sliver of sink in the centre of the hardwood lab table.

I knew then what he had tried to do to me. Only then did I understand the shushing, the pulling my pants down so he could gain access, the holding me down, the erection, the pleasuring himself, his firm but quiet voice. He knew it was wrong; I had no clue. My uncle saved me that day. He knew he saved me. I know that now.

So I sat comfortably on the shoulders of my protector when I was in the market. I didn't much understand or particularly like men, but I liked my uncle. He pointed at things and I pointed back. I kissed his fluffy big hair.

'Would your son like to buy this fresh cow's head?' one of the street vendors said as he waved the enormous grisly object above his shoulder, dwarfing his own head. Either that cow's head was enormous or this man had an unusually small head. Either way I was the consumer and he had me at 'I can take the brain out for you'. I loved brain – we loved eating brain and lungs and feet and kidneys and stomach. You name it, we ate it. If it was slaughtered halal, within the guidelines of Islam and not pork, we were all over it.

I scrambled off my uncle, which at the time felt like clambering down a giant. He couldn't lift me now and the floor wouldn't be too far. We were tough but not tall in our family.

'Come on, young man.' The man beckoned me towards him. I couldn't resist the thought of brain in my mouth.

'I never knew you had another son,' the man said to Dad.

'Yes I do.'

Dad rubbed my back and winked. We were playing the 'pretend you're a boy' game. I liked this game. We took the cow's head whole. We were going to smash it open when we got back to the village. I carried it around like a trophy. That's what boys did, right? I ate all night from one stall to the next. Not worried about fitting into a dress or my stomach protruding through the belt when it was tied tight. No, I was a boy and boys wore comfortable, loose-fitting T-shirts. I drank sweet tea with my dad and uncle till my tummy ached. Then I rode back in the cart, feeling every pebble as I sat with the cow's head at my feet. My first day as a boy was a triumph. But my eyes were heavy now; I was desperate to keep them open, not to miss a sight, not to miss a smell. My resistance made me even more tired. I nestled myself among the greens and closed my eyes.

'Bang, bang, bang!' I woke up to the sound of banging, the light streaming through the holes in the tin roof. I sat up and pressed my face against the pink mosquito net. Around me sat several of my aunts, preparing the food we'd bought in the market while my uncle smashed open that cow's head. I was a hunter gatherer. Was it a dream? It felt like one. Being a boy was much more fun than being a girl. 'Come and help me crack open your cow's head!' shouted my uncle from outside. It wasn't a dream. But I was still a girl.

Why didn't I want to be a woman? I had all the right bits, bigger than most, browner than some, but I wanted out of this body. I didn't even want to be a boy necessarily; I just wanted to be someone else, perhaps even something else. With womanhood came constraints, came shackles, came boundaries. For the first time in the market I felt none of those things. I felt free. Is that what freedom felt like? Did I have to be a man to get it? What would happen if I went there as a girl? Would the planets collide? Would it cause some sort of fireball of energy and plunge us into doom? Would I be ostracised? Would I be mocked? Would I be pelted with rotten fruit and made to leave with my head hanging in shame?

'Why can't girls go to the market, Dad?'

'Well, it's not that they can't, they just don't.'

'But why don't they?'

'Well, it's the men's job to do the shopping, they have the money.'

'So why not give the woman the money and let her get the shopping? Surely if she's doing the cooking she will know what she needs?'

'They just don't go, I don't know why. My mum never went and the younger ladies after her never went. It's just a rule.'

'But why, what kind of rule is that?'

My poor dad, always met with the W word. I was relentless in pursuit of answers. The things that other people never really questioned were the only questions I had. Blindly I followed convention – I prayed when I needed to, did my chores, completed my homework on time – I was a stickler for the rules. But I wanted to know why men sat in the living room, while the women were crammed in the kitchen; I wanted to know why Dad worked and Mum stayed at home and why not the other way around; I wanted to know if my granny died because she birthed fourteen children one after the other; and I wanted to know why I couldn't go to the market but my brother could.

Why?

'It's just a rule. We can't change it, it's just the way it is.'

We would sit beside our grandmother, back home in Luton. She gave us comfort when Mum wasn't around. When Mum was tending to my sick siblings, she was tending to us. Answering our confused questions with answers that only made sense in a spiritual hocus-pocus sort of way, specialising in explaining without explanation.

'When will Mum come back?'

'When Allah wills her to.'

She had a direct line to God five times a day; surely she could just ask him?

'Do you know when, Nan?'

'It's up to God,' she always said with reddened eyes and tears glinting on her lashes. She never had answers: she was just a presence; she was just there. The best kind of uneducated, village child bride that life had screwed up and spat out empty-handed. She had the best kind of love to give. Her sole job was to keep us alive. Not to raise us or punish us. She was just there. She never had answers for herself. And she was not equipped to answer our questions.

'Can you find out, can you call her?'

'I don't know how to use your phone, I don't have the phone number.'

You couldn't argue with the lost when we were a little lost ourselves. The blind leading the blind. But as far as she was concerned we were alive and that was her job done.

She had stories. Lots of stories. She filled every question she couldn't answer with a story instead. She had lived. Married at twelve, maybe thirteen, she wasn't a child for very long. That saying, 'if I could be a fly on a wall' – I would be a fly on her wall. But I couldn't stomach her stories so I don't know if I would be very good at it. They were well-to-do, the family she married into. Four brothers with dreams. They had land so far out into the distance, your eyes would sting trying to see its boundaries. The kind of family prospects every father looked to get his daughter married into. It was not about the man. It was about the family. My grandad had everything going for him, along with an empire that he built with his three older brothers. Nan's marriage into the family was another cog in the movement and progression of their wealth and their reputation.

The rice fields went on and on. She spoke about how much land the family owned and I could see it in my mind's eye. The men would leave while it was still cool in the morning. But Nan and her sisters-in-law would be up, huddled by the fire, crouched on the ground. The men would drink their hot tea with a handful of rice puffs in the top – filling, sweet, just enough to get them started for the day.

'The men worked hard,' she would say. 'It wasn't easy being a farmer.'

They had a routine, relying on the weather, depending on the seasons. Too much rain and the fields flooded and the buffalos couldn't go out to graze. Would the rice survive? If the buffalos didn't graze, would they make enough milk to feed the children? Was there enough rice to last the colder months? There was no quick fix.

'There were so many mouths to feed.'

The women would spend the morning tending to children, sweeping the fallen leaves, washing the dusty floors, preparing for the men to come home. They would cook a hearty breakfast of potatoes and chapatis, still one of my most favourite things to eat. Even though I don't exactly need a carb-heavy breakfast for my working day of recipe-testing and writing. As the sun peeked up through the spikes of the rice fields they would prepare food for the children.

'We would feed the kids first, so they didn't get under the men's feet.'

The men would come in and sit on their low stools, knees against their chests, legs covered to the shins with grey, smooth mud that cracked as time passed. The good stuff we pay shedloads for to make our skin lovely and smooth. Well, they got it for free. Not that it did much for their hard-working, battered feet that very rarely met a decent pair of sandals. Their plates sat unstable on the floor of the mud huts, uneven in places, marked with the handprints of wives who smothered the wet dung with their bare hands. It made a great floor until it cracked under the weight of feet on its hard, dry surface. Ready for another plastering of dung.

Heading back to the fields, the men would rush out like they'd never even been there.

'That's when we ate.'

Kids fed, children settled, men fuelled and recharged. It was time for the women to eat.

'We ate what was left over.'

Then they started work on the next meal. It was often big dishes of fish and vegetables. Chicken was a luxury – with so many mouths to feed, you only really ate meat when someone was born – new life – or someone died – goodbyes – or Eid. Fish and vegetables were their gold and that's what they ate because that's what they had, along with plenty of milk.

'We wanted for nothing. We had food, we had rice, we had milk, our kids were fed, our men ate, we had everything.'

The same again at lunchtime. The pattern followed. The kids were fed and left to sleep out of the blistering sun. The men came back, darker than when they left in the morning. Wearier than before. The mud thigh-high. Their walk slower. The women fed the men again and ate what was left over.

'We would have just the sauce left from the pots and that's what we would eat. No fish, no vegetables, just rice and sauce.'

The feminist in me wants to scream as I write. I hear this story and each time I hear it, it never changes. Nan gets older and I live a little more and still that story angers me and saddens me in equal measures.

Why couldn't everyone eat at once? What if the women ate first? Why couldn't the men come back and make their own food? The bra-burning feminist in me wants to fight. 'What if you ate first, Nan?'

'We would never do that.' She spoke for herself, with a certainty that I didn't often see in her. She spoke for herself and her sisters-in-law. They would never do that.

Seven months pregnant. 'What did you have for lunch today?' he would say, rubbing my burgeoning belly as he walked through the door, exhausted from his three-and-a-half-mile walk back from the office.

'I had an egg sandwich, with a packet of crisps, I had my vitamins and I drank plenty of water and some fruit.'

I was lying. With a debt hanging over us that we were determined to pay by the end of the year, we watched every penny. With one income, with any overtime accepted, we still lived on the edge. We had a mortgage to pay, bills to pay and responsibilities that didn't disappear with the growth of our family. He had to look after me, his family and our unborn child. The people who said 'kids pay for themselves'; they lied. That was the biggest lie. They don't pay for themselves; we paid for them like our parents did and their parents before them. They were expensive. We got everything we could for as little as was physically possible and hand-me-downs from my sister were always welcome.

So I lied: I wasn't having lunch; anything I didn't eat at lunch was money saved for another meal. I didn't tell him because he wouldn't agree to it. He would be sad and maybe even disappointed in me and definitely himself. I looked at the crisps and was tempted several times and still I resisted. Every packet saved would be a few pence shaved off another weekly shop. I didn't even buy the vitamins any more – he thought I did, but how many men actually check that sort of thing? They were expensive and after the first set I left an empty box as a decoy in the house so it looked like I was having them. We just couldn't afford them.

'My baby will be fine,' I reassured myself. 'Children in Third World countries come out healthy, my kid has every chance.' I prayed I was right. I prayed to God every night. 'Allah, please tell me I'm making the right choice.' I reassured God that the midwife said he was growing and I was hoping that tied in with what he had planned for me. 'It's going to be okay, right, God?' I asked. I pleaded for reassurance. I had not even had my baby yet and already I felt like I was failing him. He kicked every day to let me know he was just okay. I drank plenty of water to ease the hunger – I was hydrated all right – but there was no fruit in the house. Fruit was expensive and perished fast. So I didn't bother unless it was a yellow-sticker purchase. I did attempt a nap every single day, but hunger kept prodding me in the back and kept me awake, not helped by the excessive water drinking which made me pee more and the added pressure of a baby pushing against my bladder.

I was my nan four decades on. She, they, her companions in the kitchen, put everyone first, before themselves. As I sat in my soft chair whenever I was visiting her back home in Luton I would look at her sitting opposite me, comfortable. I didn't see the young, energetic, full-of-life, worked-to-the-bone mother she spoke about. She was a frail little old lady, faster than most ladies her age but bent over. It hurt her back to stand up straight these days. No wonder, given she was always picking bits off the floor. If the hips she gave me are anything to go by, no doubt I will follow suit in making the carpet my scenery just like her when I'm older.

She would speak of her days as a young mother in Bang-ladesh, doing the same things, the same routine, the same patterns. No different to the men's pattern. They moved with the seasons and their land controlled them. It was never the other way around. She too was young once. She took on sac-rifices, did what was best for her family, followed the rules and put herself last.

I was her in 2016. I was my nan. With a cooler climate and less dusty feet, I was no different. Yet I judged her through the steam that rose from my cup of tea. She should have made a stand. She should have refused. She shouldn't have settled for that. But I knew that she always put herself last so she could sleep at night, guilt-free. Even though she admitted that her hunger kept her awake. I too knew that feeling. Her empty stomach meant she had the strongest gut. She took every blow and still refused to believe she was bruised. She lay awake hungry but she smiled. The nan I saw couldn't read, write or take a diversion without getting lost. She had dark tales of death and sadness. Her eyes were always red raw with tears. She didn't read or write, but she imagined. She lost, she grieved, but she believed in something better. Through her tears she found a belly laugh. The immigrant wife, ostracised for having three girls and ostracised further for having only one boy. Bold in her pursuit for family and bitter in her pursuit for lost love. I felt sorry for her.

She was a baby once; she was a babe in her mother's arms. She smiled and giggled and learned to walk. I tried to decipher her through her words and her actions.

'Shall we take a shortcut, Nan?'

'No, we have to go this way or we'll get lost.'

'Nan, shall we get this can of beans?'

'No, it doesn't have the same picture as the one I always buy so I don't want to get it.'

'What's that on the windowsill, Nan?'

'That's your brother's toy, he must have left it when he came over last.'

'No, Nan, that's not his toy, that's a dead mouse.'

'I'll give it back to him next time he comes round.'

'Nan, can we pick the pears?'

'No, they are your grandad's pears.'

'Nan, he's dead.'

'Oh dear, he should have picked them.'

'Nan, what do you want? I'm doing a shop.'

'Can I have fita?'

'What about crumpets?'

'Yes, fita.'

'Nan, are you okay?' as we get in the car.

'It's so dark outside,' as she looks out of the car window. 'It was light a minute ago.'

'Nan, the windows are tinted.'

'Nadiya, you really should wear your headscarf at home in front of the telly, all those people can see you.'

'Nan, it's a television, it's recorded, we can see them but they can't see us.'

'That's ridiculous.' She secures her scarf.

We waited for her by the window. Nan was with us. Mum was out. Mum was very rarely ever out unless she was tending to one of my siblings in hospital.

'Come on, let's go and pray for your mum.' We all followed her to the mat she laid out. Breaking every rule: no ablution, vests on and shorts off, heads uncovered. We were certainly relaxed in our prayer procedure and attire. As you get older, wearing the right clothes and being ready for prayer becomes important. But not for us, still kids. Nan let the rules go, as she did with most of the rules where her grandchildren were concerned. She didn't say anything, so we didn't remind her. We prayed for Mum.

'Do you think God speaks English?' I asked my sister.

'I don't know, probably.' She carried on praying with open palms to her face, muttering the words. I wasn't sure how to do this. I figured if He was listening, I'd better speak in a language He understood. All that time wasted praying, better use it wisely. I had *Tom and Jerry* to watch, and with all those long minutes staring out of the window I had wasted enough time. My sister turned to me as my eyes wandered, and my knees twitched, desperate for a signal that showed me I could be off. 'Best speak in Bengali, he's probably Bengali.' He probably ate stinky fish with his hands too. It would be cool if God came from my neck of the woods. I watched with the side of my eye, and when Nan got up I wasted no time in clicking that television on.

The others scurried to the window. 'She's home.' Mum walked through the door, looking flustered. Her hair looked like she had been in a cockfight and lost badly. Her acne-scarred skin was rosy red. The only other time she went that red was when she was having words with Dad or when he was nowhere to be found. Her back wet with sweat, she pulled her top back and forth in a feeble attempt to cool down or dry, which one I'm not sure. Whatever she did to fix the dampness she undid with the tears that streamed from her face.

'You lot didn't pray for me, that's why I failed.'

I suppose when you are close to double digits in terms of the number of driving tests you've taken, you start to run out of reasons as to why you failed.

'The instructor was a weirdo.'

'There was a cat in the road.'

'It was a car I have never driven before.'

'I didn't have my tea this morning.'

'I just knew I would fail.'

'He took me on the wrong route.'

'He was a new examiner.' And of course . . .

'You guys didn't pray for me.'

She sat slumped like a melting puddle, slowly descending further and further into the sofa. My nan consoled her as she cried. 'It doesn't matter,' she comforted. 'Stop wasting your money and stop doing these tests.' My mum cried harder, till she was cried out asleep. One by one we curled ourselves into the gaps in her body as she lay there. I tucked myself into the V her legs made when they bent into the foetal position. She woke. Smiling. Unable to move from what looked like a hostage situation. As she got up we all tumbled off and dispersed. She turned to my sister. 'I could never do anything for myself, but at least if learned to drive I could do something for my kids.'

She did everything for us. She woke before we did, warming the house so we did not wake up cold, lining up our uniforms on the heater. She would take the microwave plate and pile it high with our favourite curries around the edge of a mound of steaming, mesmerising rice. She would wash us one by one, carrying us in front of the gas fire so we didn't catch a chill. She would try to make English food and when it didn't turn out the way we hoped, she would fear the worst, that we might feel a tiny pang of hunger, so she would start

again and give us rice and curry and only then was she satisfied. She did everything for us and still she didn't feel she
did enough. Her hands were dry, her eyes dark, her body
exhausted and still she didn't feel like she did enough. She
was always enough, but still she tried. If we cried, she fed us.
She fed us and we complained anyway. Even today if we say,
'Mum, you're a good mum,' her response is always, 'I wish I
could have done more.'

I cleaned my neighbour's toilet, as I retched. Not because it
was grubby but because it was someone else's. Why the hell
was I doing this?

'You know why you're doing this,' I reminded myself. I was
the housewife in every sense of the word. I was a wife and I
had a house. But I wish there was a more appropriate name for
a role that is summed up with two nouns. Throw in some
expletives, some adjectives, some connectives and few excla-
mation marks and then you have a title. Yes, I had a house,
which needed cleaning thoroughly every week and hoovering
every day, with a lot of extra cleaning as you went along. And
the house came with a garden that needed pruning and tidy-
ing until the big guns came in with their lawnmowers. It
needed tending to; after all, it was my view from the sink and
it had to be okay, not even special, just okay to look at. Three
children meant keeping them alive but with that came all the
extras, like washing, feeding, playing with them and putting
them to bed. Trips to the nursery, trips to the doctors, trips to

the dentist, the occasional trip to the supermarket and an annual one to A&E – anyone with asthma will feel our pain. Let's not forget meals to be cooked and lunches to be prepped. Leaving very little time to do much else, but somewhere in all that we had to fit in the laundry too.

So 'housewife' kind of doesn't cut it. I cleaned my neighbour's house for a little extra cash. Despite being 'just' a housewife, as many refer to us, I wanted to provide. I felt useless. Like my mother's, my hands were dry, my eyes dark, my body exhausted. But just like her a decade ago, it wasn't enough. No matter how clean the kids looked and how immaculate the house was, it was not enough. So this job was important to me because it meant I could pay for something.

I handed my husband the money.

'Look what I have.' I put it into his hand.

'What's this for?'

I was beaming with pride; it was the first time I had earned a penny for years. We put money aside so we could see a movie occasionally, a treat we would allow ourselves every few months at best.

'This will be just about enough for tickets and food, but you don't have to pay for it.'

Pushing back my hand, he insisted I keep it and spend it on myself. 'You don't have to do this.' I could feel the guilt in his voice. But no amount he earned or gave me would give me the same satisfaction as earning it myself. Despite the retching at cleaning someone else's toilet, the job was mine and I did it because being a housewife didn't suffice.

'You are enough, everything you do is enough,' Abdal would say.

Just like my mother, I was battered and bruised through life's monotony. She told herself she wasn't doing enough, just like I told myself that whatever I did, no matter how much or how long, I had to do more. My mum eventually passed her driving test and did every school run her heart desired till one day she said, 'I wish I'd never passed.' By learning to drive she had just given herself another job to do, ferrying us all around. I cleaned toilets to satisfy my need to feel useful. Even after every job in my own house was done and all I wanted to do was crash, I beamed with pride as I walked next door with my cleaning gear. We will forever never be enough and still look to find approval by spreading ourselves so thin we are on the verge of disappearing. But that passion to be more than a 'just' runs deeper than I'd thought.

We live our lives and use the generations before us as cautionary tales. All the things we shouldn't do and all the people we shouldn't be like. Then after we've lived a while we become our own cautionary tales. 'If I could go back . . .' we say. But there is no going back. There is looking back with anger, with suspicion, with fondness. But there is no going back.

If my nan could go back she would pray harder for her baby boy not to die. But God gave her another, for her worship, for her belief in the Almighty, for her gratitude.

If my mother could do things differently she probably

would have stayed on longer at school. She had six kids; that was her life, and she never really lived for herself. She breathed because it was habit; she breathed for us. But eventually she passed her driving test. She did a maths course, her first step back into education after leaving school as a teenager back in Bangladesh. She was a student, just like her children. She felt embarrassed but I know she also felt quietly empowered. It gave her the confidence that would see her into old age, the confidence that she should have had years before. But as they say, better late than never. Her leap meant she finally got herself a job, independence and, most of all, money of her own.

If I could go back, I would eat the cake she said I couldn't have.

I would slap the boys who smashed my fingers in the door.

I would perhaps refrain from the occasional 'why'.

I would not scrub my skin raw to see if it was white underneath.

I would tell my mum the trousers didn't fit and ask her to get a size that fitted, rather than pin my trousers all year, using myself as an unintended human pin cushion.

I would ask for straighteners for my hair.

I would have worn my hijab later on in life, because I want to know what it feels like to have the wind run through my hair.

I would have thrown a brick through the window of the local pervert who would try to lure us into his house with sweets.

I would have gone to university.

I would have looked on the map to see how far Leeds really was.

I would have smiled more and fought less.

Every part of my being hated being a woman. So much so, I looked like a boy and my sister accused me of being a lesbian. I listened to my nan's stories and watched my mum eat alone in the kitchen. I watched my aunts cook while the men sat. We served the men, we cleared up after them and then we served ourselves lukewarm food. I watched myself from within my walls while my brothers flew.

I hated being a woman. Everything about my existence and that of the women around me sickened me. They were always beneath someone and never on top. They were somewhere in the hierarchy but never at the apex.

Women are power amongst the weak. They cook, they create, they feed, they sustain. Women are resilience, they are strength, they are brick walls. They are courageous. They bear children and bury them. They bleed and bed men. They please and disobey. They ask and they answer. These are my women: the ones that bore me, the ones that nurtured me, the women that bring me down and the ones that hold me up.

I know now I was meant to hate being a woman then so that I could love being one today.

―╱╲―

Acknowledgements

I want to thank all the people for humouring me when I first thought that this book was a good idea to write. Thanks to Lindsey Evans and Kate Miles for going back and forth and then some more to get us to where we are right now and to everyone else – Lindsay Davies, Siobhan Hooper, Jessica Farrugia, Jo Liddiard, Dan Kennedy, Emma Lahaye, Heather B and Tina Paul – who worked on the book throughout.

For every time I have had a comatose moment of 'I can't move', 'I won't speak' or 'why am I doing this?', thank you Anne for reminding me of my reasons, my thoughts and my vision.

And most of all, thank you to the people who helped shape me to make me the person I am today:

To all the people I have had the pleasure of working with and coming across on this journey who have been kind to me, as well as those who have been less so – the good shapes us, but the bad gives us the fire, and that fire burns strong!

My nan, Anwara Begum – your name should always be in lights and in the sun. In the shadows too long, you deserve to feel the warmth on your face. Without your love we would have so little to say.

My parents – I moan about you all the time, but you are who you are and, as you stand with your traditional values, unwavering, I stand beside you, also unwavering, different in every way but still beside you.

My sisters – my friends, the only people I can love and hate in equal measure. Together we are unbreakable, always questioning, bound by love.

My brothers – thank you for always seeing the bright side. No matter what, you know how to drag us out of the shade and under a rainbow!

My in-laws – my extension to a family that I once feared so much. Thank you for the fear; it keeps me on my toes!

My children are the lights of my life – thank you for choosing me as your mother. For so long I have enjoyed threatening to tell you too much detail about your birth stories but I thank you for asking God to make me your mother. I thank you! I will always tell those stories, embarrass you and make you wish I would shut my mouth, but thank you for picking me. The pleasure will always be mine.

Acknowledgements

To my husband, Abdal – the biggest thank you. Our story is still relatively short, with less history compared to that of my family and no actual biological tie between us. But ours is the most important one of all. After my story is told, the memories will fade; the children will move on; they will live their own lives. Just like we live ours. We will be what is left. We are the shape of our past but we are shaping our future. We will have stories to tell and, with some luck and prayer, three beautiful people to return into the world.

When I said I was broken: 'But how can you be broken, if all
    I see is light shining through?'
When I said I was falling: 'Not if I'm holding on.'
When I said I can't: 'You're already doing it.'
When I said, why me? 'It was always you.'

We will be left.

Index

Ali, Jamir (Nadiya's father) 2–3,
33–4, 83, 187
at Bangladesh market 304–7,
311–14
as Baba 15–21, 26
cooking 232–4, 259, 260–3
family 31
haircutting 303–4
and Jakir 49–51
marriage 39–40, 155–6
and money 251
and Nadiya 94, 149, 276
Nadiya's birth 4–9, 25
and nail painting 59–60
and Nan 86–8
surname 11, 12–13
and Yasmin 55

Bake Off 230–1, 269, 283
baking 263–6, 268–9, 270

Bangladesh 3–4, 15
markets 304–7
Nadiya's wedding 115–17, 118
Begum 11, 12, 13–14, 15, 25
Begum, Asma (Nadiya's
mother) 11, 22–5, 35–6,
276, 293, 327–8
cooking 155–6, 162–3, 232,
256–7, 258–9, 266
driving tests 323–4, 327, 328
family 31
and grandkids 82
handesh 162–3
marriage 39–40, 155–6, 323
and money 251
as mother 8, 175–6, 207–8,
254, 255, 324–5, 327
Musa's birth 177, 179–84
Nadiya's birth 4–5, 25
Nadiya's jobs 219–22, 249,
251

Index

Begum, Asma (*cont.*)
  and nail painting 59–60
  and Nan 135–6
  and Nana 22–5
  surname 11, 13–14
  and Yasmin 54–5
Begum, Jasmin (Nadiya's sister)
  21–2, 35–41, 66
Begum, Nadiya *see* Hussain,
  Nadiya
Begum, Sadiya (Nadiya's sister)
  10, 41–6, 66
Begum, Yasmin (Nadiya's sister)
  51–9, 66
bullying 59–65

cooking 232–5, 250–71

Dhadha (Nadiya's paternal
  grandad) 12–13
Dhadhi (Nadiya's paternal
  grandma) 32

eyebrows 102, 288–91

Facebook 275, 278–9, 281, 291–2

The Great British Bake Off
  (GBBO) 230–1, 269, 283

Hussain 11, 12, 13
Hussain, Abdal (Nadiya's
  husband) 116
  and Dawud 192
  family 144–54, 165, 186, 257
  marriage 115–27, 229, 318–19,
    326–7
  Musa's birth 178, 179, 184,
    185–6
  Nadiya's baking 268–9
  name 103–4, 109–10
  phone calls 111–12, 113–14
  text messages 100–3, 104–8,
    111
Hussain, Dawud (Nadiya's son)
  172–3, 186–93, 205–6
Hussain, Jakir (Nadiya's
  brother) 47–51, 66, 73
Hussain, Maryam (Nadiya's
  daughter) 173–4, 195–6,
  197–202, 204, 205, 207
Hussain, Musa (Nadiya's son)
  171–2, 205–6
  birth 176–86
  and Dawud 186–8, 189, 190,
    191, 192
Hussain, Nadiya
  at Bangladesh market 304–7,
    311–14
  baking 230, 263–9
  birth 3–10
  bullying 59–65
  call-centre job 102–3, 111–12,
    214–15, 227
  chauffeur job 220, 227
  cleaning job 228–30, 325, 326

cooking 234–5, 238–9, 241,
    256–59, 263–71
as daughter-in-law 140–1,
    142–65
and Dawud 186–93
eyebrows 102, 288–91
and father 2, 15–21, 26, 90,
    94, 149, 263, 276
first name 10–11, 25
glasses 106, 216–17
hair 302–3
and Jakir 47–51
and Jasmin 35–41
and Marmite 152–4
marriage 115–27, 227–8
and Maryam 195–6, 197–8,
    199–201, 205, 207
and milk 150–1
and mother 22–5, 182, 276
as mother 193–4, 241, 255–6,
    318–20, 325–7
Musa's birth 176–86
name 10–15, 25–6
and Nan 71–96, 120–1, 133–9
and Nana 21–3, 89, 136
panic disorder 122–3, 124–5,
    199, 201–5
periods 89–94, 95
prayer 159–61, 241, 322
as presenter 238–41
and Sadiya 41–6
sexual abuse 308–11
and Shakir 65–6, 224–7

and siblings 3, 29–66
and social media 275–98
surname 11–15, 25–6
university 110, 222–4, 253–4
work 213–42, 246–52, 253–6
writing 235–8, 241
and Yasmin 51–9
Hussain, Shakir (Nadiya's
    brother) 65, 66, 224–7,
    259–61

influencers 293–5
Instagram 276, 288–91

Jabbar, Dr 294
jeans 279–80

Kookoolis, Mrs 14–15, 26

Marmite 152–4
Marshall, Mrs 264–5
mental health 284–5
    panic disorder 122–3, 124–5,
        199, 201–5
mothers 193–4, 207–9, 318–27

names 10–15, 109–10
Nan (Nadiya's maternal
    grandma) 71–88, 91–5,
    120–1, 133–9, 256, 314–18,
    321–3, 324, 327
    chapatis 83–4, 96
    handesh 163

Nan (*cont.*)
   persistence 293
   putting herself last 315–18,
      320–1
Nana (Nadiya's maternal
      grandad) 9, 21–5, 79, 89,
      120, 136, 137

panic disorder 122–3, 124–5, 199,
      201–5
periods 89–94, 95
prayer 159–61, 241, 322–3

Ray, Tamal 283–4
reality television 230

sexual abuse 308–11
Smith, Delia 263–4
SMS 100–4
Snapchat 279, 280

social media 101, 275–98
   Facebook 291–2
   Instagram 288–91
   Twitter 284–7
   YouTube 292–8
surnames 11–15

text messaging 100–3
Twitter 275–6, 284–7

university 110, 222–4, 253–4

women 301–2, 329
   as mothers 193–4, 207–9,
      318–27
   putting themselves last
      315–18
writing 235–8

YouTube 292–8

Recipe Index

cakes, my Madeira 272–3
chapatis 96–7
cheese, special leftover
    chips 243–4
chicken, sweet and sour chicken
    curry 128–31
chips 243–4
chocolate, eyebrow rocky
    road 299–300
cod, tenga 27–8

eggs their way 210–11
eyebrow rocky road 299–300

fish
    tenga 27–8
    tuna patties 67–70

fritters, handesh 166–9

handesh 166–9

Madeira cake 272–3

rice fritters, handesh 166–9
rocky road 299–300

special leftover chips 243–4
sweet and sour chicken
    curry 128–31

tenga 27–8
tuna patties 67–70